Anglo-American Policy toward the Persian Gulf, 1978–1985

Power, Influence and Restraint

Books by the Author and Published by the Press

Richard Nixon, Great Britain and the Anglo-American Alignment in the Persian Gulf and Arabian Peninsula: Making Allies Out of Clients

The Decline of the Anglo-American Middle East, 1961–1969: A Willing Retreat

The Military Conquest of the Prairie: Native American Resistance, Evasion and Survival, 1865–1890

Anglo-American Policy toward the Persian Gulf, 1978–1985

Power, Influence and Restraint

Tore T. Petersen

sussex
ACADEMIC
PRESS
Brighton • Chicago • Toronto

2 4 6 8 10 9 7 5 3

First published in hardcover 2015, reprinted in paperback 2016, by
SUSSEX ACADEMIC PRESS
PO Box 139
Eastbourne BN24 9BP

and in the United States of America by
SUSSEX ACADEMIC PRESS
Independent Publishers Group
814 N. Franklin Street, Chicago, IL 60610

and in Canada by
SUSSEX ACADEMIC PRESS (CANADA)

British Library Cataloguing in Publication Data
A CIP catalogue record for this book is available from the British Library.

Library of Congress Cataloging-in-Publication Data
Petersen, Tore T., 1954–
Anglo-American policy toward the Persian Gulf, 1978–1985 : power, influence and restraint / Tore T. Petersen.
pages cm
Includes bibliographical references and index.
ISBN 978-1-84519-371-3 (hardcover : acid-free paper)
ISBN 978-1-84519-750-6 (paperback : acid-free paper)
1. Persian Gulf Region—Foreign relations—United States. 2. United States—Foreign relations—Persian Gulf Region. 3. Persian Gulf Region—Foreign relations—Great Britain. 4. Great Britain—Foreign relations—Persian Gulf Region. 5. Islam and politics—Persian Gulf Region—History—20th century. 6. United States—Foreign relations—1977–1981. 7. United States—Foreign relations—1981–1989. I. Title.
DS326.P487 2015
327.41053609′048—dc23
2014032423

MIX
Paper from
responsible sources
FSC® C013056

Typeset and designed by Sussex Academic Press, Brighton & Eastbourne.
Printed by TJ International, Padstow, Cornwall.

Contents

Cast of Characters

Alam, Asadollah, Iranian Minister of Court.
Al-Zawawi, Qais, minister of foreign affairs Oman.

Baker, James, White House chief of staff, 1981–85.

Callaghan, James, UK prime minister, 1976–79.
Carrington, Lord Peter Alexander Rupert, British foreign minister, 1979–82
Carter, Jimmy, US president 1977–81.
Carter, Rosalynn, US first lady, 1977–81.
Casey, William, director CIA, 1981–87.
Church, Frank, United States senator

Deaver, Michael, Wite House deputy chief of staff, 1981–85.

Eisenhower, Dwight D., president of the United States, 1953–61.

Faisal ibn Abd al-Aziz Al Saud, king of Saudi Arabia, 1964–1975.

Haig, Alexander, US secretary of state, 1981–82.
Haldeman, H. R., chief of staff White House, 1969–1973.
Healey, Denis W., British minister of defense, 1964–70.
Heath, Edward, British prime minister, 1970–74.
Helms, Richard M., United States ambassador to Iran, 1973–1976.
Hesseltine, Michael, minister of defence UK 1983–86.
Home, Lord (Alexander Frederick Douglas-Home), British foreign secretary 1960–1963,
thereafter prime minister to 1964, foreign secretary 1970–74.
Howe, Geoffrey, UK secretary of state 1983–1990
Hurd, Douglas, minister of state foreign affairs, 1979–1983
Hussein I, ibn Talal, king of Jordan, 1952–1979

Johnson, Lyndon B., president of the United States, 1963–1969.
Jordan, Hamilton, White House chief of staff, 1979–81.

Kennedy, John F., president of the United States, 1961–1963.
Khalid bin Abdulaziz al Saud, king Saudi Arabia, 1975–82.

Khomeini, Ayatollah Ruhollah, leader of Iran from 1979.
Kissinger, Henry A., National Security Council advisor to president Nixon and afterwards president Ford, 1969–1975 and secretary of state from 1973 to 1977.

Lucas, Ivor, UK ambassador Oman, 1979–81.

McFarlane, Robert, US national security advisor, 1983–85.
Meese, Edwin, counselor to the president, 1981–85, attorney general, 1985–88.
Moberly, John, assistant undersecretary of state UK .
Morris, Willie, British ambassador to Saudi Arabia, 1970–1972.
Murphy, Richard, country director US Department of State Arabian Peninsula.
Muskie, Edmund, US secretary of state, 1980–81.

Nasser, Gamal Abdul, president of Egypt, 1954–1970.
Nixon, Richard, president of the United States, 1969–74.
Noyes, James E., United States deputy assistant secretary of defense.

Owen, David, UK secretary of state, 1977–79.

Pahlavi, Mohammed Reza, shah of Iran, 1941–1979.
Precht, Henry, country director Iran, US state department, 1978–80.
Pym, Francis, UK secretary of state, 1982–83

Qabus, bin Said, sultan of Oman since 1972.
Qaddafi, Mu'ammar, leader of Libya.

Parsons, Anthony, UK ambassador to Iran, 1974–79, special advisor to Thatcher 1982–83.
Reagan, Nancy, US first lady 1981–89.
Reagan, Ronald, US president 1981–89.
Regan, Donald, US secretary of the treasury 1981, White House chief of staff, 1985–87.
Rothnie, A. K., British ambassador to Saudi Arabia, 1972–1974.
Rush, Kenneth, United States acting secretary of state from 1973.

Sick, Gary, principal White House aide Persian Gulf, 1977–1981.
Shultz, George, US secretary of state, 1982–89.
Stockman, David, US director management and business, 1981–85.
Sullivan, William, US ambassador to Iran, 1977–79.

Taymur, bin Said, sultan of Oman, 1932–1970.
Thatcher, Margaret, prime minister UK, 1979–1990.

Trezise, Philip, Assistant United States secretary of state for economic affairs, 1969–1971.

Vance, Cyrus, US secretary of state, 1977–1980.

Weinberger, Caspar, US secretary of defense, 1981–87.
West, John, US ambassador Saudi Arabia, 1977–81.
Wilson, Harold, British prime minister 1964–70 and 1974–76.
Zaid bin Sultan Al Nahyan, sheikh leader of the UAE.

Acknowledgements

I wish to thank the Faculty for Humanities and the Department of History for partially funding the research for this book. Anthony Grahame, Editorial Director at Sussex Academic Press has for the third time efficiently guided one of my manuscripts to publication. He has also been great support for other scholarly matters, for this I am most grateful. Special thanks to Ole Aksel Øveraas and Elise Hov for their work in the National Archives, Kew.

List of Abbreviations

AEI   Associated Electrical Industries.
AIPAC   American Israeli Public Affairs Commmittee.
ARAMCO   Arabian American Oil Company.
AWACS   Airborne Warning and Control System.
BAC   British Aircraft Corporation .
BOAR   British Army on the Rhine.
BP   British Petroleum.
CAB   Cabinet papers, The National Archives, Kew.
CF   Country File.
CFNSF   Country File, National Security File.
DEF   Defense.
DEFE   UK Ministry of Defence.
CIA   Central Intelligence Agency.
FCO   Foreign and Commonwealth Office.
FO   Foreign Office records, Public records Office, Kew.
FRUS   Papers Relating to the Foreign relations of the United States.
GOI   Government of Iran.
GPO   United States Government Printing Office .
JCL   Jimmy Carter Library, Atlanta; Georgia.
LARG   Libyan Arab Revolutionary Government.
LBJ   Lyndon Baines Johnson.
LBJL   Lyndon Baines Johnson Library, Austin, Texas.
Mc   memorandum of conversation.
NA   The National Archives, Kew, England.
NARG   National Archives, Record Group, College Park, MD.
NCL   Remote Archives Capture project in Jimmy Carter Library.
               to be cited as NCL.
NIOC   National Iranian Oil Company.
NLF   National Liberation Front for Occupied South Yemen.
RMNL   Richard Milhous Nixon Library, Yorba Linda, California.
RN   Richard Nixon .
RNNSC   Richard Nixon National Security File.
RWRL   Ronald Wilson Reagan Library, Simi Valley, California.
NSABMCF   National Security Affairs; Brzezinski Material, Country File;.
               Jimmy Carter Library.
NSC   National Security Council.
NSF   National Security File.

OPEC	Organization of Petroleum Exporting Countries.
PDRF	President's Daily Report File, Jimmy Carter Library.
PFOAG	The Popular Front for the Liberation of the Occupied Arab . Gulf.
POL	Political Affairs and Relations.
PRC	Public Republic of China.
PREM	Prime Minister's Office, The National Archives .
PRSY	People's Republic of South Yemen.
SAF	Sultan's Armed Forces, Oman.
SDI	Strategic Defense Initiative.
SHSC	Special head of state correspondence.
TOS	Trucial Oman Scouts .
UAE	United Arab Emirates.
WHORM	White House Office of records Management, Ronald Reagan . Library, Simi Valley, California.

List of Illustrations

Photo reference numbers beginning NLC are courtesy of the Jimmy Carter Presidential Library; NAI (National Archives Identifier) numbers courtesy of the Reagan Presidential Library.

Cover illustrations
[Front] President Reagan addressing the British parliament, 8 June 1982.
[Back] Photograph of the four presidents (Reagan, Carter, Ford, Nixon), 8 October 1981.
(NAI 198531 and NAI 198522)

Plate section (after page 72)
President Jimmy Carter hosts a state dinner at the White House for Prime Minister James Callaghan, 10 March 1977.
(NLC-WHSP-C-00623-12)

President Jimmy Carter and Prime Minister Margaret Thatcher, 13 September 1977.
(NLC-WHSP-C-2705-20A)

The Shah of Iran, Empress Farah, President Jimmy Carter and First Lady Rosalynn Carter, on a podium, 15 November 1977.
(NLC-WHSP-C-03804-10)

President Jimmy Carter's infamous New Year's Eve toast to the Shah of Iran, 31 December 1977.
(NLC-WHSP-C-03795-06A)

President Jimmy Carter hosts a luncheon for king Khalid of Saudi Arabia, 27 October 1978.
(NLC-WHSP-C-08132-18)

Chancellor Helmut Schmidt, Prime Minister James Callaghan, President Jimmy Carter and President Giscard d'Estaing in Guadeloupe, 5 January 1979.
(NLC-WSP-C-08899-16)

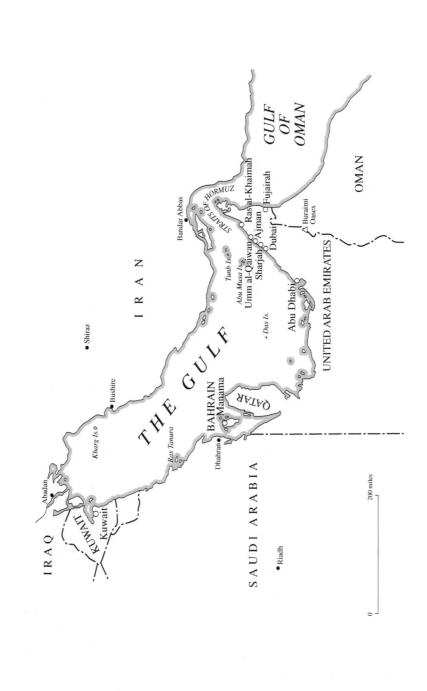

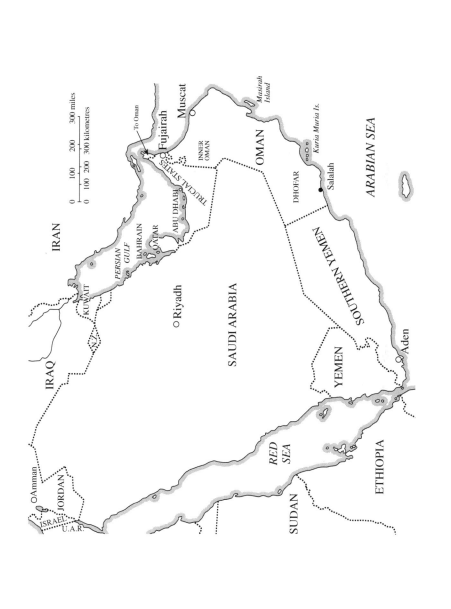

Introduction

James Morris in his *Pax Britannica* trilogy gives a graphic and poignant description of the last British colonial civil servant, having finally returned to England after having lived most of his life overseas: "He is not a young man now, in his fifties, perhaps, and he is slightly stooped, as a succession of fevers has warped his spine. But he is slim. Stringy, rather rangy, and his face is so heavily tanned, not simply a sunburn but a deep, ingrained tincture of brown, that physically he scarcely looks like an Englishman at all. (. . .) He is a foreigner in his own capital. He is a true exotic among the cosmopolitans. He is the last of the British empire builders, home on leave and hating it."[1] The formal empire may have ended, and with it the civil servants from the Colonial Office. But after the announcement of the British leaving the Persian Gulf in 1971, formal positions were replaced by informal ones. Britain still ran much of the political, economic and military life in the lower Gulf and also in the Arabian Peninsula. The deeply tanned British bureaucrats that remained were no longer employed by Whitehall, but acted as administrators for the sultans, sheiks and emirs, as employees of the locally owned British business or oil company, or as British Loan Service Personnel from the UK Department of Defence, leading, training and officering the local armed forces. While their paymaster was different, and their employer private, most of them continued to serve the interests of London. The transition from formal to informal empire was almost seamless, British influence remained large and almost paramount in the region. While the Conservative government of Alec Douglas-Home and R.A. Butler fought a rearguard action to maintain its informal empire in the Gulf after the Suez crisis, some of the more ardent proponents of a change in policy began questioning the utility of remaining, as exemplified by the 1964 decision to grant South Arabia independence, but to keep the Aden base. But even keeping the base was a long-term doubtful proposition, as Butler observed to the Cabinet on April 20, 1964:

> To the extent that future United States/United Kingdom interdependence in round-the-world strategy may require land-based facilities, we should look for points where the local political scene has no anti-colonialist or anti-Western complexes, or, preferably, where there are no inhabitants at all.[2]

Almost instantly after the announcement to quit the Gulf, any local loyalty towards Britain evaporated, and those Arabs favoring a continued British presence realized that soon no one would be there to protect them. The process of withdrawing from fixed positions was greatly accelerated when Labour returned to power in October 1964. But while withdrawing from formal positions was the new policy, even Labour was loath to give up British influence in the Persian Gulf and Arabian Peninsula. One of the major avenues to maintain influence was arms sales, which became a key element in British policy after 1964, so much so that being an arms merchant at times gave the appearance of being the only remaining aspect of British policy.

As Iran's minister of the court Asadollah Alam noted after meeting the British ambassador after the British withdrawal from the Gulf on August 7, 1972: "The British are so forlorn that nothing interests them these days save commerce and arms deals."[3] But in contrast to the British withdrawal from Aden, Britain did not leave chaos behind in the Persian Gulf. The UAE (United Arab Emirates) federation must be counted as a success history, as well as British policies in Oman. This despite the fact that some observers have alleged that Britain deliberately allowed the rebellion in the Dhofar province to fester in order to prolong British influence in Oman. Whatever the case, the British certainly took their time about it before finally defeating the Dhofari rebels in 1975.[4]

But it is important not to confuse rhetoric with reality. Britain was not weak and did not have to withdraw from the Persian Gulf for military reasons. On the contrary, Britain had *to appear weak* when withdrawing from the Gulf to make it politically possible and acceptable to British Parliamentary and public opinion, and to soften local criticism for Iran occupying Abu Musa and the Tunbs Island. These islands belonged to Sharjah and Ras al-Khaimah, two of the future members of the UEA, sheikdoms that Britain was obligated to defend by treaty. For supposedly being in a withdrawal mode and at the end of their imperial tender, the Heath government (1970–1974) acted surprisingly similar to the imperialists of old – the sheikhs were practically instructed to federate into the UEA. Buraimi is also a case in point, having brought Anglo-American relations close to breaking point in the 1950s; it was a continuing running sore in Anglo-Saudi relations until 1972. But after the British withdrawal from the Gulf, Buraimi was simply dropped by the Heath government, which refused further involvement in the issue despite king Faisal's strictures about demanding control of the oasis. So much for Faisal's increased international stature and position, which did little to impress the British.[5] The Islands were practically given away as a down payment for access to the lucrative Iranian market, and their age-old ally sultan Taymur of Oman was resolutely deposed when he refused to do the bidding of the British. Thereafter, the Heath government would for all practical purposes run the administration of the successor to Taymur sultan Qabus, direct his military operations and evict foreign companies from Oman for the benefit of British companies. Oman, then, in the early 1970s was an exclusive British enclave.

The British, despite liquidating most of its fixed positions in the Persian Gulf and the Arabian Peninsula, successfully made the transition from formal to informal empire in the region. Even the Labour government, at the height of withdrawal, managed to a large degree to control events in the Persian Gulf, despite the numerous territorial disputes that emerged in the wake of the withdrawal decision. This is because all roads to a negotiated solution went through London. But London was more than a political center for the Gulf States. As Christa Salamandra observes, it has also been the capital for the Gulf Arabs abroad since 1970. "Strong affinities between members of Britain's conservative diplomatic, financial and cultural establishment(s), wealthy London-based Middle Easterners and the ruling families and elites of the Arab Gulf buttress Arab London's culture industries."[6] Military ties are also strong beyond buying British arms, though perhaps somewhat symbolic; king Abdullah of Jordan and sultan Qaboos of Oman received their training from the British military academy at Sandhurst.

Margaret Thatcher's premiership was in many ways the culmination of these trends. Under her guidance there was a sharp increase in British influence not only in the traditional British enclaves of the Persian Gulf sheikdoms, ensured by taking British arms sales efforts to new heights, but also by deepening British military commitments to the UAE, Oman and, surprisingly, Saudi Arabia. And of course by effectively utilizing the increased American security commitment to the Gulf in the wake of the Carter doctrine, to Britain's benefit. In meetings with both the Carter and the Reagan administration Thatcher's mantra was: We are your friends, you are entitled to our support and you can rely on us.[7] But the declarations of support came at a price; if Britain was ever in need of American support, Thatcher expected it to be forthcoming. Furthermore, the prime minister easily sensed when vital American interests were at stake, and took care to accommodate the United States on such occasions, but she held equally firm against the United States for central British concerns. During the Falklands war, for instance, the Americans repeatedly urged negotiations, wanting to avoid Argentine defeat and humiliation; in the end, they were all, including the president, firmly rebuffed by Thatcher. In the Persian Gulf and Arabian Peninsula, Thatcher saw no reason to end the British presence, despite an increased American commitment, but instead effectively used the newfound American engagement in the region to deepen British influence and commitments. Interestingly, Thatcher's policies towards the Persian Gulf and Arabian Peninsula have been largely ignored by the scholarly literature.[8] But now we must turn to the American side of the coin.

Richard Nixon, for all his flaws, laid the foundation of American foreign policy from the 1970s, through the era of Carter and Reagan, possibly to this very day. Believing that the United States was confronted by a new international environment when he became president, with the Soviet Union having reached an approximate parity with American military strength, the growth of China and strong economic competition from West Germany and Japan, Nixon sought to put the international system on a new footing – a footing where the United States could keep its global preeminence.[9] Carter and Reagan, and I strongly suspect all presidents thereafter, followed the basic outlines of these new ideas in American foreign policy made by Nixon. Throughout his career as president and thereafter, Nixon promoted the concept of a global structure of peace. This was more than a mere slogan for Nixon, the idea was to develop a secure balance among the great powers – hence the opening to China and detenté with the Soviet Union, leading to great power restraint, and concomitanty giving more responsibilities to regional powers that were American allies. In the Persian Gulf, Iran and to a lesser degree Saudi Arabia fit the bill: it was a twin pillar strategy. Nixon announced the doctrine bearing his name in July 1969 that henceforth the United States would support its allies with economic and military assistance and the coverage of the American nuclear umbrella, but not American soldiers. Just like the British, Nixon had no restraints inselling massive amounts of arms to its allies. None of the Anglo-American allies in the Persian Gulf and Arabian Peninsula had the required educational level or adequate infrastructure to run their newly imported western arms. Hence large numbers of British and American experts were imported to run the military machines, creating structures of dependencies between the United States and their allies in the Persian Gulf. For Britain, it was an efficient way of maintaining influence.

Carter and Reagan would, as we shall see, more or less follow Nixon's scripts, with twists of their own making. After the disgrace of Watergate Nixon worked assiduously for his own political rehabilitation and indeed came into his own during the Reagan administration. Nixon's archive in Yorba Linda is a treasure-trove of documents on this period, and includes his correspondence with Reagan (a source which, according to the Yorba Linda archive, has hitherto been unused by historians). Carter's grand strategy sought reciprocal accommodation with the Soviet Union and the leadership of its European allies (England, Germany and France), developing a cooperative context where China and Japan would also fit in. Despite public rhetoric to the contrary, Carter continued American arms sales, to Iran in particular which received more American military equipment under Carter than under Nixon. Reagan, was willing to accommodate the Soviets with serious negotiations, after forcing the Communist regime on the defensive, by political, economic and military pressures. Reagan continued the policy of massive American arms sales inherited from Nixon and Carter, keeping the established structures of dependencies intact. Unfortunately for Carter, the Iranian pillar in the Persian Gulf crumbled under his leadership, the shah being ousted in favor of radical Islam under the leadership of Ayatollah Khomeini. It is fascinating to learn from the archives how the United States was at times unable and at other times unwilling to help its most important ally in the Persian Gulf, the shah, to weather the gathering storm from Islamic revolutionaries. Britain, having a major economic interest in Iran, also refused to assist the shah, who was initially refused entry into the United States, and permanently refused entry into Britain. The treatment of the shah shows a certain callousness and ruthlessness from American and British policy makers, leaving an old ally with little or no support when he struggled to remain in power, and effectively shunning him thereafter. There will be many more examples of such attitudes as the story unfolds.

Quietly and quickly, after the fall of the shah, Oman became key to the western effort in the Persian Gulf, and has in my view remained so to this very day. Whatever the faults of Anglo-American politicians, it is evident that they had learned a lesson or two from the contretemps in Iran and earlier debacles in the Middle East. British and American leaders took care to keep its engagement in the sultanate below the radar, and there is very little on the western interests in Oman that was volunteered to newspapers and television. Furthermore, while British and American interests had at times clashed in the past in the Middle East (the Suez crisis comes to mind with the tempestuous early 1950s preceding it), in Oman while often competitive local British and American representatives have learned to live together, if not fully in harmony, then relatively peacefully. It is the central thesis in this book that while the United States increased its engagement in the Persian Gulf and Arabian Peninsula after the Soviet December 1979 invasion of Afghanistan, Britain with Margaret Thatcher at the helm actually deepened and increased its involvement in the region under the cover of the Carter doctrine. There was much less need to worry about the Soviets any more, since Carter had publicly stated he would take care of the bear; Britain was thus freed to focus fully and freely on local issues and opportunities for selling British products. This Thatcher and her government did with a vengeance. The historic *Al-Yamamah* deal with Saudi Arabia in 1985, the largest arms deal in the world to date, selling advance fighter aircraft to Saudi Arabia, was worth £5.2 billion on signature, ballooning to over £90 billion over the next two decades and created 50,000 jobs.[10] Similarly, Thatcher exploited the opportunities that presented themselves by the Carter doctrine, to increase British engagement in the United Arab Emirates and to an even larger extent in Oman. Diminished British influence in the Persian Gulf as a result of their withdrawal from fixed bases in 1971 had by the mid 1980s evaporated. British influence was stronger than it had been in a very long time. In order to understand how this came about and how Thatcher was able to exploit the opportunities presenting themselves, we must turn to the antecedents – the Nixonian foundations of American foreign policy.

I

The Nixonian Foundations of American Foreign Policy

"And another thing – this 'new world order' doesn't amount to a tinker's damn. I mean it. Every time we see the end of some kind of era in the world, we call it a new world order. Bullshit. The world is dangerous, unpredictable place; force will always have to be used; and collective organizations, whether it's the UN or whatever, will never work when it comes down to protecting national interests. And it always comes down to national interests. The only collective body that has ever worked was NATO, and that was because it was a military alliance and we were in charge."[1]

On November 17, 1973 the president during the height of the Watergate crisis held a press conference on the question of his personal finances: "And so, that is where the money come from. Let me say just say this, and I want to say this to the television audience: I made my mistakes, but in all my years of public life, I have never profited, never profited from public service – I have earned every cent. And in all my years of public life, I have never obstructed justice. And I think, too, that I could say that in my years of public life, that I welcome this kind of examination, because people have got to know whether or not their President is a crook. Well, I am not a crook. I have earned everything I got."[2] Despite the president's assertions, Nixon's body language conveyed the opposite of the intended message; his performance was anything but convincing. In fact, for many commentators and historians the 'I'm not a crook' press conference was a confirmation of a president engaged in shady practices. Fawn Brodie observes: "When Richard Nixon resigned, the London *Spectator* observed that in the United States the presidency had come full circle, from George Washington, who could not tell a lie, to Richard Nixon, who could not tell the truth." In other words, Nixon was a pathological liar and as Brodie insists: "He had no emotional investment in the truth."[3] Nixon's leadership style compounded his political problems. Just prior to the 'I'm not a crook' speech, the president met with the Congressional Republicans, many of them annoyed by the belated calls for support and cooperation. Stephen Ambrose observes: "Nixon had ignored them for years, had refused to campaign for them, had sucked up campaign funds from their districts and left nothing for them, had asked their support and giving them nothing – and now he wanted them to save him. Their feeling was that they had been and were being used by someone who had never done anything for them, and never would."[4]

The consensus among historians is that Watergate drained Nixon of support and the ability to govern. Keith W. Olson explains that "During 1973 and 1974, Nixon faced other problems, unrelated to the cover-up, that further lessened his credibility." These problems included vice president Spiro Agnew pleading no contest to "charges of tax evasion and accepting bribes during his governorship of Maryland", Nixon's questionable tax deductions "for the donation of his vice presidential papers to the National Archives", and seemingly lavish public spending to improve the president's private residences in Florida and California. "These headline issues, combined with the steady conviction of White House aides for their part in primary campaigns, the illegal fundraising, the break-in, and the cover-up, created the appearance of an administration out of touch with morality and honesty. In the public's eyes, Nixon had no reserve of integrity to draw upon in his appeal for public support."[5] Stephen Ambrose explains: As the problems with Watergate compounded, taking Nixon's time and draining his energy, Henry Kissinger stepped forward to "hold foreign policy together." By January 1974, Nixon's control of foreign policy had deteriorated completely: "Nixon's preoccupation with Watergate and his own future was such that he could only give his attention to foreign policy in fits and starts. Kissinger covered for him."[6]

It is easy to make fun of the former president, with his penchant of referring to himself in the third person singular as RN, his continuous quest for self-aggrandizement, and his pestering and hectoring aides and associates of ways on how to promote the president.[7] Leaving the RN usage aside, Nixon had perhaps a better understanding and perception of the office of the president than many of his contemporaries, critics and later historians. More importantly, Nixon to a large degree built the foundation of future American foreign policy up to the present time. Peeling back the self-promotion, rhetoric and posturing it is possible to discern several elements of the Nixonian foundation of American foreign policy. The opening to China and détente with the Soviet Union is considered Nixon' greatest foreign policy successes, but were only two figures, albeit major ones, on the broadly based international canvas the president was painting. His ambition was nothing less than putting the international system on an entirely new footing. Nixon's new foreign policy approach was complex and multi-layered. Firstly, in his grand design, which the president consistently referred to as a global structure of peace, the new approach to the Soviet Union and China was part of a design to weave together international cooperation to the extent that the system encouraged great power restraint. More power and responsibility would then devolve to regional powers. To give ideological justification to this grand plan, and the changing American international role, the president promulgated a doctrine carrying his name. He announced that the United States would adhere to its treaty commitments, but regional American allies would have to provide the manpower to protect themselves and their interests. In the Persian Gulf, Iran, in particular, and Saudi Arabia were to serve as American pillars in the region. To enable these local powers to purchase sufficient military hardware to be credible local policemen, Nixon deliberately broke up the long and successful cooperation between the West and the oil companies. As a result, increased oil prices gave Saudi Arabia and Iran the necessary income. Nixon cared more about the security of the oil supply than oil prices. Besides, the main economic global competitors of the US – Germany and Japan – bore the brunt of the costs of the increase in oil prices. Since none of the American third world associates had the infrastructure or education level to service their new sophisticated western, largely American military machinery, huge numbers of American and British nationals had to be imported and engaged to keep all this military hardware operational. At the same time that Nixon sought to upgrade former clients in the Gulf to allies, he created structures of dependencies whereby Iran and Saudi Arabia became more dependent on the West for its markets, technology, spare parts and Anglo-American expatriates not only to run their armed forces, but also much of their civilian society. In the Gulf, following the British November 30, 1971 withdrawal, for instance, British nationals commanded the armed forces of the different sheikdoms, ran their civil service and in addition controlled their economies. While the shah strutted on the international scene promoting Iranian largesse, in his hearts of hearts he must have known that he was and remained a client. Significantly, when his regime was crumbling in the fall of 1978 he closeted himself with the British and American ambassadors, hoping then, as in 1953, that his western puppet masters would save him.[8]

Whatever else that may have been said or believed about Richard Nixon he was consistent in his quest to build a global structure of peace while president and afterwards. In fact, Nixon claimed that peacemaking was his main concern as president. In his inauguration speech on January 20, 1969, he said: "The greatest honor history can bestow is the title of peacemaker. This honor now beckons America . . . If we succeed, generations to come will say of us now living that we mastered our moment, that we helped make the world safe for mankind. This is our summons to greatness."[9] With his penchant for the snappy phrase, the inaugural speech continued: "Let us take as our goal; Where peace is unknown, make it welcome; where peace is fragile, make it strong; where peace is temporary, make it permanent."[10] In his report to Congress on foreign policy in 1970, Nixon observed: "I have often reflected on the meaning of 'peace', and have reached one certain conclusion: Peace must be far more than the absence of war. Peace must provide a durable structure of international relationships which inhibits or removes the causes of war."[11] The president outlined the main priorities of his foreign policy in his next annual report to Congress in February 1971. The fundamental goal of American foreign policy was "to build a durable structure of international relationships." With the international system in transition, the United States was forced to adapt to changing circumstances. "We need a vision so that crises do not consume our energies, and tactics do not dominate our policies." For Nixon, this led to the inescapable conclusion for American foreign policy: "Today we must work with other nations to build an enduring structure of peace" – that is a "global structure of peace" which the president defined as "A peace that will come when all have a share in its shaping. A peace that will last when all have a stake in its lasting."[12]

The quest for peace combined Nixon's penchant for the grandiloquent with his namedropping:

> We have not achieved perfect peace, which philosophers have been writing about for centuries and which Immanuel Kant described as "perpetual peace". This idea always had enormous appeal. But it will never be achieved, except at diplomatic think tanks and in the grave. During my last meeting with Leonid Brezhnev in the Crimea in 1974, I jotted down this note on a pad of paper: "Peace is like a delicate plant. It has to be constantly tended and nurtured if it is to survive. If we neglect it, it will wither and die."[13]

We should be grateful to the president for giving us a window into the non-importance of summits and to the pretentiousness of it all. But Nixon was not much of a tenderer or nurturer and his political garden soon became over-grown and full weeds, his delicate plant lost in the overgrowth of political reality. The same idea colored Nixon's last meeting with Mao in 1976: "Mao asked me the key question: 'Is peace America's only goal?' I replied that our goal was peace, but that peace was more than the absence of war. 'It must be a peace with justice,' I told Mao."[14] In his memoirs, the president observes: "What I was trying to do, however, was to construct a completely new set of power relationships in the Middle East – not only between Israel and the Arabs, but also among the United States, Western Europe, and the Soviet Union."[15]

In his resignation speech Nixon claimed that he had always worked for peace:

> I have done my very best in all these days since to be true to that pledge. As a result of these efforts, I am confident that the world is a safer place today, not only for the people of America, but for the people of all nations, and that all our children have a better chance than before of living in peace rather than dying in war.
>
> This, more than anything, is what I hoped to achieve when I sought the presidency. This, more than anything, is what I hope will be my legacy to you, to our country, as I leave the presidency.[16]

Nixon was preoccupied by the verdict of history, writing numerous books after his resignation to polish his image and re-establish his reputation, revealing himself as a shallow but persistent thinker. Stephen Ambrose's verdict of Nixon's book *Real Peace*[17] is a fairly accurate description of most of the former president's writing: "*Real Peace* was a string of generalizations and quips that were suitable to a political speech but lacking substance; simplistic assertions, given in short snappy sentences that would have wowed an audience in a speech, made the author look superficial when read on page after page" (. . .) The Result was (. . .) an army of pompous phrases marching over the landscape in search of an idea."[18] But Ambrose and other academics like me were not the intended audience for Nixon, rather the political classes and enlightened public. In this sense, he succeeded magnificently in reaching large audiences and re-establishing his reputation after the nadir of Watergate, so much so that he was on the cover of *Newsweek*, May, 19, 1986 under the headline: "He's back; The Rehabilitation of Richard Nixon."[19]

In his book *Leaders* Nixon leaves no doubt about the importance he attaches to the role of personalities in politics: "In the footsteps of great leaders, we hear the rolling thunder of history." The president compared himself to and modelled himself after French president Charles De Gaulle who when confronted with an issue or a problem:

> using his immense capacity for the mastery of detail, would learn everything there was to know about it. He would then withdraw from his advisers to study and contemplate his decision in solitude. He understood how vitally important having time to think can be for a leader, and at his insistence his staff reserved several hours a day for undisturbed thought.[20]

In office; Nixon did his best to emulate De Gaulle, withdrawing to his hideaway office in the Executive Office Building, curtains drawn, the fireplace going in the heat of an Washington summer, with air conditioning at full blast, the president pondered his foreign policy options in splendid isolation.[21]

For all its contretemps, and it is hard to resist poking fun of Nixon, the key element to Nixon's global structure of peace is his concept of great power restraint. To give the full flavour and justice of this very Nixonian concept, it will be helpful to quote the briefing paper to the president prior to his May 1972 Tehran visit:

> Iran's strength, vitality, bold leadership, and willingness to assume regional responsibility, are a classic example of what the United States under the Nixon Doctrine values highly in an ally. (. . .) The US–Iranian partnership is a crucial pillar of the global structure of peace the US is seeking to build. Your [Nixon's] trips to Peking and Moscow exemplify your effort to develop a secure balance among the great powers. Great-power restraint – which we are seeking to build into the system – devolves more responsibility onto regional powers. The US is counting on Iran to make a major contribution to regional and Third World stability, in the Persian Gulf and indeed in the Middle East and the whole non-aligned world.[22]

Oil was of lesser importance in American relations with Iran. After Nixon's Tehran visit in May 1972, the American–Iranian communiqué grandiloquently stated that the American president and Mrs. Nixon were summoned by "His Imperial Majesty Shahanshah Arya Mehr and Her Imperial Majesty the Shahbanou of Iran" and "were received with exceptional friendliness and warmth by their imperial majesties and by the government and people of Iran." Significantly, after a *tour d'horizon* of the world, nothing less would suffice; the lofty personages deemed it below their dignity to discuss oil politics, testifying to the unimportance of oil in American relations with Iran.[23] This *tour d'horizon*, became as we shall see, a trademark of the shah – refining it again and again in his meetings with American leaders.

The operative concept of Nixon's idea of a global structure of peace was the Nixon doctrine which the president enunciated in Guam in July 1969; the United States would honor its treaty obligations and provide nuclear cover to its allies and economic and military assistance in lieu of American troops. Ostentatiously, the doctrine was intended to cover the American withdrawal from Vietnam, but it also had global implications. Reducing American commitments, the Nixon doctrine called for close American allies to substitute for the United States. In the Persian Gulf, Nixon believed that Iran, and to a lesser degree Saudi Arabia, fitted the job description as regional policemen.[24] Nixon himself was very clear that his doctrine was not a cover for an American retreat: "The Nixon doctrine rather than being a device to get rid of America's world role is one which is devised to make possible for us to play a role – and play it better, more effectively than if we continued the policy of the past in which we assume such a dominant position."[25] To fulfil Iran and Saudi Arabia's new role as regional policemen, Nixon deliberately broke up the successful post-war partnership between western oil companies and western governments, enabling them to finance the necessary military hardware from mostly American and British sources for their new role. The president gave priority to security of supply and not price of oil. With this stroke, the president achieved three things, firstly a structural dependency of Iran and Saudi Arabia on the United States and Great Britain, since neither country had the infrastructure nor the educational level to run their newly important sophisticated military machinery. Huge numbers of American and British nationals were required to keep Iran and Saudi military machines running, turning the Nixon doctrine on its head, increasing the demands of American military personnel rather than decreasing, which was the stated effect. Britain, at the same time, was busy liquidating its position in the region, withdrawing from its last bases in the Persian Gulf on November 30, 1971. But as with the United States, there was an increase in British personnel in the Gulf. In reality, there was a transition from Britain's formal empire with fixed positions to an informal empire, where British influence remained strong, if not paramount. The British added a bold new twist to the Nixonian foundation of policy – the projection of weakness. Britain severely cut down its military presence when leaving its Persian Gulf bases on November 30, 1971 in order to appear unable to prevent the shah of Iran's occupation of the Abu Musa and Tunbs islands. Britain was pledged to protect these islands but in a secret agreement with the shah was in collusion with Iran to divest them from the rulers of Ras al-

Khaimah and Sharjah, Lilliputian sheikdoms that later federated into the United Arab Emirates under the tutelage of Whitehall. Secondly, by seemingly upgrading Saudi Arabia and Iran to allies, their support was more beneficial than from clients falling in line with regional policy objectives. Thirdly, since Japan and Germany had become serious competitors to the United States, but unfortunately in contrast to the United States, had to import practically all their oil, increasing energy prices was an effective way of soaking up their surpluses and reducing their competiveness versus the Americans.[26]

Following the ignominy of Watergate, and resignation in disgrace, Nixon was eager to rehabilitate himself and to maintain influence on the direction of American foreign policy. Nixon's foreign policy assistant from 1990 to 1994 observes: "His post-presidential years were spent trying to affect the course of events and guide American policy so that what he had accomplished for the country during his career was not squandered."[27] Nixon got his chance when president Carter normalized American relations with China in December 1978, writing Carter on December 20, 1978. The former president dismissed the chance of a PRC (Public Republic of China) attack on Taiwan in the immediate future: "I believe the U.S. should publicly go on record that any use of force against Taiwan would irreparably jeopardize our relations with the PRC." If Carter himself felt unable to do so, Congress should not be opposed from protesting. "If the Congress does proceed in that manner I would urge you not to oppose such action publicly and that you privately inform the Chinese of the problem. They will strenuously object, but they will understand because they need us far more than we need them. They also will be impressed by the fact that those who are most strongly pro-Taiwan are also those who are most strongly anti-Soviet."

It would furthermore be important to explain to American allies and friends "that Taiwan was a special case and that the U.S. firmly stands by all its treaty and other commitments and under no circumstances will we renounce a treaty simply because we determine our interests are no longer served by it. (. . .) The Philippines, Indonesia, and Iran in different ways present difficult problems because of their corruption and in varying degrees their denial of human rights. At this time in view of the Taiwan decision; I believe it is important to publicly and privately give them unqalified support. It would be ironical to qualify our support to any country which allows some human rights at a time when we have dramatically moved toward normalization with cooperation with a nation which allows none – the PRC. (. . .) From a purely partisan political standpoint, I would hope you would not take my advice. But I feel that the stakes for America and the world are too high for partisanship as usual. You have a supreme opportunity to lead the nation and the world into a new era of prosperity, peace and justice. To paraphrase Charlie Wilson – what is good for you is good for America, and if it results in many happy returns for you in 1980, you will deserve it." Nixon ended the letter by assuring the president that his letter was private and the former president had no intention of publishing it.[28] Carter replied with a handwritten letter only two days later: "I appreciate your excellent letter, which is very helpful to me."[29] Nixon wrote Carter again following his 'malaise' speech: "This is just a note to say I have had a great deal of empathy for you during this rather difficult period. (. . .) While I disagree with some of your energy proposals I admire the effective way you presented them in your television address. (. . .) Needless to say, as a partisan I want to see a Republican elected in 1980. On the other hand, as an American I want to see our President do well, particularly in the international area."[30]

The election campaign of 1980 and subsequent election of Ronald Reagan opened up greater vistas for Nixon to influence the president and American foreign policy. The former president did not restrict himself to private communications only; 1980 saw the publication of Nixon's most hard-line book to date, *Real War*.[31] The book, according to Stephen Ambrose, "was exactly what the right wing of the Republican Party, and its leader, Ronald Reagan, wanted to hear. In the 1980 campaign, the incumbent President was a Democrat, and thus fair game."[32] For Nixon, courting Reagan was not enough; he took care to stroke senior figures in the future president's team. Edwin Meese, then director of the transition team and later in a White House leadership position, received a personalized copy of *Real War*. Meese thanked the former president profusely: "I am sure it [*Real War*] will become a rich source of reference matter to those of us who entered the world arena. I am particularly grateful to you for your counsel during the long campaign. I would like to think that we might continue to benefit from your advice." The Reaganites saw the importance of keeping up the good side of the former president, Meese concluded that: "we will be doing our very best to merit your continued support."[33]

After the election, Nixon sent the president-elect a long memorandum about staffing the presidency, policy and not the least Nixon' role in the new administration. Giving his gratulations, the former president disclaimed any selfish motives: "As one who has been there and who seeks or wants absolutely nothing except your success in office, I would like to pass on to you some candid observations based on past experience and on intimate knowledge of some of the people you are considering for major positions." As with the publication of *Real War*, Nixon was keen to show how fully he was attuned to Reagan's political priorities. "As you know, I believed before the election that, while foreign policy was to me the most important issue of the campaign, the economic issue was the one which would have the greatest voter impact. Now I am convinced that decisive action on the inflation front is by far the number one priority. Unless you are able to shape up your home base it will be almost impossible to conduct an effective foreign policy."

Nixon made a number of personnel recommendations, many of whom would serve in the Reagan administration, including Caspar Weinberger, secretary of defense and George Shultz, secretary of state from 1982. But here we will focus on the former president's pitch for Alexander Haig as secretary of state. "Whoever is appointed Secretary of State must have a thorough understanding not only of Europe, but of the Soviet Union, China, Japan, and the Mideast, Africa and Latin America. He must also share your general views with regard to the Soviet threat and foreign policy generally. These requirements pretty much limit those who could be considered. Haig meets them all. (. . .) He would be personally loyal to you and would not backbite you on or off the record." Nixon concluded his recommendations with a further expression of selflessness: "As far as my own personal situation is concerned, I do not, as you know, seek any official position. However, I would welcome the opportunity to provide advice in areas where I have special experience to you and to members of you Cabinet and the White House staff where you deem it appropriate. President Eisenhower said to me when I visited him at Walter Reed Hospital after the election of 1968, 'I am yours to command': I now say the same to you. I trust that that can be our relationship in the years ahead."[34] In a handwritten note only five days later, Reagan replied: "I can't thank you enough for the guidelines you gave on personnel – this will be done."[35]

In line with Nixon's concept of a global structure of peace, the former president suggested material to Reagan's inaugural speech. "This is a time not just to defend freedom but to extend it to those who want it wherever they may be – not by the force of arms, but by the power of our example. (. . .) Wars and the fear of war have plagued us over the past 30 years. The time is now for total mobilization of our resources to bring the world the blessings of peace, with the same dedication that we mobilized our efforts to wage war." With this, Nixon neatly combined Reagan's hard-line rhetoric with his idea of a global structure of peace.[36]

Haig was controversial, and when the new secretary of state went into rhetorical overdrive, charging among other things that the Soviets were "wet-nursing third world terrorists", a public backlash caused the White House to distance itself. Nixon rushed to defend his recommended appointee. On March 26, 1981 he wrote the president: "The press flap over the Haig controversy understandably must cause concern to you and even more to members of the White House staff. (. . .) As you have so well demonstrated over your career, the major mark of a big man is his ability to enlist and tolerate other big men on his team." The draft version of the letter continued: "The world is too dangerous to be satisfied with pip-squeaks in any of the important foreign policy positions." Nixon concluded with a ringing endorsement of Haig: "The world is too dangerous to be satisfied with any but the best in the top foreign policy positions."[37]

Haig wanted single-handedly to formulate and implement foreign policy, being the sole spokesperson in foreign affairs for the President. When Haig attempted to take charge, he was thwarted, much to his surprise. The president was not amused: "I discovered only a few months into the administration that Al didn't want anyone other than himself, me included, to influence foreign policy while he was secretary of state. He was never shy about asserting his claim".[38] The incomprehension was mutual, Haig observes in his memoirs: "But to me, the White House was as mysterious as a ghost ship; you heard the creak of the rigging and the groans of timbers and sometimes even glimpsed the crew on the deck. But which of the crew had the helm? Was it Meese, was it [James] Baker, was it someone else? It was impossible to know for sure."[39] Given Haig's experience from the Nixon administration, it is strange that he voluntarily gave up daily access to the president. One historian has described the Nixon White House as a shark tank, where aides fiercely struggled for presidential favors and access, a sign of power in this competitive environment. In the exquisite atmosphere of aquatic predators and Watergate poisoning, Haig thrived. He advanced from aide to National Security Advisor, Henry Kissinger, to White House chief of staff, to, in the eyes of many, *de facto* President, when Watergate crippled Nixon. Some works on the Nixon administration strongly suggest that Haig had a devious side, and that he may have been (wrongly as we know in the aftermath) the famous *Deep Throat* feeding secrets to *Washington Post* journalists Carl Bernstein and Bob Woodward. Haig observed Kissinger outmaneuver Nixon's Secretary of State, William Rogers, for power and influence. With these experiences in mind, Haig voluntarily relinquishing daily access to president Reagan can only be explained by Haig considering the president a political and personal lightweight, holding him in little regard and not needing to pay much attention to Reagan.[40]

But Haig was difficult to defend. Nixon's choice for secretary of state had a knack for alienating friends and foes alike. The British foreign minister noted early in the Reagan administration's tenure: "that Haig has been diminished by recent events in Washington. He appeared curiously unsure of himself in Rome: not the same man who had assured Lord Carrington in Washington in February that 'no tricky Dickies from the White House' would run US foreign policy. Moreover his habit of constantly referring in meetings to difficulties within the Administration struck Lord Carrington as unwise, unhealthy, and damaging to the reputation of the Administration in the closest councils of the Alliance."[41] Haig not only complained to the British but his relations with senior White House staff were 'abrasive'.[42] Undersecretary of state, William Clarke, felt compelled to apologize to the British about Haig: "At the end of the meeting with Lord Carrington this afternoon, Judge Clark had two minutes entirely private conversation. Clark's purpose was to say to Lord Carrington – apparently as an explanation of, and apology for, some of Haig's recent actions statements – that Lord Carrington should know that Mr Haig had been under considerable strain." The apology was deftly handled by the British foreign minister: "In reply, Lord Carrington was effusively complimentary about Mr Haig."[43] While Haig was forced to resign in the summer of 1982, I have found nothing in the declassified record that his mentor, Nixon, are coming to his defence. In any case, however a failure from Reagan's point of view Haig turned out to be, it did not seem to diminish Nixon's effectiveness and influence with the new Republican administration.

Nixon kept up a steady stream of communication with Reagan in all matters large and small, it seems with the express purpose of courting the current occupant in the White House. When the former president returned from a trip to China in the fall of 1982, it spawned a 25-page memorandum to the chief executive. Undersecretary of State William Clarke noted in a covering memorandum to Reagan of September 25, 1981: "Nixon's report is quite interesting and useful as an indicator of Chinese thinking (. . .) [on] the prospects for US–PRC relations and the US–USSR relations."[44] Nixon concluded his report: "What we must recognize is that over the next ten years our major goal should be to do everything possible along with the Japanese and our western European allies to assist the Chinese in their economic programs. Juvenile talk about "playing the China card" should be knocked off. We should make it clear to the Chinese and to the world that even if there were no Soviet threat, we should consider it in our interest to help China to become economically strong so it will better be able to resist any threat posed by the Soviet Union or any other potentially aggressive power."[45] But Nixon did not restrict his communications only to foreign policy or president Reagan. Before the 1982 mid-term election he gave the president this advice: "I do not know your people well – except for 3 or 4, but from all reports they are honest, competent, and personally loyal to you. However, campaigning is just not their bag. You need at least two or three nut cutters who will take on the opposition so that you can take the high road."[46] At the same time, Nixon continued to polish his own public image, and in 1982 he published *Leaders*.[47] This book and *The Real War* were best sellers, and as Jonathan Aitken observes, Nixon "used them as his calling card in the international arena. Over 3,000 copies of *The Real War* and 2,500 copies of *Leaders* were sent as personal gifts to opinion formers in every part of the world. In Britain alone, more than 750 signed copies of these volumes arrived on the desks of Ministers, Members of Parliament, journalists and academics."[48] *Newsweek* had the former president on the cover on May 19, 1986, with the headline: "He's Back", describing a very active former president who "tends his political network and cultivates a new generation of reporters at quiet dinner over fine wine." But this was not enough, for in addition Nixon was writing his seventh book, to "help guide the nation into the 21st century."[49] Nixon, of course, was well aware that his influence was the sum of his public and private utterances. In the Reagan era, Nixon pursued a very public schedule. In the 'nut cutter' letter above, the former president explained that he had summarized on pages 334 to 336 his view on leadership in his last book *Leaders*, urging Reagan to take a look. "The big man [president] is hired for the big decisions, not to fritter away his time on small ones."[50] And it worked, Reagan wrote Nixon on March 11, 1983, commenting on the beneficial effects of *Real War*: "You have done a great service in alerting our nation to the steady, relentless nature of Soviet military expansion, and the need to devote more of our resources to defense. (. . .) Like you, I believe we can halt this one nation arms race and accept genuine, mutual arms reduction only if we show our strong, bipartisan resolve not to let the military balance tip against us. I have appreciated your help in this effort and urge your continued support."[51] But it came at a cost, for not all had forgotten Watergate or was willing to forgive Nixon his transgressions. The *Washington Post* observed on November 12, 1982: "But humble origins and a brain devoid of content are no bar to grandeur in our nation, praise be God, so it is right that Richard Nixon should surpass even Spiro Agnew and his other merry lads in American affections now."[52]

Before the 1985 November Geneva summit, Nixon went into overdrive, writing a playbook for Reagan: "As you meet General Secretary Gorbachev, I think it is important for you to have some surprise cards of your own ready to play. It is vital that we test the new Soviet leadership's attitudes in order to gauge the range of fresh possibilities that may exist. Personal initiatives by you, free of the bureaucratic trappings that so often encumber communication between governments, could prove decisive." Nixon concluded the letter by stating that he was at the president's disposal to discuss all and any initiatives "on which you feel I can be helpful."[53] The playbook even included a document titled, "Elements of a Joint Communique", that should include a major reduction in the parties respective nuclear forces, and reduction in future nuclear tests. Nixon's communique included even a sop to the Russians worried about Reagan's Strategic Defence Initiative: "The parties will undertake joint research and analyses to determine whether and how defensive technologies might eventually be introduced on a cooperative basis to diminish reliance on the threat of offensive nuclear weapons."[54] Nixon even wrote the script on how Reagan should handle himself at Geneva: "The rash of contradictory statements on and off the record by officials purporting to speak for the Administration have disserved the President. (. . .) premature publicity is also detrimental in another way. Background statements, apparently emanating from lower level bureaucrats, have indicated in detail what agreements are likely to be made at Geneva. Speculation that the President is prepared to make agreements even on such issues as annual summits removes the element and suspense which is essential in getting the maximum out of an announcement of an agreement when one is made. Particularly where a minor agreement is concerned, the element of surprise is needed to make it newsworthy at all. Above all, the President should not be placed in the position where all that he does at the summit is to sign agreements which pip-squeaks in the bureaucracy will gleefully later claimed to have worked out in advance. (. . .) It is vitally important that the impression be created that the President is the one in charge and that he is not being programmed by his subordinates."[55] Reagan's response was effusive: "I have read and reread your thoughtful overview of where we stand with the Russians going into this meeting and appreciate your providing me with one of the most thoughtful analyses of contemporary Soviet behaviour I have read." Reagan explained that he wanted to engage the Soviets in a broad dialogue and seek to establish a "more cooperative relationship."[56]

Nixon kept up a steady stream of letters, advice and memorandums during Reagan's presidency, combined with appropriate doses of sycophancy and flattering as when responding to Reagan's birthday wishes: "Nineteen eighty-seven is an especially significant year for me because it was just over 40 years ago that I began my political career as a freshman member of the 80th Congress. As I look back over the past four decades, there is nothing that is more heartwarming than your continued expressions of friendship."[57] The process continued with Reagan's successors and Nixon remained the supreme political animal virtually to his dying day.

CHAPTER
II

Jimmy Carter in the Oval Office

"Ever since my boyhood days on the farm, I have enjoyed the solitude and beauty of the early morning hours. As President I established a routine of rising early, around six o'clock, and going to the Oval Office a half-hour later. I would begin my day with coffee, an open fire in the winter, the morning newspapers, and the overnight report from the Secretary of State, all of which were waiting for me when I arrived."[1] Carter's successor Ronald Reagan did not have the same enjoyment from the beauty and solitude of the early morning, usually receiving his White House operator wake-up call at 8 a.m.[2] Carter's national security advisor, Zbigniew Brzezinski, had the president rising even earlier, White House operator waking the president at 5.30 giving him the time, temperature and Washington weather. The president entered the Oval Office half an hour later, drinking coffee and reading the president's daily brief and newspapers in winter in front of the fire place.[3] In his diaries, published in 2011, the morning routine differed, the president claimed to get up usually at 6:30 to enjoy the early morning solitude Carter style, at the same time multitasking to enrich his cultural life: "In the inner White House office we established a high-fidelity sound system, and for eight or ten hours every day I listen to classical music. Records are changed by Susan Clough, my secretary."[4] But Carter may have embellished the truth a little on his strong Protestant ethic of a work habits. Ronald Reagan's personal assistant, Jim Kuhn, would later observe: "Some critics unfairly contrasted Reagan's work habits to those of Carter, (. . .) When you work in the White House, you learn much about its previous residents, and I was told by reliable sources that Carter would actually retreat to his study and go back to sleep on the couch."[5]

Despite all the condiments, Jimmy Carter's main interest and concern was Jimmy Carter, mercilessly exposed by his former speechwriter James Fallow, in an article in the *The Atlantic*, "The Passionless Presidency." Fallow observed Carter speaking in Chicago: "He was speaking with gusto because he was speaking about the subject that most inspired him: not what he proposed to do, but who he was. Where Lyndon Johnson boasted of schools built and children fed, where Edward Kennedy holds out the promise of the energies he might mobilize and the ideas he might enact, Jimmy Carter tells us that he is a good man. His positions are correct, his values sound." No detail was too small to concern this president, personally reviewing all requests to use the White House tennis court. No wonder, according to Fallow: "The central idea of the Carter administration is Jimmy Carter himself."[6]

Carter both complained and bragged about the workload and his capacity to work. On December 18, 1978 he wrote in his diary: "Paperwork this week is unbelievable. I work from 5:00 a.m. and can't clean out my in-box before I'm exhausted, and have something scheduled every night." Adding to the stress was "a horrible attack of hemorrhoids" . . . "I could hardly bear the pain." Alleviating the latter was strong pain killers and an injection of Demorol, while speed-reading classes eased the workload. On top of it all the presidential couple tried to learn Spanish: "The last thing Rosalynn and I do every day is to read a chapter in the Bible in Spanish." On the other hand, the amount of work was easily manageable. For the weekend October 29 to 30, 1977, at Camp David, Carter noted: "I read four books over the week-end and had plenty of time to watch movies, play tennis, ride bikes, swim, and have long bull sessions with the top staff people."[7] Whatever else he did, Carter was not in the slightest doubt of his own importance: "Had my seventh press conference, which I enjoy and believe they give me an opportunity to both educate the American people and give them a sense of participation in government."[8] When he gave his now infamous crisis of confidence speech on July 15, 1979, the president alluded to the same themes: "I have promised you a president who is not isolated from the people, who feels your pain and who shares your dreams and draws his strength and wisdom from you." But the message was far from uplifting, the United States faced a 'nearly invisible' threat: "It is a crisis of confidence. It is a crisis that strikes at the very heart and soul and spirit of our national will. We can see this crisis in the growing doubt about the meaning of our own lives and the loss of a unity and purpose for our nation."[9] Carter was concerned that his was a departure from the Imperial Presidency: "I tried in many other ways to convince the people that barriers between them and top officials in Washington were being broken down. A simpler lifestyle, less ostentation, more accessibility to the press and public – all these suited the way I had always lived."[10] But for all his empathies and eagerness to work for the American people, Carter was a demanding task master. The following quote is an example of his leadership style (and the Carter Library is studded with similar notes):

"Phil [JC's personal assistant]–
Find form for 15 min speech re Persian Gulf. Zbig has base text.
Zbig will get State; Defense to sign off on it.
Expedite
    JC
cc Zbig"[11]

His leadership style created problems of their own, but was initially in response to what at the time was seen as the excess centralization of the Nixon White House. H. R. Haldeman was Nixon's chief of staff and this is his own job description: "Every President needs a son of a bitch, and I am Nixon's. I am his buffer and I am his bastard. I get done what he wants done and I take the heat instead of him."[12] Nixon wanted a tightly organized administration, laying down the law to the Cabinet on June 29, 1971. "From now on, Haldeman is the lord high executioner. Don't you come whining to me when he tells you to do something. He will do it because I asked him to and you're to carry it out."[13] In order to distance himself from Nixon and to ensure a wide range of advice, the president was determined to be his own chief of staff. On this Robert A. Strong comments: "Carter's attraction to this type of organization was only partly a matter of symbolism. He genuinely enjoyed being at the center of a complex array of policy problems and placed himself in that position because it suited his intellectual curiosity, his desire to solve national problems, and his methodical work habits, It did not, however always serve his political interests." But the activism came with a price: "Having the president as the active decision-maker on a large number of issues reinforced the public perception of a chief executive bogged down in detail and unable to distinguish between important and trivial presidential tasks."[14]

Carter set up an elaborate apparatus to deal with foreign policy. There were regular weekly Monday lunches with vice president Walter Mondale, Friday breakfasts with the principals, foreign minister Cyrus Vance, secretary of defense Harold Brown, and national security advisor Zbigniew Brzezinski, Mondale and Hamilton Jordan the president's chief domestic advisor. The system was outlined in detail by Brzezinski to Carter, where the president was at the top of the apex: "in overall charge, through frequent and direct contact with the Secretary of State, the Secretary of Defense, and Assistant for National Security Affairs, and also through written reports staffed through the formal NSC system." Brzezinski thereafter goes on to describe the internal workings of the National Security Council, to which the president added in his own handwriting: "Reports reviewed and modified or approved by the President." The principals – Vance, Brown and Brzezinski – had their own lunch "to resolve sub-Presidential issues."[15] But that was not the end of the eating, the president even had a regularly scheduled Thursday luncheon with his wife. "As usual, at lunch with Rosalynn we discuss issues parallel to the ones I discuss with my major foreign and domestic advisors, plus a few personal matters, quite often financial in nature; our family interrelationships; White House entertainment; guest lists for state dinners and other events; and she brings me correspondence of interest to both of us."[16] Rosalynn claims their lunch was on Wednesday, but in any case both of them explain that it was a weekly affair: "I made lists of subjects so that when I went to the Oval Office, I had an agenda."[17]

Huge amounts of papers, studies and reports were thus grinding through the bureaucracy. But what came out of it? The Carter administration was largely proactive in its responses to foreign policy challenges, and as far away from the George W. Bush doctrine of preemptive strikes and war as it possibly could come.[18] Despite the seemingly sophisticated foreign policy apparatus, the administration did little and perhaps realistically had little chance to prevent the major crises that erupted in 1979, in Iran and Afghanistan – crises that seemingly caught the administration off guard, not being able to develop effective policies to meet these challenges, and giving the public the impression of engulfing the Carter presidency. While Carter's policy of restraint, particularly in connection with the Iran hostage crisis, had scores of detractors, but so did the George W. Bush preemptive wars, so there is, perhaps, something to be said for an administration that was reluctant to use force. Walter Mondale lauded the president at the Carter administration's farewell dinner: "We told the truth. We obeyed the law. We kept the peace."[19]

Even when in his hometown, a large apparatus travelled with the president: "While I'm in Plains I have a fairly large staff. I get a briefing each morning from the State Department, a separate one from the CIA, dispatches fairly frequently from the National Security Council, telephone communications with my staff in the White House."[20] But despite of or perhaps because of the elaborate system, high Carter officials had difficulties in trying to cope with the demands placed on them, as Brzezinski admits in his memoirs: "The general reader probably cannot imagine the extraordinary pressures of time under which those engaged in shaping America's global policy operate. The President's advisers are like jugglers: moving from meeting to meeting, from topic to topic, dealing with developments as they occurred in an increasingly disorganized world."[21] Operating under these conditions gives little room for long-range thinking and planning and confirms the picture of an administration largely reactive to crises. The whole system was designed to keep the president involved in foreign policy making on a daily basis.[22] Not only the stresses of time but an often obsessively involved president reinforced the structural impediments against strategic thinking and planning.

Carter's sometime pettiness, obsession with detail and his main concern being about Jimmy Carter, may have had something to do with the problems the president encountered in foreign and domestic policy. Brzezinski clearly liked and admired his boss: "His memory was phenomenal, his reading voracious, and his thirst for knowledge unquenchable." But the president could also be extremely pedantic; correcting spelling errors on staff memos, gave Brzezinski a list of his staff's minor security violations that the president had learned from the security office: "it showed the extent to which he was still a Navy lieutenant who very much enjoyed keeping the ship in trim and proper shape." The national security advisors thought the president's leadership style warranted even more serious criticism. "Moreover, he [Carter] involved himself excessively in too many secondary matters, and to make matters worse, he resisted, and quite sharply at times, any effort by me to promote genuine delegation of authority." [23]

Still, initially, the system worked quite well, as Brzezinski observed to the president on December 28, 1978: "I believe that as we enter 1979, you, quite literally, have [a] historic chance to start shaping a new global system, with the United States as its predominant coordinator if no longer paramount power. The fulfillment of that opportunity depends critically on how you play the China/Soviet Union issues, and also on how you respond to the deteriorating situation along the Indian Ocean."[24] Carter, with the strategic underpinnings from his national security advisor sought to refine the Nixonian concept of the global structure of peace to develop his own version of an American grand strategy. American policy towards the Soviet was, according to Brzezinski, reciprocal accommodation in which several policy strands were part; containment, resistance to Soviet indirect expansion, ideological competition, and, most important of all, "creation of a framework <u>within which</u> the Soviet Union can accommodate with us, or face the prospect of isolating itself globally." This approach had the added benefit of fitting the "U.S.–Soviet relationship into a cooperative context of U.S.–European–Japanese and now also Chinese, relations." While seeking a cooperative and reciprocal relationship with the Soviets, but if such a relationship failed to materialize "as it has been on Africa, Cuba, and the Persian Gulf, we are prepared to assert our interests." Carter's human rights policy was part of the strategy: "It means affirming our position on human rights, which greatly increases the moral appeal of the United States and provides an effective response to Soviet ideology."[25] As we shall see, Reagan would to a large extent continue in this grand strategic vein. Brzezinski in this instance was inspired by concepts developed by Nixon previously. Nixon's global structure of peace rested on three pillars; the first being great power restraint which Nixon sought to build into the international system with his openings to the Soviet Union and China. Secondly, on the Nixon doctrine where the US would continue to provide military and economic assistance as well as coverage under the American nuclear umbrella, but not American troops. Thirdly, more responsibility would then evolve to American allies. Iran being the perfect example under Nixon.[26] Even though, particularly with the American emphasis on human rights, United States relations with the shah and Iran (as we shall see below) was more complicated and, perhaps, more convoluted than under Nixon, Carter nevertheless failed to develop any alternative. Despite being somewhat unhappy with the relationship, Iran remained an American pillar in the Gulf under Carter before the shah was forced into exile.

There are indications that Carter sought to establish a quadripartite leadership group of the western powers, the United States, of course, the United Kingdom, France and Germany, with himself as a kind of chairman of the board or *primus inter pares*, with Valery Giscard d'Estaing, president of France, German chancellor Helmut Schmidt, James Callaghan, prime minister United Kingdom as his peers. The height of this cooperative effort came at the Guadeloupe summit meeting, January 5–6, 1979, between the principals mentioned above. Life was still good, international affairs fairly tranquil, even problematic Iran seemed manageable, the US expecting to have a mostly friendly regime there even after the departure of the shah. Vance briefed the president prior to the Guadeloupe summit: "Your meeting with Schmidt, Giscard and Callaghan comes at time of growing readiness on [the] part of Western nations to cooperate in solutions for common problems," cooperation that went beyond the traditional NATO alliance. "They will look to you for guidance and leadership." The summit provided an excellent avenue for Carter to assert his leadership: "The Guadeloupe meeting offers you an invaluable opportunity to expand your personal relations with Giscard, Schmidt and Callaghan; to explore with unusual freedom and candor problems of common concerns; to build a better understanding of each other's political imperatives; and, finally to maintain their confidence in the undiminished strength, authority and creativity of the United States."[27] While recent OPEC price increases would probably bring higher inflation and slower growth, the problems should not be overdramatized Vance argued: "However, we still anticipate a better-balanced global payments pattern in 1979, the key to which is a reduction in the Japanese and German surpluses and the US deficit – primarily because of a slowdown in the US growth rate." But the crisis in Iran escalated dramatically whilst the president was at Guadeloupe,[28] contributing to lesser success of the meetings than anticipated and in the long term whittling away at Carter's leadership of the western quartet. But this was not readily apparent when the summit ended, and is also reflected in the letter from Carter to Callaghan: "I found our talks most helpful and am grateful once again for the opportunity to personally exchange thoughts. As you know, our periodic private discussions are important to me. Let me express once more my best wishes for the New Year. I draw confidence from the spirit which we started the year in Guadeloupe."[29]

But with a problem there usually comes an opportunity. Brzezinski, the conceptualizer, noted after the fall of the shah: "This political and psychological crisis can only be contained by forceful and purposeful U.S. action." The United States should "develop a consultative security framework for the Middle East, "basically with regimes friendly to the US. "Saudi Arabia, because of its wealth and its weakness, is in a category by itself and requires special attention." Brzezinski envisioned the new security relationship en par with the Truman Doctrine, the Marshall Plan and NATO. However such an effort, while urgently necessary, would be costly in time and money.[30] But this was not to be.

The British ambassador to Washington, Nicolas Henderson, reported of the eventful year 1979 in his annual report: "When Carter himself, in an extraordinary mid-year exercise of televised self-analysis, spoke of the "spiritual and political malaise afflicting the country", he touched off a debate about the morale of the American nation. His critics accuse him of trying to shift responsibility for what they describe as his own failure of leadership onto an unresponsive people. In addition, the president faced serious challenges on his oil policies: "He knows that if he is to reduce oil consumption and hence the US's dependence on OPEC he will have to let oil prices rise to market levels, impose heavy taxation on the consumer and stimulate an ambitious programme of alternative fuels."[31] Richard Thornton is caustic about Carter's oil policies, claiming the crisis of 1979 was almost a repeat of the 1974 oil crisis, and for the same purpose to slow down the economies of Germany and Japan to the benefit of the United States: "The principal means employed to make the adjustments was to raise still higher the price of oil, but evidence suggests that the scheme got out of control, only partially accomplished the desired outcome, and actually backfired on the president."[32] Here Carter seems to have pilfered a page from Nixon's playbook, but the execution left something to be desired. Carter readily admits in his memoirs that US domestic oil prices had to rise in order "to stimulate American production and encourage conservation, but the increase needed to be brought about in a predictable and orderly fashion, so that consumers of petroleum products would be protected from unreasonable fuel bills issued by an uncontrolled semimonopoly."[33] The West, the United States and the United Kingdom assigned the blame for their oil woes to the different Arab potentates, who willingly played their part, as Linda Blandford notes: "We picture them coasting out of Harrods or the Playboy Club, wallets exploding, desperate to unload their petrodollars."[34] In the end Carter failed to gain a second term as president, a failure John Dumbrell attributes squarely to the president himself: "By November 1980, the American people had simply endured too many Presidentially-defined crises from which the President seemed unable to rescue them."[35] But far greedier than the Arab producers were the western governments which used the oil crises to impose heavy taxes on their own consumers, to a much larger degree than OPEC had ever done, hiding behind the fig leaf of protecting the environment. The president's mishandling of the 1979 energy crisis points to the larger problems of his leadership, are for lack of a better term, the paradox of American power – a paradox neatly outlined by Robert Gates, secretary of defense under George W. Bush and Obama, in his recent memoirs. Gates claims that visiting Jeddah in August 2007, he and the United States were chided by king Abdullah for being weak, not willing to chastise Iran. Gates responded angrily: "I also told him that what he considered America's greatest weakness – showing restraint – was actually great strength because we could crush any adversary. I told him that neither he nor anyone else should ever underestimate the strength and power of the United States: those who had – Imperial Germany, Nazi Germany, Imperial Japan, and the Soviet Union – were all now in the ashcan of history."[36] Precisely. The power is there, always has been, what is needed is its proper application. And this might be Carter's unintended addition to the Nixonian grand strategy: failure to apply American power properly or to any demonstrable effect or to a demonstrable positive result for the United States. Leaving morals aside, the question being, of course, how to deploy its tremendous arsenal to the American advantage.

The debacle following revolutionary Iran's seizure of the American embassy in Tehran is a case in point. Khomeini's followers, who took American embassy personnel hostages on November 4, 1979, claimed that the American embassy in Tehran was a den of spies. In reality at that time there were only three CIA agents in the embassy, and only one of them spoke Farsi.[37] The CIA presence was hardly more than a bare minimum, but it fitted the conspiracy theories of the opponents of the United States, creating a strawman for all their anger and frustration by making the United States much more powerful than it actually was at the time in Iran. One wonders what kind of benefits successive American administrations drew from this incorrect portrayal of US power and influence. On the other hand, when the United States really applied itself, as in the Carter administration's increased engagement with Oman (see chapter IX) the Americans had almost unlimited power to bear, potentially completely drowning out the British presence in Oman. But that was perhaps one of the key problems for president Carter as a foreign policy maker: American power was tremendous but also an unwieldy instrument to apply properly. In Iran and Oman, president Carter clearly had difficulties in administrating the proper dosages. For all his bluster of being anti-Nixon, emphasizing human rights, Carter to a large degree aped Nixon's policies down to increasing oil prices to help local allies, particularly Saudi Arabia whose rulers were in constant need of stroking, and squeezing the main American international competitors Germany and Japan. Then, as with Nixon, America's western allies imported practically all oil they used domestically, in sharp contrast to the limited quantities imported by the US which in addition was blessed with a large domestic production where the allies had none. Increased energy prices would therefore soak up much of Japan and Germany's economic surplus to the benefit of the United States. The effort backfired badly, as we have seen courtesy of Richard Thornton's arguments, because of the president's poor execution of the policy. Concomitant with these efforts, national security advisor Zbigniew Brzezinski was busy producing memorandums trying to conceptualize the administration's policies and explain what Carter was really up to. In the end Carter's failures by far outweighed any successes he may have achieved. Carter presided over the breakdown of détente, in contrast to Nixon and Kissinger who used the American opening to China as an inducement for the Soviets to improve relations with the US. Carter suffered the ignominy of China playing him against the Soviets, by invading Vietnam after Deng Xiaoping had visited the United States and informing a non-protesting president of China's intention to do so. The president was thereafter seen as at a minimum, tacitly at least, giving the green light for the Chinese attack on Vietnam. Carter's conduct of foreign policy was marked by poor alliance and client management. For example, relations with German chancellor Helmut Schmidt soured, while the president handled American relations with Iran badly. And all this in combination with an oil policy that misfired both internationally and domestically, and failure to adequately address the issues confronted by the rising of Islamic fundamentalism. Islamic fundamentalism was not one size fits all: homegrown in Iran; used in a domestic power struggle in Saudi Arabia; state sponsored in Libya and Pakistan; while Islamic fundamentalists were American allies in Afghanistan after the Soviet invasion.

There is no denial that the end of 1979 was a turning point for the Carter administration: The last two months of 1979 saw dramatic expressions of radical or fundamentalist Islam. In rapid succession, Iranian students occupied the American embassy in Tehran, followed by the occupation of the Holy Mosque in Mecca by Saudi Islamic fundamentalists (an act claimed by the new Iranian leader Aytollah Khomeini and his followers to be instigated by the Americans, to which incensed Muslims burned down the American embassies in Tripoli and Islamabad in addition to attacking the American consulate in Karachi, the American Library in Lahore as well as the British consulate in Rawalpindi). The year 1979 ended with the Soviet invasion of Afghanistan and the rise of the anti-communist but pro-Islamic mudjahedin guerillas. Fundamentalist Islam takes many shapes and forms. In addition to the well known Iranian example, the occupiers of the Mecca Mosque were grandsons of the tribal chieftains that fought against king Saud when he forcefully united Saudi Arabia in the 1920s. In Libya and Pakistan the regimes ruthlessly used Islam to mobilize anti-western sentiment and solidify their own positions, while in Afghanistan, as long as the Soviets remained, the guerillas were *de facto* allies of the West.

The Soviet Union invaded Afghanistan in December 1979. The invasion as such is of little concern to us here and in the context of this study only important in so far its affects Anglo-American relations in the Persian Gulf. One obvious consequence was the Carter Doctrine which the president announced in his June 23, 1980 State of the Union address: "An attempt by an outside force to gain control of the Persian Gulf region will be regarded as an assault on the vital interests of the United States and will be repelled by any means necessary, including military force."[38] Brzezinski would later claim that the United States enticed the Soviets into Afghanistan by secretly supporting the Mujahedin six months prior to the invasion in order to give the Russians their Vietnam.[39] But in a memorandum to the president immediately after the invasion Brzezinski discounted the policy of creating a Soviet "Vietnam" in Afghanistan; the guerillas were to poorly organized and led, without sanctuaries, organized army and central government as in North Vietnam, furthermore. "They have limited foreign support in contrast to the enormous amount of arms that flowed to the Vietnamese from both the Soviet Union and China."[40] Many writers see it as the natural order of things that the US replaced the UK in the Persian Gulf with the announcement of the Carter doctrine. Thereafter, the United States would move with full force into the region; in this thinking there is direct line and connection between the Carter doctrine and the first Gulf war in 1991. After the Carter doctrine the remaining vestiges of British influence would mostly wither away. What is less well understood is that Britain under the coverage of the American umbrella actually extended its presence and influence in the Persian Gulf; a case in point is the Anglo-Saudi arms deal of 1985.

While Brzezinski has the reputation he was not the only strategic thinker in the administration. Secretary of state Cyrus Vance sent a memorandum to the president on January 29, 1980, entitled, "Blueprint for the Implementation of Your State of Union Message." On the United Kingdom Vance noted that the British easily aligned themselves with the new found American interest in the Persian Gulf, with the deployment of extra naval units and assisting the Carter administration in getting access to Oman. "The UK is planning more active and frequent naval and air deployments to the region and we will be coordinating our respective plans to ensure they are mutually reenforcing." At the same time the Americans were to respect the local culture: "Emphasize American willingness to cooperate with all Islamic countries, American understanding of Islamic values, and American sensitivity to Islamic concerns about levels of US presence in the region." This was to be combined with a public relations campaign in the United States in support of Islamic values. But this was not all, there was also a charm offensive to be conducted abroad: "We will continue our efforts to strengthen ties with all Islamic states, including the radical Arabs such as Libya, Iraq, and Algeria." And this comes right after the attack and burning of three American embassies in the Moslem world within a month at the end of 1979.[41]

Whatever problems the United States had in the Middle East, Islam was not to blame as the president noted in a speech on February 7, 1980: "I have been struck . . . by the human and moral values which Americans as a people share with Islam. We share, first and foremost, a deep faith in one Supreme Being. We are all commanded by him to faith, compassion and justice. We have a common respect and reverence for law . . . On the basis of both values and interests, the natural relationship between Islam and the United States is one of friendship . . . We have the deepest respect and reverence for Islam."[42] With every crisis or problem there usually comes an opportunity. Margaret Thatcher had no intention of letting the British position in the Persian Gulf wither on the wane. On the contrary, her stated goal was to make Britain great again. She forcefully and cleverly exploited the Carter doctrine to strengthen Britain's position in the Persian Gulf.

III

Margaret Thatcher
takes Charge

Preceding Reagan by more than five years, ever since her election as leader of the Conservative Party in 1975, Thatcher's first priority was to strengthen the British economy which was combined with a strong opposition to the Soviet Union. As her biographer John Campbell explains: "Thus the struggle for the British economy was part of a struggle against Communism."[1] Margaret Thatcher expounded on her governing philosophy when meeting American legislators on December 17, 1979, that her approach "to all her policies was dominated by the belief that people in the West were privileged to live in free societies, with freedom under the law, which promoted human dignity and economic prosperity. All that she did was dominated by her determination to protect and extend those freedoms." Furthermore, the United Kingdom fully supported the US, Thatcher citing the British position towards Iran. "The special relationship was indefinable, but it existed and gave the Americans the right to expect to be able to count on Britain."[2] From these more philosophical underpinnings came a more assertive British foreign policy, as noted in an American briefing paper for the upcoming June 1980 Venice summit: "To counter the Soviet threat in the Gulf area, Britain is considering a return to an 'East of Suez' role, beefing up naval forces in the region and possibly returning to naval bases used during Britain's previous presence in the region. The British are also assisting US defense efforts in the Gulf by joining in the upgrading of Diego Garcia and helping the United States find additional facilities."[3] But while Thatcher would accelerate British arms sales, the Labour government had been no slouch. By 1979 British arms production employed about 300,000 workers or one per cent of the labor force, and accounted for about 3.5 per cent of total British exports.[4] While Carter might be enjoying his early morning snooze in the Oval office and was believed to have a rather lax personal style, nobody ever accused Thatcher of not working enough. Some suggests that she could have benefitted from more sleep, rest and more vacation time instead of driving herself too hard at the cost of political effectiveness.[5] One of her biographers note: "She had no idea how to relax. She had no hobbies, no hinterland and no close friends with an 'old shoe' quality of comfortable familiarity. Recharging her batteries was a practice she had never heard of. She kept going at full throttle on a combination of extra adrenalin and extra work."[6] But politicians whatever their color or stripe always claim they work hard. Nixon, for instance, wanted to gain political credit for his work ethic, writing his speech writer William Safire: "It has been suggested to me that we capitalize upon the work habits of the President-elect: long hours of work, delayed dinners, eighteen-hour days, late reading, no naps, perfunctory and very short lunch and breakfast times (frequently five or ten minutes)."[7] Few if any politicians turn down chances for reelection or promotion, however exhausted they claim to be; their claim to hard work should therefore be taken with a grain of salt.

But her philosophy clearly had also a practical content, British trade with the Middle East increased dramatically after 1981, often spurred by a prime minister taking a keen interest in promoting British exports to the region. The key was Saudi Arabia, which took nearly £2,000 million of British exports in 1987, the most important being sales of British military and civilian airplanes. The foundation was the announcement on September 26, 1985 of a British sale to Saudi Arabia "of no less than 132 British military aircraft, including seventy-two Tornados."[8] This was the so-called *Al-Yamamah* deal, the largest ever to British manufacturers to date.[9] Needless to say, this deal must have been a tremendous boost to British influence in Saudi Arabia. Thatcher, like the Conservative governments of yesteryear (Macmillan comes to mind when he restored relations with Saudi Arabia in January 1963 resulting in a tremendous increase of British influence on the Arabian Peninsula), now drew a rabbit of similar size from her handbag. Mark Phythian argues that the Saudis, despite Reagan ramming AWACS (Airborne Warning and Control System) through the senate in 1981, turned to Britain because of the conditions attached to American arms sales and the role of the American Israeli Public Affairs Committee (AIPAC).[10] But this deal presaged a long and often tempestuous Anglo-American relationship over Saudi Arabia, going all the way back to Britain being pushed out of the kingdom after 1945 and all the vicissitudes over the Buraimi oasis. However, rapprochement over Saudi Arabia began with the Anglo-American air consortium in 1965.[11] *Al-Yamamah* should properly be regarded as the continuum of the 1965 air consortium.

The prime minister often took personal charge to promote the sale of British military equipment. One prime example is how she pushed the sales to the United Arab Emirates, complaining of the bureaucracy's lackluster performance. "She wished to see that whatever was necessary to win the order was done."[12] Writing sheikh Zaid on December 22, 1981, the prime minister was grateful that the sheikh was willing to receive the delegation led by the minister of state, Douglas Hurd, on such a short notice: "As Mr. Hurd will explain to you, this contract is extremely important to us not just [as] a matter of trade but for the contribution it will make to the development of our defence industry and therefore our ability to help you in the future."[13] But this was part of a larger British sales effort: "The Prime Minister has made it clear on several occasions recently that she and her colleagues attach importance to increasing the sale of British defence equipment overseas." The effort was three-pronged: a progressive removal of constraints on sales, including a more relaxed attitude towards human rights violations in the buyer country; an increased sales effort; and, finally, " a review of our arms procurement policy with a view to simplify specifications to make equipment more readily saleable overseas."[14] Increased sales was not only about exporting more, it certainly had a political component. "Together with our programme of military training assistance, arms sales are a cost effective way of providing continued support for pro-western regimes." Sales could also be used to sustain friendship and good political relations for Britain.[15] Few if any British prime ministers had made the connection so explicit as Thatcher: the connection between buying British military equipment and receiving UK military assistance. In fact, to get British military assistance you had to buy British military equipment.

In her memoirs the prime minister had some interesting observations on Britain's place in the world, explaining the effect of the Suez crisis on British perceptions on their global position. Prior to the crisis the British leadership had exaggerated its power to influence world affairs, but after the crisis British policy makers were perceived to have less power and influence than was actually the case. "The truth – that Britain was a middle ranking power, given unusual influence by virtue of its historical distinction, skilled diplomacy and versatile military forces, but greatly weakened by economic decline –seemed too complex for sophisticated people to grasp."[16] The prime minister is perhaps too modest, not only taking upon herself the role of arms sales woman supreme but also seeking to keep and restore and possibly even expand British influence as much as possible. A case in point is the almost turning around of British influence in the United Arab Emirates, as the British ambassador, David Roberts, explained in his annual report to Carrington of 1980, who noted after a certain erosion of British influence after the withdrawal in 1971, recent events had almost completely reversed the process. Behind this was the prime minister who forcefully intervened to change the lackluster performance of the British men on the spot in the UAE, and also to prevent France from stealing a march on British arms manufactures. "She wished to see that whatever was necessary to win the order was done."[17]

According to Roberts, when the Iran–Iraq war broke out in September 1980, both Britain and the UAE feared that hostilities might spread to the other side of the Gulf. Oman had given Iraq permission to use its territory to launch offensive operations against Iran. Sultan Qaboos had a willing accomplice in the ruler of Ras al Khaimah, who was eager to recover the Tunbs islands from Iran, after the shah had snatched them in 1971. On October 1, 1980 ambassador Roberts learned that France had promised to give the UAE assistance in case of an attack from Iran. Ten days later, Carrington authorized the ambassador to give similar assurances on behalf of the British government, and also to send in secret a MoD team to assess UAE defensive needs. This was followed up by visits in rapid and coordinated sequence first by John Moberly

from the Foreign and Commonwealth Office, providing the necessary political assurances, thereafter the Director of Military Assistance Office, general
Perkins, who started a process to upgrade UAE air defenses to the highest state
of readiness, to finally, "the Chief of Defence Staff, Admiral of the Fleet Sir
Terence Lewin, who visited the Emirates from the 3rd to the 5th of November
on a long planned trip and splendidly reinforced the effect of the previous
visits." According to ambassador David Roberts the rulers of the emirate
uniformly sang praises for the British effort: "Shaikh Zaid himself set it out in
most detail. Our help was a little tardy but most welcome. It was only tardy
because they had expected their oldest friend to be first in the field. But now
we had restored the traditional relationship; and they preferred help from us
to that of the French or the Americans. They would always remember what
we had done for them." The rulers were much relieved, having felt much to
their dismay a loss of British interest after 1971, in favor of commercial policies: "They could not accustom themselves to the overthrow of the highly
successful Pax Britannica which had maintained security from any external
threat for over 150 years." The renewed trust in Britain provided, of course,
an excellent opportunity to sell British military equipment to the emirates.
"Similarly, on the commercial front, we might at the right moment apply judi-
cious pressure in favor of a British bid for some important contract in the
construction or oil industries."[18]

Miers in the Foreign and Commonwealth Office argued that Britain should
no longer leave Abu Dhabi in benign neglect: "We must cultivate the ruling
family of Abu Dhabi more than in recent years." The planned 1981 visit of
prime minister Thatcher could do some good for British commercial
prospects, telling the local leadership flat out "about the need not to see our
offers of military co-operation rewarded by undue preference for the defence
equipment of our rivals."[19] As Roberts noted in his annual review for 1980, the
Iran–Iraq war was not only a problem but also an opportunity for Britain: "The
war which began in late September between Iraq and Iran advanced our relations more than any event since the visit of the Queen in early 1979. (. . .) The
UAE let us know by unorthodox channels that they hoped for some assurance
that, if the war spread to them, we would help. They wanted moral rather than
material support at that stage." The British response was, as we have seen,
rapid and positive, assuring the UAE "that if they were attacked we could offer
direct aid to defend them. Shaikh Zaid himself and others stated that we had
restored in their eyes our old position, which our withdrawal from the Gulf had
seemed to diminish if not extinguish."[20]

Prior to Thatcher's meeting with United Arab Emirates oil minister, Mana
al Otaiba, the briefing memorandum deemed it important that "it will be valuable if he can hear from the Prime Minister a firm expression of our
determination to help our old friends in the Gulf in whatever ways we can and
not to let it be thought that we have in any way lost interest in the Gulf states,
their defence, their commercial markets or their regional concerns."[21]
Incidentally, UK commitments went much deeper and longer than the 1981

British assurances to the UAE. The Reagan administration was advised in January 1984 of UK measures in case of expanded Iran – Iraq hostilities. British Gulf partners were pledged intensive efforts in mine counter-measures in addition to "a more active role in providing security for offshore oil facilities in the Gulf, since Britain has trained commandos to deal with North Sea oil rig security measures." Sheikh Zayid informed the British that he counted "on dispatch of British troops to the UAE at a moment's notice in a crisis."[22] The events above provided an excellent starting point for Thatcher's April 1981 tour of the Persian Gulf.

The Persian Gulf visit was intended to strengthen Britain's political and economic role in the Persian Gulf and Arabian Peninsula. "This will be the first visit to Saudi Arabia and the Gulf States by a British Prime Minister. It will be much welcomed and will increase a great deal of interest in the region and beyond, as well as among our NATO allies. It is designed to demonstrate the degree of importance we attach to our relations with the countries of this region of vital strategic significance to us. It is an area where British influence was once paramount, but where an initiative of this kind is now necessary to counteract efforts which our competitors, particularly the French, have been making at our expense to secure influence and large contracts." While the Labour Party announced departure from the Persian Gulf was in reality greatly exaggerated, as Britain was left with much residual influence even after departure, the Tories now planned a more assertive British presence in the region. The Soviet invasion of Afghanistan and the Gulf war had left many of the regimes in fear of their own security, needing British support, but an unobtrusive support to avoid fanning the flames of anti-western sentiments. "Apart from serving local, and thus indirectly western, security interests, the practical assistance which we could offer will improve our chances of winning substantial orders for British defence equipment." Apart from the broader political and strategic contexts, Thatcher's main purpose was to sell as much military hardware as possible.[23]

As the prime minister herself noted about the Persian Gulf sheikdom's: "It was also important that they should have the right military equipment and be trained to use it. In this our old defense links reinforced our commercial interest." Thatcher was very conscientious during her entire Gulf tour to seek and provide commercial opportunities for British companies.[24] When meeting Sheik Khalifa, prime minister of Abu Dhabi on April 22, 1981, Thatcher strongly pitched for selling Hawk aircrafts, a pitch she had earlier made to sheikh Zaid. "It was the best training aircraft of its kind in the world. It was being adapted so that it could be used in a combat role as well as a trainer. The Prime Minister had put her own authority behind the offer. It mattered greatly both to our own industry and to our ability to support our friends." Thatcher urged Khalifa to close the sale this very day, the sheikh replied "that he was very keen to maintain traditional links in this field with the UAE and the United Kingdom. The UAE would therefore be very happy to purchase the Hawk aircraft. The details could be finalized as soon as the Prime Minister wished.

The Prime Minister said this was a most generous mark of friendship between the two countries. Shaikh Khalifa said that even if his Government had known nothing about the aircraft, they would have purchased it simply on the basis that it came with the Prime Minister's recommendation." This is almost needless to comment. Arab leaders understood all too well the connection between purchasing British military hardware and getting British military protection. The United Kingdom pledged assistance in training UAE military personnel, as well as strongly hinting that there were more useful military equipment that could be profitably considered by the emirate. In addition, she plugged equipment for the oil industry based on the performance of British companies in the North Sea.[25] Although lower key, the prime minister continued her sales pitch in Oman, this time for Tornado aircraft.[26]

In Saudi Arabia she pushed for Tornados and Hawk aircraft. The meeting started, however, with prince Fahd pleading for the restoration of the old intimacy in the Anglo-Saudi relationship. "If a new bilateral accord could be developed, it would have an effect on the international situation generally."[27] Thatcher was dressed for the occasion, as Douglas Hurd, minister of state at the Foreign Office who accompanied her, observed in his memoirs: "The Prime Minister looked superb in the costume specially devised for a female prime minister visiting Saudi Arabia, which transformed her into a modern version of the late Queen Alexandra."[28] While in Qatar she pushed for Rapier missiles. Thatcher assured the Qatari prime minister sheikh Khalifa bin Hamad al Tani that she would take a personal interest in any agreement: "Substantial difficulties or complaints would be dealt with by her office." Thereafter she made a pitch for British Petroleum: "The British oil industry's experience in offshore development was enormous. We had gone from scratch to self-sufficiency in the North Sea in 12 years. BP would not let the Qatar Government down. Moreover, the British Government would keep a close and continuing eye on their work. The Government, after all, held 40% of the company's shares." But the saleswoman prime minister did not end with that, concluding the meeting: "The Prime Minister said that, finally, she would like to mention for the record that we had high hopes for getting the construction of the Ras Laffan Power station. Our record in power station construction was also very good."[29] Taken together, Margaret as arms sales woman supreme is almost embarrassing in her fever pitch for British military and civilian sales.

Thatcher reported her impressions of the Gulf to the new American president Ronald Reagan on April 27, 1981: "The position in North Yemen is confused: Consolidated, it could prove the best barrier to the extension of Soviet influence northwards from the PDRY [People's Democratic Republic of Yemen]. But the Saudis, whose influence there is strong, are curiously complacent and indecisive." The prime minister thereby knowingly or not touched upon the key feature of Saudi foreign policy – they hardly had one, except for bitching to their western benefactors demanding solutions that fit Saudi specifications and protection against their enemies. (The 'blame game' does not a foreign policy make.) Thatcher explained to Reagan that Qaboos impressed her, citing his achievements of ten years in power. "I told him that we would continue to help him with manpower, at his request. He and his country is very important to us." British relations with the UAE and Qatar were good, their "problems, if any, are those of very rapid development, including populations whose size is growing fast and whose composition is changing." The prime minister encouraged and supported the Gulf Cooperation Council of the nations mentioned above as well as Saudi Arabia, Kuwait, Bahrain and Oman, and was pleased to report to the president that British relations with all them were in good shape. "I was glad to be told in Abu Dhabi that they would be ordering some of our trainer/strike aircraft. Our ability to make a contribution to the defence of the area in an emergency, even in the modest scale we have in mind, depends crucially on our being able to sell our defence equipment. This order was a great encouragement. We shall be following it up energetically throughout the area."[30] Thatcher was not only reasserting the British position in the Gulf, but it was also a not so subtle rejoinder against the increasing American presence in the region, a presence that increased dramatically after the Soviet invasion of Afghanistan and the announcement of the Carter Doctrine. But the process had begun earlier than that. With regard to the American embassy in Manama, Bahrain reported as early as March 8, 1978: "America's interest in Bahrain is almost exclusively a function of its location in the oil-rich Persian Gulf, we and our allies need this region's oil, and its money, and fostering local conditions in Bahrain, and in the other Gulf States, which assure continuing access to oil, investment funds, and export profits will be a major US concern for years to come." Bahrain was also the point of access for the American Navy's Middle East force.[31] For the United States, the underlying assumption was that the British security presence in the lower Gulf was fading; still, early in the Carter administration, the United States sought to complement rather than supplement the British presence.[32] When meeting Thatcher on December 17, 1979, Carter said that: "The United States Administration would like to expand its discussions with the UK Government on the need for an increased presence in the area of the Persian Gulf and on increased use of Diego Garcia. In the Gulf, they would welcome the support that the UK could give, with the benefit of its long links in that area, and they would like to consult the British on possibilities for providing bases for a US presence."[33]

While seeking to maintain influence, British officials had but little respect for much of what they observed in the region. Anthony Parsons of the Foreign Office toured the Persian Gulf in early June 1979. His comments are not untypical: "Riyadh is one of the most dreadful hellholes I have seen, and I do not lack experience of hellholes. It is cross between a vast building site and a municipal rubbish heap, sprawling endlessly. The bazaar was filthy and flyblown. Wealth abounds and poverty seemed confined to the pullulating Yemeni immigrant workers. (. . .) The UAE is a vast practical joke perpetrated by western greed on willing billionaire victims." But the British position in the area was secure. "Commercially, we are still doing extremely well, a prime example of long established British influence paying off."[34]

As the Americans moved into the Persian Gulf, the British were acutely aware that in order to maintain influence recourse to the methods of yester-year had to be avoided at all costs. "To resume a tutelary or policing role, backed up by a military intervention capacity, even if we shared this with our Western partners, would carry little appeal for our friends in the Arab world, embarrass or inhibit our broader relationship with the Third World and, as seen in Iran, would be unlikely to counter unrest arising from internal strains in any country." This meant that any British role should be low-key: "Direct military interest by the West should be discreet and unprovocative." But an accelerated withdrawal carried its own risks, and undermine the self-confidence of pro-British regimes. "The next steps towards disengagement will have to be gradually and subtly negotiated over a period."[35] That is, under Thatcher at least, the British planned to stay a long time in the Persian Gulf.

Reagan, when becoming president, was met with a substantially upgraded American military presence in the Persian Gulf, despite both Egypt and Oman objections to a permanent US presence or bases in their country. The United States had a flotilla of ships in the Indian Ocean carrying equipment for 12,000 marines and munitions for nine air force squadrons and four army brigades supplies that could be rapidly transferred to points of crisis, greatly reducing the time required to deploy American troops in the Persian Gulf. In addition, the United States had access agreements with Oman, Kenya and Somalia.[36]

Much has been made by many writers of the close relationship between Margaret Thatcher and president Ronald Reagan, their ideological affinity, and their personal friendship that blossomed into a restoration of the special relationship after years of alleged neglect during the Carter years.[37] But as Alan Dobson points it was not without foundation, for there were fifteen Anglo-American summits when Reagan was president.[38] The president himself has contributed to the belief of a special Anglo-American understanding in the Thatcher/Reagan era. The president called Thatcher after her fellow Conservatives had forced her into involuntary retirement in early December 1990: "I wanted her to know that my heart was with her, and that I thought England owed her a great debt and was going to miss her. I told her that the United States and many other countries would miss her as well. (. . .) We disagreed from time to time, but the disagreements went away when we had a chance to talk. (. . .) Yes, she was an ally. But more than that she was a friend. It helps to avoid problems when you know each other and can pick up the phone. It helps to have a rapport and a chemistry in a relationship. They say that the United States and Britain have a special relationship. Well, our friendship was very special."[39]

But Carter did not neglect the special relationship, he simply wanted to put it on a different footing as we have seen by his efforts culminating during the January 1979 Guadeloupe summit. Carter enjoyed the closest personal relations with Thatcher's predecessor, James Callaghan. The special relationship was thus well and alive when Carter was president, while contrary to earlier impressions the Thatcher/Reagan was not without problems of its own. Richard Aldhous argues that Thatcher was clearly subordinate in the relationship: "Certainly Reagan was always pleased to have Thatcher on the team if her position fitted into his overall strategy for the cold war. At other times, when they disagreed, he simply brushed her aside. In the end she always remained a junior partner, a fact that she – more than most – rarely forgot." Besides, for all their ideological compatibility the early Thatcher/Reagan years were fraught with discord and often highly contentions disputes: there were major Anglo-American disputes over the trans-Siberian pipeline, the Falklands war, the American invasion of Grenada and Reagan's Strategic Defense Initiative (Star War), and disagreements over the president's policy of abolishing nuclear weapons.[40] The president's detached style did not potentially make the personal aspect of relations easier. For instance, when meeting Thatcher on July 20, 1981 Reagan hardly said anything himself but let his advisors do the taking.[41] The personal aspects of the Anglo-American relationship should, perhaps, not be overestimated. Lyndon Johnson evidently did not like British prime minister Harold Wilson, describing the premier once as "the little creep camping on my doorstep."[42] The far from perfect relationship at the president/PM level, however, did little to disturb close Anglo-American relations in the Johnson era; the United States was an eager and willing underwriter of the pound and the British role east of Suez.[43] On the other hand, the consequences of disagreements during the Thatcher/Reagan era should probably not be exaggerated, as Alexander Haig reports after particularly difficult negotiations with Thatcher over the Falklands on April 8, 1982: "As the evening ended at No. 10, Mrs. Thatcher gave me her hand, 'Only true friends could discuss such an issue as this with the candor of feeling that has characterized this dinner,' she said. Then she laughed and said, 'We are nice to other people.'"[44]

Aldous, writing in *The Difficult Relationship*, is not overmuch concerned with the Persian Gulf and Arabian Peninsula; a case can be made that while Thatcher bowed to the undeniable facts of the discrepancies of Anglo-American power in terms of the issues referred above, the prime minister took advantage of these 'losses' for British influence in these areas to expand the influence of the United Kingdom in the Gulf. [45] Junior partner or not, when Reagan phoned the prime minister suggesting further mediation when British forces were poised to capture Port Stanley, the capitol of the Falkland Islands, Thatcher snapped back: "I didn't lose some of my finest ships and some of my finest lives, to leave quietly under a cease fire without the Argentinians withdrawing."[46]

Grenada was another point of contention, when Reagan ordered the invasion of this Commonwealth island without consulting and only informing Thatcher after military operations had begun, the British grew testy, particularly because the Thatcher government was made to look like an American 'poodle'. Geoffrey Howe, UK Secretary of State at the time, observed afterwards: "The truth is that the government had been humiliated by having its views so plainly disregarded in Washington."[47] Percy Cradock, foreign policy advisor to Thatcher observed: "We had been made to look silly and the value of the US connection greatly degraded."[48] Henderson sent back a sobering assessment of Anglo-American relations on November 27, 1981: despite the ideological harmony between Thatcher and Reagan it had "not established greater harmony of policy."[49]

But Thatcher was not alone in snapping, Robert McFarlane, then US National Security Advisor, wrote Robert Armstrong on November 7, 1983: "While we genuinely regret that circumstances did not permit more timely consultations, I must tell you in all candor that the British Government's public reaction to our effort to restore democracy and order to Grenada has caused us profound disappointment. The Prime Minister's statement on 30 October that 'Western democracies . . . do not use force to move into other people's countries' was unusually harsh. The infliction of such public criticism by one of our closest allies during a moment of national anguish over the tragedy in Beirut was doubly wounding." This missive was in contrast to US support of Britain during the Falklands war, even to the extent of potentially damaging US relations with Latin America. The US accepted private criticism: "We deeply respect the careful and profoundly well-informed views of your government on a broad array of questions. But public differences only serve to diminish British–American solidarity which has serve our mutual interests so well."[50]

Be that as it may, Thatcher, like predecessors, eagerly sought the chance to visit Washington as early as possible in the new president's tenure, believing, perhaps too optimistically, that good personal relations could help overcome political problems. Thatcher's Cabinet secretary Robert Armstrong minuted on the eve the first Thatcher – Reagan meeting, taking evident pride that Reagan wanted to meet the British prime minister first of all European leaders: "It is of particular importance that she will be the first leader from among the European allies to visit President Reagan. The visit will provide a valuable opportunity to exploit the Prime Minister's high standing in the USA; while the policy of the new Administration is still at a formative stage the Prime Minister should in this way be able to gain American understanding for our policies and in some measure to influence American policies in our direction."[51] In this Thatcher followed in the tradition of several British prime ministers. Harold Macmillan for instance assiduously courted John F. Kennedy after his inauguration, writing in a memorandum: "I must somehow convince him [Kennedy] that I am worth consulting not as an old friend as (Eisenhower) felt but as a man who, although of advancing years has young and fresh thoughts."[52] While one should not underestimate the value of good Anglo-American relations and the Reagan/Thatcher relationship came out quite well, the president naturally was foremost concerned with promoting the American national interest, as Thatcher worked to improve the standing of Great Britain in the world.

IV

Ronald Reagan: Leadership Style and Foreign Policy

He grew more puzzling the more I studied him. I only came out of this despair when I found out that everybody else who had ever known him, including his wife, is equally bewildered.
[Historian Edmund Morris who began work on Ronald Reagan's still unfinished biography in 1985].[1]

Historians are still puzzled by Reagan. According to Michael Schaller; "Reagan lived a politically charmed life in a world he thought he fully controlled but only dimly understood." On the other hand, John Lewis Gaddis credits Reagan with ending the cold war.[2] The press reported Reagan to be lazy, unintelligent and dependent on his aides, delegating freely and thoughtlessly, having little or no idea of what his free-wheeling associates where up to. The Iran/Contra scandal was a prime example of Reagan's lax leadership style. Reagan had little or no interest in details and said the strangest things. During the campaign in 1980, he claimed trees polluted more than cars. How could this simple minded seventy year old end up as president? Why would any old man with such limited abilities expose himself to the rigors of campaigning and governing as president? An office usually not lacking for the want of well-qualified and intelligent applicants. How did this ex-actor end up there? Reagan's Hollywood background was for many commentators in itself disqualifying.

But as president, Reagan was extraordinary effective. He won two national elections with increasing margins, and dominated the political process. This is impressive since the president's powers are limited, having to work with a system, believed to be largely ungovernable. Faded party loyalties make Congress into countless ad hoc combinations of 435 Congressmen and 100 Senators. Reagan controlled the chaotic political scene to a much larger degree than his predecessors and successors.[3] He pushed through massive rearmament; the Strategic Defense Initiative (SDI or Star Wars); limitations or cut-backs in most other governmental budgets; substantial tax reform; scrapped a whole class of nuclear missiles; and forced radical change in the

Soviet Union with concomitant improvement in Soviet-American relations and reduction in areas of regional tensions (Afghanistan, Nicaragua, Angola etc.).

Why then the massive critique against Reagan? The answer can be found at four different levels. To many critics it was inappropriate that a former actor became president; others disagreed with Reagan's conservative policies; some believed that Reagan's successes was caused by good staff work, and attributed his failures to the advice and action of bad staff, most notably through the institution of chief of staff, and, finally, the negative picture painted by the early memoir writers of the Reagan administration: David Stockman, Alexander Haig and Donald Regan.[4]

Being an actor is not more disqualifying for the presidency than being a rich man's son, teacher, lawyer, football player and law student, or peanut farmer as were the occupations of Reagan's predecessors from Kennedy to Carter. Besides, more than anything Reagan was a professional politician, having national name recognition since his days with General Electric in the mid-1950s. Reagan addresses the critique in his memoirs: "For years, I've heard the question: 'How could an actor be president?' I've sometimes wondered how you could be president and not be an actor." Reagan's training as an actor taught him how to conduct himself at public functions. Journalist Richard Ben Cramer, in his book on the 1988 election, gives an amusing contrast between Reagan and George Bush acting in their official capacity. I ask the reader's indulgence for the length of this quote, but it certainly says something about public appearances:

> You'd think he [George Bush] would have learned from Reagan, watching him for six years. You watch Reagan do something public, anything, like walk across the lawn to his chopper: every movement is perfect. There he goes . . . with his big western walk, shoulders back, hands swinging easy at his sides, the grin raised to perfect angle, then one hand aloft in a long wave . . . and every instant is a perfect picture. It doesn't even matter if they're screaming questions at him. At any one millisecond, as the shutter clicks, the President is perfect: relaxed, balanced, smiling, smooth.
>
> Now watch Bush make for his chopper: hey, he knows that agent! – not part of his detail, but he met him on the last trip to Houston, got a kid who wants to go to West Point, wrote a letter for him. So Bush twists around and waves to the agent – lets him know he's seen him, bends his head back to Bar[bara Bush], and pointing at the agent, that's Keith, the *agent*, remember? "MR. VICE PRESIDENT! MR. VICE PRESIDENT!" a photographer is yelling, and it's Fred, the *Life* guy, who was on the trip to Cleveland last week, so while he is talking to Bar, and pointing at the agent, he makes a face to Fred, to let him know he doesn't have to shout. He *knows* him, see. Fred's a friend! And there's Steely waiting at the chopper stairs, Jack Steel! Known him for – God! Twenty-five years? And so he's got to goose Steely, let him know he's glad to se him, ougtha ask him, but the engine is so loud, and the wind 's whipping his hair in his face, which he is screwing up to yell, as he

pauses – gotta ask him – trying to balance, crouching in the engine wind, one foot up on the stairs: "Hey! How's your *son*? . . . YOUR SON? . . . " And at any one moment, as the shutter clicks, Bush looks like a dork.[5]

Appearances matter, and especially for an American President who is both head of state and head of government. Functions which in Great Britain are divided between Queen and Prime Minister. It was as head of state, the ceremonial aspects of the presidency, that Reagan excelled, advantages gained from his actor background. Bush, as we have seen, did not achieve the same success with his public appearances, and perhaps as a result of that, he has been derided as 'a lap dog', in columnist George Will's memorable phrase, or a wimp by others. For all the criticism directed at Reagan, nobody has faulted him with Bush's alleged problems. The President was acutely aware of the public dimension of his presidency, so much so that Don Regan, Reagan's one time chief of staff, complains in his memoirs that Ronald Reagan was too little concerned with detail (a point to be discussed below) and preoccupied with the 'outer presidency'.[6]

Reagan, some critics claim, was not able to function unless 'scripted' by his aides. Countless lawmakers have complained that Reagan did not engage in serious discussions, but mindlessly read from cue cards. Donald Regan noted: "Every moment of every public appearance was scheduled, every word was scripted, every place where Reagan was expected to stand was chalked with toe marks." But Reagan the professional actor was extremely careful about his public appearances to ensure the best possible effect and contact with the audience. Close aide Michael Deaver had the President's appearances as his main responsibility. Reagan did not need cue-cards in closed meetings, but it made life easier for him and it betrays a certain intellectual laziness. Besides, being partially deaf on both ears, the president had difficulties hearing at larger meetings, unless he was directly addressed. Under these circumstances cue-cards were a useful supporting tool.[7]

Acting taught Reagan to control difficult situations. A well-known Reagan critic explains:

Reagan's later control of volatile situations comes as clearly from his announcing days as from his film training. His canniness in debates, his handling of potentially embarrassing moments, his coolness in crisis (. . .) Reagan's years of handling audiences in every conceivable situation gave him an easiness of carriage under stress that touched the heroic in his reaction to being shot in 1981. (. . .) Reagan not only kept his head but reassured others around him.[8]

Prominent liberal Democrat Clarke Clifford once called Reagan an 'amiable dunce'. Reagan's conservative politics and attack on the Democratic New Deal welfare state were intensely disliked by most of his critics. The opposition is more effective if the conservative standard-bearer, in addition to despicable policies, is lazy, unintelligent, incapable, and yes, almost senile. American journalists and social scientists vote overwhelmingly Democratic, raising questions about their objectivity when describing Reagan.[9]

Reporter Lou Cannon is the most notable proponent for the good staff/ bad staff thesis, but the theory has also other adherents.[10] When Reagan was served by a good staff, most importantly chief of staff, he was successful, but a bad chief of staff may cause disasters. James Baker was chief of staff during Reagan's first term, and carefully cultivated the press. Cannon's report on him is glowing, calling him the best chief of staff in White House history. When Baker departed, the road to Iran/Contra, according to Cannon, was the chosen pathway, a move the astute Baker would have prevented. Baker was a friend of Vice President George Bush, who had watched Baker privately blame the president for most of the failures, while claiming credit for most of the successes of the Reagan administration. Bush, when elected President, was determined to find a more selfless chief of staff, someone who "would take the heat, dish out covering and retaliatory fire, and make sure the president got all the credit. He wanted a chief of staff that would salute smartly at any request. (. . .) Someone who would, above all, be loyal".[11] Baker's successor as chief of staff, Donald Reagan, received much of the blame for the Iran/Contra scandal. Regan's lack of consultation and self-aggrandizement, according to Cannon, antagonized Republican Congressmen. While Baker carefully culti-vated the media, Regan did not, upsetting Cannon and other journalists as important sources of information dried up. Cannon, therefore, is hardly an objective critic of Reagan's chiefs of staff. Besides, chiefs of staff are not self-less. Regan, in the end, much like Baker, was far more concerned about his own reputation than the president's, railing at the vice president and president: "I deserved better treatment than this", when after protecting him for months against an avalanche of critics, Reagan fired him.[12]

Cannon attributes too much power and influence to the chief of staff, because chiefs of staff are expandable. As Eisenhower fired Sherman Adams, Nixon fired H. R. Haldeman, Bush fired John Sununu, Reagan fired or let go James Baker, Donald Regan, and Howard Baker. Stephen Ambrose claims in the introduction to the Haldeman diaries, that Nixon's chief of staff was the most powerful and influential filling this job, but chiefs of staff rarely have much influence on policy. They serve as a transmission belt to and from the President, shielding the President by taking much of the blame for the presi-dent's policies.[13]

There are no indications that Don Regan's role as chief of staff differed significantly from other chiefs of staff. In fact, when Regan desperately tried to avoid the blame for the Iran/Contra debacle, he was tainted with the scandal anyway. To begin damage control, Ronald Reagan established the President's Special Review Board (later called the Tower report after its chairman John Tower) to assess administration policy. The report was a damning indictment of Regan as chief of staff: "He must bear primary responsibility for the chaos that descended upon the White House". The Tower report description of the Reagan White House led one British journalist to observe: "The Tower

Commission produced its picture of a comatose President and his wild aides, and there was no rebuttal".[14]

However, there are strong indications the Tower Commission got it wrong. Reporting the testimony of Reagan's former National Security Advisor, Robert McFarlane, to Congress, *Time* magazine observed:

> Many accounts of Iranscam, notably the damning Tower commission report, depict the President as a woolly-minded, out of touch leader who permitted a band of overzealous aides to conduct secret and possible illegal operations right under his nose. The White House has done little to dispute that characterization, and for good reason: An inattentive Reagan who knew little of the weapons sale to Iran and nothing of the funneling of arms to Nicaraguan rebels seemed better than a President who played an active role in the affair.

McFarlane claims that Reagan overrode strong objections from Secretary of Defense, Caspar Weinberger, and Secretary of State, George Shultz, instructing McFarlane to proceed secretly with the Iranian initiative. But the president evaded responsibility by blaming Don Regan, overzealous aides, or by leaving the impression that his own lack of attention and laziness permitted unsupervised aides to pursue illegal policies. In any case, this testifies to the unimportance to the chief of staff compared to the President.[15]

The Tower report spreads the blame evenly; the president had such a compassionate attachment to the hostages and was so inattentive to detail that he embarked on illegal policies, without hardly realizing it. Furthermore, he did not use the NSC-apparatus properly by submitting his policy to review. But the whole point was secrecy, Reagan did not want to involve the cumbersome and not so secretive National Security Council. McFarlane is criticized for failing to keep all parties informed, in particular Secretaries of State and Defense. They, on their side:

> [S]imply distanced themselves from the program. They protected their record as to their own position on the issue. They were not energetic in attempting to protect the President from the consequences of his personal commitment to freeing the hostages.

Most likely, Reagan simply told them to mind their own business. Shultz admits as much in his memoirs. Besides, the whole Tower report reeks of memories of Watergate. By seemingly making full disclosure, impeachment is avoided, but many details are presented in a confusing manner, contradictory signals given, and the issue disappears in a sea of fuzziness. Theodore Draper notes: "The Tower Report is at its worst in its verdict on what was wrong with President Reagan's handling of this affairs. The emphasis is put on his "management style" instead of his "political decisions".[16]

Memoirs by David Stockman, Alexander Haig and Donald Regan depict the president as extremely passive, giving no orders and having little or no control over aides and associates. Their portrayal has undoubtedly made a major contribution to the public and press perception of Reagan. However, a president so conspicuously absent as claimed by the authors is obviously incapable of running the country; any successes must be credited to the memoir writers and not Reagan. But these memoirs are flawed sources to Reagan and his administration. The authors resigned under embarrassing circumstances or were fired by the president. After Stockman's now infamous leaking of the administration's economic secrets (see note 12), he received a dressing down from the president, and I remember him crying on national television afterwards in an apparent act of contrition. Donald Regan had before becoming Secretary of the Treasury been a successful Wall Street executive. "My public service cost me the most acute public discomfort of my life", Don Regan writes and "the friendship of the only man [Reagan] to whom I had ever willingly subordinated myself."[17]

The memoirs are extremely critical of Reagan, but sometimes when describing single episodes they show a skillful and effective president. Stockman's president is a man of limited intellect, with only the most shallow knowledge on the economy. The budget cuts and control of Congress should therefore be credited Stockman, and not Reagan. But then Stockman writes:

> The tax cut was one of the few things Ronald Reagan deeply wanted from his presidency. It was the only thing which he threw the full force of his broad political shoulders. Getting the tax cut passed was one of the few episodes involving domestic policy and legislative bargaining in which he firmly called the shots. By intimidating and overpowering the whole of the nation's politicians, he got what he wanted.[18]

Incidentally, when reading this I began to suspect there was more to Reagan than the standard portrayal of the lazy, unintelligent right-wing nut by most of the president's critics. Stockman was a radical *laissez faire* ideologue, who wanted to dismantle the welfare state, cutting subsidies and social welfare programs. Stockman's ideal state would only preserve peace and the legal system, an ambition that by far exceeded Reagan's vision of America. When increased defense spending and tax cuts threatened to let the federal deficit out of control, Stockman pressured the President to increase taxes to bring the deficit down. But Reagan held firm and refused.[19]

Like Stockman, Haig describes an episode that put the President in a different light. Toward the end of the Carter administration it pledged to sell AWACS (airborne warning and control system) advanced radar planes to Saudi Arabia. An obligation 'inherited' by the Reagan administration, but facing strong opposition, in particular from the Jewish lobby, believing the sale a threat to Israeli security. The United States government thought the sale important in order to maintain influence in a crucial part of the Middle East. However, 54 Senators wrote the President not to force the issue on Congress. At that point Reagan became involved:

> Reagan himself became fully engaged in the process, and in one of the most effective Presidential lobbying efforts of recent times, put the full weight of his office and the full force of his personality into the fight.

The president proved persuasive, the Senate voting 52-48 in favor of the sale.[20]

Donald Regan complains of lack of presidential involvement and explicit goals. During his four years as Secretary of the Treasury, he never met the president one-on-one. As head of Merrill Lynch, Regan was trained in management by objective and explicit written standards. The president never told him what his economic policy was; Regan had to figure it out by reading the president's speeches and the newspapers. Doing so, he discovered "that there was a remarkable consistency in the president's public utterances". When chief of staff, Regan was struck by the president's seemingly passive leadership style, but still, things happened: "Common sense suggested that the President knew something that the rest of us did not know".[21]

Almost in spite of himself, Regan portrays a hard-working and intelligent chief executive. The President handles himself superbly when meeting other heads of state, and during international economic summits. Returning to the residency, Reagan regularly took work with him – "briefing papers, communications from foreign and domestic leaders, decision-making documents to be read and signed. He never failed to deal with every single item, whether it amounted to five pages or five hundred". In addition, several packets of material were delivered to him every night.[22]

When elected president, Reagan had more than fifty years of experience from the communication industry, from his early radio sports-casting days to newspapers, Hollywood stardom, and later TV-personality, qualifying him for the presidency in the age of mass communication. Reagan the actor was used to be corrected and guided on the set and still be the star, and therefore did not grudge his aides and associates press coverage or acclaim. He had a knack of making people comfortable, putting them at ease, and not being intimidated in the presence of the president or the White House. Speech writer Peggy Noonan noted: "He had a tact and delicacy so great that I suspect no one has ever been embarrassed in his presence". Reagan would do whatever necessary for people to like him, and because his kindness was so well-known, "people were afraid not to like him. They were afraid to get mad at him because his goodness was so famous, such an accepted part of the inner air of the place, that to dislike him was tantamount to admitting a serious inner flaw". But Reagan is no pushover, as one-time aide, Martin Anderson, explains:

> Reagan is one of the toughest men I have ever known, far tougher, for example, than his predecessors Carter, Ford, and Nixon. Once Reagan has determined what he thinks is right, and what is important to do, then he will pursue that goal relentlessly.
> The personal feelings of others and their emotional distress, while something he

is always sympathetic to, will never alter his course. What others would be cursed for, Reagan does in a friendly, even-handed way that disarms criticism. Perhaps it is because he never acts with malice and he never takes pleasure from the discomfort of others. But if it is necessary he will cause that discomfort, freely and easily.

Reagan may be unique in that he is a warmly ruthless man.[23]

Martin Anderson had previously worked for Nixon, who because of the demands of a hard-fought election, neglected planning for personnel till after the election was won. Anderson recalled going to meetings, being the only person in the room supporting Nixon's policies.[24]

Determined to avoid Nixon's predicament, Reagan began early in the campaign of 1980 to plan the new administration. Candidates were carefully screened and indoctrinated:

Ronald Reagan came to office with a remarkable coherent agenda and set of policy priorities. His priorities to significantly to increase defense spending and cut spending in virtually all domestic policy areas lent themselves to a narrow focus and simple set of priorities served as a litmus test and guide to action that was a great help in recruiting personnel for the administration. Personal and ideological loyalty were the primary criteria for appointees. The coherence of values led to an administration with much more unity than has marked recent administrations with more disparate policy agendas and personnel.

Stockman, Haig and Regan went through the same screening and indoctrination process as other members of Cabinet, despite their claims to the contrary. The President elect took a lively interest in appointments, but in such an indirect manner, that, according to Cannon, "distanced him so much from actions and appointments that he appeared not to be responsible if they turned out badly". Reagan usually went to great lengths to support aides in trouble, ensuring their loyalty.[25]

During the campaign Reagan established 48 policy task forces, which produced detailed reports from welfare reform to missile defense, from economic policy to foreign relations. At the inauguration, Reagan had a blueprint or a battle plan on how to proceed. To implement policy, Reagan organized Cabinet councils, or sub-units of the Cabinet for "deliberate consideration of major policy issues which affect the interests of more than one department or agency". Such a system allowed "second level policy to be dealt with below the presidential level and it would help keep the focus of the administration on the central Reagan agenda". The combination of his personnel policies, task forces and Cabinet councils, helped Reagan govern effectively without being overwhelmed by the heavy burden of the modern presidency. Extensive delegating also contributed to the 'teflon' effect, that is nothing stuck to the president, but his aides and associates took the blame for unpopular policies.[26]

While most historians have shown little enthusiasm for Reagan's overall policies, their evaluation of his foreign policy has fared no better. Walter

LaFeber complains that during the first five years of his presidency, Reagan's foreign policy was his military budget. The president was so dimwitted that his National Security advisor had to show Reagan "simple government-made instruction movies" because of his ignorance of foreign policy fundamentals. Robert J. McMahon believes that Mikhail Gorbachev's reforms were more important in ending the cold war than American policies. The defense build up was dangerous; it might have provoked Soviet counter-reactions, even nuclear war. Michael Schaller thinks that Reagan's foreign policies rested on myths and symbols, rather than facts and programs. Raymond L. Garthoff seriously questions the thesis that Reagan forced the Russians on the defensive and ended the cold war.[27]

But Reagan did, in fact, have a foreign policy. A policy to be realized in successive stages. The first stage was rebuilding American military and economic strength, to achieve superiority over the Russians. Reagan writes:

> The great dynamic success of capitalism had given us a powerful weapon in our battle against Communism – money. The Russians could never win the arms race; we could outspend them forever. Moreover, incentives inherent in the capitalist system had given us an industrial base that meant that we had the capacity to maintain a technological edge over them forever.

McMahon's thinks the defense build up could have provoked strong Soviet counter-measures, but Garthoff shows that while taking advantage of opportunities presenting themselves, the Soviet leadership was essentially cautious (and very much so when pressured), and responded to Carter's (1980 budget) and Reagan's rearmament programs by hinting at substantial concessions for a return to détente.[28]

The next stage was to strengthen and revitalize American alliances, NATO being the most important. Relations with most European powers were strained (to be discussed below) during the later years of the Carter administration and early years of Reagan's presidency, but in 1983 the allies solved most of their difficulties and downplayed the others. Only when the these two stages were realized would the United States engage in serious discussions with the Soviet Union: Negotiations not only to limit and contain further Soviet expansion, but according to National Security Decision Directive (NSDD) 75 of January 17, 1983, to "reverse Soviet expansionism by competing effectively on a sustained basis with the Soviet Union in all international arenas". To counter the Soviet threat and expansion during the late 1970s and early 1980s into Afghanistan, Nicaragua, Cambodia, Ethiopia, Angola and Mozambique, the United States engaged in a political, economical and military competition. Politically, the United States promoted democracy and the free enterprise system in a global propaganda campaign. Economically, the United States sought to restrict credits and transfer of advanced technology to the Soviets, and encouraged the West to seek alternative sources of energy to Soviet oil and gas. Militarily, rebuilding American defenses, the US aided anti-Soviet guerrillas (the Reagan doctrine) and other covert operations. The final stage was directed against the perceived static and anti-American third world. The United States would no longer seek accommodation, but undermine Communist regimes like Nicaragua, while promoting the free enterprise system. Implicit in this policy, Robert W. Tucker insists, was a strong commitment to human rights against tyranny in any form, whether left- or right-wing.[29]

Reagan was the chief propagandist against the Soviet Union. Two of his speeches in particular stand out in setting the president's ideological agenda. To the British parliament in June 1982, Reagan said:

> It is the Soviet Union that runs against the tide of human history by denying human freedom and human dignity to its citizens. It is also in deep economic difficulty.

The president in a reverse dig at Lenin's famous quip urged a global crusade for democracy against communism in order that "Marxism-Leninism would be tossed to the ash heap of history". The second speech was given almost a year later to a group of evangelical Christians in Florida, where Reagan compared the Soviet Union to an evil empire. Reagan was only the point man in a world-wide American effort to sell democracy and the free enterprise system, employing Voice of America, Radio Free Europe, Radio Liberty and the United States Information Agency (USIA).[30]

The United States declared an economic war against the Soviet Union, where each action in itself was, perhaps, of lesser significance, but in sum constituted a serious challenge to the economic well-being of the Russian empire. The first battle on the economic front was over the trans-Siberian pipeline, a huge project between European companies, their governments, and the Soviet Union. Scared by the oil crisis, western Europe sought alternative sources of energy. A 3,500-mile pipeline from western Siberia, north of the Arctic circle, was to supply seven countries in western Europe with natural gas. Initially, providing only a small part of Europe's total energy consumption but this was estimated by the end of the 1980s to increase to between 15 and 20 per cent. The United States feared a Soviet economic stranglehold of Europe. European and American companies would provide credits, engineering, critical supplies and $10 to $12 billion in hard currency annually, to purchase western goods and advanced technology. In a period with high unemployment (in mid-1982 it was 14 per cent in Great Britain, 9 percent in France, almost 8 percent in Germany [the highest level since 1954], and up to 10 per cent in the United States), the pipeline would create good jobs.[31]

Reagan wanted to restrict trade that gave the Soviets interest rates below market price, earned hard currency, and access to western technology. On December 29, 1981, American companies were therefore prohibited to participate in the construction of the pipeline. The President explained the rationale behind this policy to Margaret Thatcher, the British Prime Minister, in a cable of March 8, 1982. In her memoirs, the Prime Minister noted:

The American argument was that not only was the USSR economically weak, it was suffering from an acute shortage of foreign exchange. Europeans and other governments which provided the Soviet Union with subsidized credit were cushioning their failing system from economic realities which would have otherwise have forced its reform.

While Thatcher granted Reagan some points, she became livid when he unilaterally on June 18, 1982, extended American sanctions to licensees and subsidiaries of American firms located in Europe. Thatcher and other European leaders objected for two reasons; that American sanctions would force the break of contracts retroactively and by the extension of American extra-territorial authority. "The European irritation was increased still further by the news that the Americans were intending to renew grain sales to the USSR on the pretext that this would drain the USSR of hard currency – but transparently because it was in the interest of American farmers to sell their grain".[32]

The controversy was resolved when the United States lifted the sanctions against the pipeline in return for European agreement on four principles that should govern economic policy towards the Soviet Union: that the West would no longer provide credits to the Soviet Union below market rates; the West would withdraw support of the pipeline; the West would coordinate policies and seek to limit transfer of high technology to the Soviets; and, finally, the West would seek to develop alternative energy sources and supplies to the Siberian pipeline.[33]

Peter Schweizer insists that the Reagan administration engineered with Saudi Arabia a drastic fall in world oil prices, denying the Soviet Union crucial income in hard currencies. Saudi Arabia was a 'swing-producer', that is by raising or lowering its oil production it could raise or lower world oil prices. At the same time the Saudis were pressured from Iran and Iraq and looked to the United States for protection. A protection willingly granted, the implicit bargain saw Saudi Arabia bring world oil prices down. The 1970s, the years of the oil crisis, were a bonanza to the Soviet Union: hard currency earnings from oil export increased 272 per cent, while the volume of exports increased only 22 per cent. Each time the price of oil went up one dollar per barrel, the Soviets earned one billion dollars. But the reverse was also true, the Soviets lost one billion dollars, when the oil price declined one dollar per barrel. Thus when Saudi oil production rose, world oil prices tumbled from 30 dollars a barrel in November 1985 to 12 dollars a barrel barely five months later; for Moscow over 10 billion dollars evaporated overnight, almost half of its hard currency income. Many of the imports from the West became too expensive, making it exceedingly difficult for Gorbachev to finance his reforms.[34] While the Reagan administration gives the impression of having caused the fall in oil prices, and this author (but memory is a treacherous thing) believes to remember Donald Regan bragging on national television: "Believe me, we planned it this way", the Reaganites were also aided by extenuating circumstances. The dramatic rise in oil prices since 1969 led to the deepest recession since the Great Depression, reducing demand for oil in the industrialized nations. In addition, new oil fields in the North Sea and Alaska were set in production. At the same time, oil was substituted by other energy sources like coal and nuclear power, and demand slackened by energy efficiency and conservation reduced the choke hold the oil-producing countries in the Middle East had on western economies. Oil historian Daniel Yergin notes: "Yet suddenly, instead of the feared shortage, there was a surplus of production capacity over market demand-in short, the makings of a massive glut." It was in this situation that Saudi Arabia, with one-third of total free world reserves, could determine world oil prices by raising or lowering its production.[35]

Reagan's military challenge to the Soviet Union was a massive arms build up, and the Strategic Defense Initiative (SDI) or Star Wars. The president opposed the prevailing military doctrine, MAD (mutually assured destruction), a terror balance where each superpower could destroy the other by a massive nuclear attack. Reagan was the driving force behind SDI, which would create a 'shield' against incoming Soviet nuclear missiles. The plan is also an example of the president's leadership style, since neither Shultz nor secretary of defense Caspar Weinberger was informed or consulted about the launching of SDI. The initiative was made in a speech by Reagan on March 23, 1983, less than two weeks after his 'evil empire' speech. While some commentators have denied any connection between the two, the president thereby linked his political and military pressure on the Soviet Union. Star Wars was greeted by waves of laughter and heaps of sarcasm by Reagan's many critics, but proved a major ingredient in the successful disarmament talks with the Soviets in 1987. The Russian economy went into a tailspin in the 1980s, particularly lagging in computer and micro-processing technology, central aspects of the SDI program.

There was a real danger that the United States would move ahead quantitatively and qualitatively in these areas. Soviet ambassador to Washington, Anatoly Dobrynin, reports that the Soviet leadership was outraged. And while Russian scientists were skeptical about the feasibility of SDI, "their views hardly carried much weight at that emotional moment. Our leadership was convinced that the United States had scored again and treated Reagan's statement as a real threat". While presenting SDI in an idealistic light, to avoid nuclear war and do away with nuclear weapons, the Reagan administration was well aware that if the Soviets wanted to catch up, it would impose a fearsome burden on an already overstretched economy. This at a time when Soviet leaders anticipated reduced military outlays. Reagan argued, when meeting Thatcher, that "there had to be a practical limit as to how far the Soviets could push their people down the road of austerity".[36]

SDI, therefore, pressured the Russians to give concessions after confessions in the disarmament talks. They argued that after the United States began placing intermediate missiles in Europe (in response to previously placed SS-20 Soviet intermediate missiles), that they would not return to the bargaining table until the Americans had removed their missiles. Thereafter, according to a political scientist who has studied the process:

> When that approach failed, the Soviets said that they would return to the bargaining table, but only to talk about space weapons: when that failed, they agreed to resume START [Strategic Arms Reduction Talks] and INF [Intermediate-range Nuclear Forces] talks, but only if they were linked to a ban on SDI; when that failed, they agreed to 'delink' the negotiations and reach a separate INF accord, but only covering Europe, when that failed, they agreed to ban medium range missiles world wide.[37]

When Reagan took office Russia was overextended in Afghanistan, Nicaragua, Cambodia, and Ethiopia. Angola and Mozambique had not become the expected Kremlin beacon of socialism, but a drain on Soviet resources. The Reagan-doctrine applied mainly to Afghanistan, Nicaragua and Angola. The Soviets had since 1979 been involved in a protracted war in Afghanistan. Total Soviet losses were relatively small; 13,000 killed and 35,000 wounded for the entire war 1979–1989. But the war cost the Soviets much in international prestige and treasure, and even more so when the Reagan administration stepped up aid to the Afghan Mujahideen, and encouraged them to take the war to Soviet territory. These small-scale raids raised serious concerns in the Soviet leadership about American intentions. American military actions against Libya in 1981 and 1986, and the occupation of Grenada in 1983, demonstrated that the Soviets were unwilling to give anything but moral and rhetorical support to third world pro-Soviet regimes under western attack.[38]

Reagan and Pope John Paul II agreed on June 7, 1982 on a clandestine campaign to encourage the dissolution of the communist bloc. Their focus was on Poland, which in December 1981 had declared martial law to crush the independent labor union Solidarity. The president and the Pontiff wanted to destabilize the Polish government and keep Solidarity alive. The labor union's survival was assisted by a cooperative effort by the Vatican, the CIA, the AFL-CIO and European labor movements, providing money and equipment until Solidarity was legalized in 1989. Reagan and the Pope believed that a free Poland would seriously threaten the integrity of the Soviet empire. In addition, the United States pursued covert operations aimed at encouraging reform movements in Hungary and Czechoslovakia, offering economic aid to Warsaw Pact nations according to their willingness to protect human rights and undertake political and free market reforms.[39]

The Reagan doctrine and other covert operations had their share of unsavory aspects. American and international law were sometimes overlooked, most notably in the Iran/Contra affair at home and refusal to accept the International Court of Justice ruling against the United States when it mined Nicaraguan harbors. Furthermore, the United States disregarded human rights violations in El Salvador, Pakistan, South Africa and Zaire (which served as a transit to anti-communist rebels in Angola), and turned a blind eye to its own policy of non-nuclear proliferation towards Pakistan's pursuit of nuclear weapons, because it was a major supply route to Afghan insurgents – the very same insurgents tacitly accepted by the United States as being the leading source of illicit heroin to the United States and Europe. The international mujahedin from Arabia and elsewhere would later fight in Bosnia, Algeria, post-Soviet Azerbaijan and Tajikistan, as well as post-communist Afghanistan. After the war, when western military aid petered out, Afghan rebels vented their hostility to the West against western aid workers. *Newsweek* reported a bizarre incident, when 5,000 Afghan refugees burned down a center for widows and orphans, because the women committed the fiendish crime of washing themselves with soap. Among the Islamic heroes from Afghanistan were some of the immigrants from six Arab countries who detonated the massive truck bomb at the World Trade Center in New York in February 1993, killing six Americans and injuring a thousand, causing more than half a billion dollars' worth of damage, culminating, so far, with the 9/11 attack in 2000. The carnage has spread to Europe and there seems to be no end to various shapes and forms of fundamentalist Islam, all of them hostile to the West and most, if not all, extremely violent. The Reagan doctrine led to association with dubious characters, such as the Argentine generals before the Falklands war and General Manuel Noriega of Panama. When a list of more than a hundred Soviet agents in Iran fell into the hands of CIA chief William Casey, he, in spite of the hostility of the Iranian regime to the United States, relayed the information to Iran. The Iranians rounded up the agents and executed them.[40]

The unresolved hostage crisis in Iran was a main contributor behind Carter's loss in the 1980 presidential election. But apart from a very strong rhetoric, Ronald Reagan did not have much of a success in fighting terrorist attacks on the United States. When he met the returning American hostages from Iran, the newly elected president pledged "swift and effective retribution" against terrorists. But the reality was different, as Joseph T. Stanik points out: "Over the next five years terrorist aggression against Americans became increasingly violent, and after each incident Reagan stated that the responsible party would be held accountable for its deed. Yet he did not act." During the same period 660 American civilians and military personnel were killed and wounded by terrorists.[41] On the positive side of the ledger, the Soviets were hurt by American pressure. The Soviet leadership had spent much time and effort to gain superpower parity with the United States, and American acceptance of such. They therefore responded with bitterness and anger to Reagan's military build up and anti-communist campaign. Many historians, though, discount the President's contribution in dismantling the Soviet empire. William Pemberton's comments are typical:

> It is possible, however, that rather than having some deep insight into the Soviet Union Reagan was fortunate enough to be in power when that nation changed for reasons he did not understand and did not influence.

Reagan, according to Pemberton, was immaterial in dismantling the 'evil empire': "The cold war ended mainly because the Soviet Union had to change internally to save itself." But Mikhail Gorbachev had no intentions of reforming himself or the Communist Party into oblivion. The reform impulse came from the KGB and the military who were afraid of losing out in the arms race to the United States; reforms would consolidate and maintain party rule. Significantly, Gorbachev was the protégé of former KGB chief Yuri Andropov, and the KGB has never been a seed bed for democracy. Misjudging the extents of the problems and depths of public dissatisfaction, combined with heavy American pressure, Gorbachev found that once on the tiger's back it was not easy to find a safe place to dismount. Despite numerous challenges to the Soviets, Reagan cautiously applied military power. There are strong indications that the United States did not take military action against Libya, until Moscow signaled that it had written off the country. Besides, being diplomatically isolated and strategic vulnerable, Libya and its leader Colonel Muhammar Gaddafi was perfectly located to send a signal about American intentions in its fight against terrorism.[42]

While his anointed successor, George H. W. Bush, presided over the break up of the Soviet empire and the unification of Germany, there is little doubt that much of the credit belongs to Ronald Reagan. There is also little doubt that Reagan by focusing on the cold war was instrumental in forcing positive changes even in backwaters of the Soviet–American confrontation of the most intractable conflicts. A good example is how American policy assisted in guaranteeing independence for the last African colony Namibia, forcing withdrawal of 50,000 Cuban troops from Angola and moving South Africa away from its apartheid government.[43] Unfortunately, the president had a somewhat cavalier attitude towards the rise of Islamic fundamentalism and despite its fiery rhetoric his administration's fight against terrorism was mostly a lackluster affair.[44] Ronald Reagan was probably least successful in the Middle East, he placed American servicemen in harms way in Beirut (where the American embassy was bombed) and the Persian Gulf (where the American 'ally' Iraq attacked USS *Stark* killing 37 American sailors – which the President wrote off as an accident) with little to show for the sacrifice of American lives apart from the Iran/Contra scandal. In addition, Reagan passively watched the mushrooming of Israeli settlements in the occupied territories complicating American attempts to broker an Arab–Israeli peace treaty. While American intentions are somewhat unclear, the Reagan administration willingly or at the very least tacitly accepted a deepening British presence in the Persian Gulf. For a discussion how this came about we must turn to a discussion of events themselves in the Gulf, beginning with the crumbling Anglo-American pillar in Iran.

V

Iran: The Pillar Crumbles

When the shah of Iran visited the US for the first and only time during Carter's presidency in November 1977, the Iranian monarch was quite impressive. Chief aide to the president, Hamilton Jordan, would later record:

> Of all the people we had seen during that period – Sadat, Schmidt, Callaghan. Giscard, and scores of others – the Shah was clearly the most impressive. At their first bilateral meeting in the Cabinet Room at the White House, the Shah had conducted a *tour d'horizon* of the world, describing with great accuracy the problems facing the West, the strategic importance of Iran, and the entire nature of the U.S.–Iran relationship. He spoke for almost an hour without notes. It was more than a presentation – it was a performance.[1]

Then again, he had been practicing the speech for a long time, always concluding with the importance of Iran. The speech had been polished by several dress rehearsals when meeting previous American presidents, but with Nixon in particular. The *tour d'horizon*, however impressive, did not prevent the president from lecturing the king of kings on the lack of human rights in Iran, leaving the light of the Aryans visibly shaken.[2] Still, the visit had gone well in the eyes of the Carter administration: "By the time the Shah's visit was over, we felt reassured about the political situation in Iran and fortunate to have this strong leader as an ally."[3] This points to the key dilemma in Carter's policies towards Iran: for all his emphasis on human rights and limiting arms sales, the president and his advisors failed to develop an alternative policy towards Iran, being saddled with Nixon's policy of making Iran into an American pillar in the Persian Gulf. The Carter administration being somewhat unhappy with the edifice without being able to create constructions of their own in the region. Clearly, the president's push for human rights was one factor in the shah's decision to liberalize his domestic policies – a policy that partially contributed to the downfall of his regime. Carter and his associates on the other hand have in the aftermath of the Iranian revolution downplayed the role the president's human rights policies played.[4]

The *shahanshah* was deeply troubled by the human rights emphasis in Carter's foreign policy and in early March 1977 he fired the following diatribe in *Newsweek*: "I cannot believe that U.S. would be so shortsighted as to cut off its arms sales to my country. That would create a widening breach between you and the primary force for stability in this area . . . If America refuses to sell us arms, if you say that only you and the Russians are entitled to have major armaments, you will be treating us like slaves . . . and if my country is servile, if it cannot maintain true independence, what do I care if it becomes Communist? . . . If you do not want to sell me arms, I would have to reconsider my policies. (. . .) So who will suffer but yourselves? Because if you do not refuse me, I can buy $5 billion worth of arms and $5 billion worth of goods a year from the U.S. over the next five years. Who else can do that?"[5] This was basically the only other arrow in the shah's arsenal in addition to the speech, pleading for American support, which in the view of the *Ayamehr* ment that Iran should be able to buy whatever it wanted from the American arsenal. And why not? After Nixon had visited Tehran in May 1972, the president permitted Iran to buy without restrictions, bar nuclear weapons from the American arsenal. The shah bought on a grand scale, supported by rapidly increasing oil revenues. Between 1972 and 1977 Iran purchased arms to the tune of 16,2 billion dollars. The Iranian defense budget increased by 680 percent in the same period. Unfortunately, Iran had neither the infrastructure nor educational level to run its new sophisticated military machine. The presence of American and British military advisors ballooned to help the shah run his newly acquired military machine. It was a foreign presence that caused much resentment among the Iranians and became an important contributing factor to the ensuing revolution in the country.[6]

In the beginning, the shah and the new American president were off to a rocky start. On July 30, 1977, Carter noted in his diary that the shah had sent an angry message for the month-long delay in presenting the sale of AWACs to Congress: "He was thinking about withdrawing his letter of intent to purchase these planes from the United States. I do not care whether he buys them from us or not."[7] The great irony, despite Carter's emphasis on human rights and wanting to restrict arms sales, as Scott Kaufman observes: "As it turns out, the Carter administration during 1977 and 1978 provided more military assistance to Iran than Presidents Richard Nixon or Ford."[8]

Brzezinski claims that the fall of the shah and subsequent events in Iran "was the Carter Administration's greatest setback." But the blame for the debacle did not belong to the president or his national security advisor: "As the crisis unfolded, it became evident to me that lower echelons at State, notably the head of the Iranian desk, Henry Precht, were motivated by doctrinal dislike of the Shah and simply wanted him out of power altogether."[9] In addition much of the blame belonged to the shah, who "proved weak, vacillating and suffering from a paralysis of will."[10] Henry Precht in turn blames Brzezinski for unrealistically supporting the shah and ignoring Iranian opposition long after the king of kings for all practical purposes was finished. What they both agreed on was the weakness of the shah, in Precht's sarcastic account of a ruler losing his grip on power: "Would the British and especially, the Americans please tell him what to do?"[11] James Bill exonerates Precht: "He was one of the few in Washington who understood the fragility of the shah's power."[12] The king of kings blamed the west: "In power, I believed that my alliance with the West was based on strength, loyalty and mutual trust. Perhaps that trust had been misguided." While the public image of the shah was of an independent ruler with great power pretentions, he had never overcome his client status. Lacking clear instructions from his patron, the *shahanshah* floundered: "I never knew from one day to the next what U.S. policy was, or how reliable it was."[13]

President Carter blames his ambassador to Iran, William Sullivan, "who apparently lost control of himself, " and "seemed unable to present an objective analysis of the complicated situation in Iran." The president "was well aware that he had been carrying out some of my directives halfheartedly, if at all." Still, Carter did not fire Sullivan, explaining that secretary of state Cyrus Vance "insisted that it would be a mistake to put a new man in the country in the midst of the succession of crisis we probably faced." In this way, Vance too is deftly brushed with the Iranian debacle and not Carter. Sullivan, Carter complains, was aided and abetted by the State Department, in his obstructionism. [14] But ultimate authority rests with the president, and it was his responsibility to conduct American policy towards Iran. Sullivan, on his side, blames the Carter administration for not having any "policy whatsoever" towards Iran.[15]

But there is plenty of blame to go around, David Owen foreign minister of the United Kingdom when the shah fell, claims that the British failed to handle the *Ayamehr* properly but came to believe in the shah's "carefully constructed self-image", and furthermore: "We failed to remember how weak he was before he took on the airs of an autocrat. We were far too deferential before his charade of leadership while he vacillated month by month. We failed to infuse him with the decisiveness and ruthlessness which were necessary not just for survival but for his country's rejection of an Islamic revolution."[16] Scott Kaufman puts the blame squarely at the top: "There was a lack of leadership from the White House."[17] Interestingly in an earlier work Kaufman agrees with Carter that Sullivan pursued policies at odds with the president.[18]

But the beginning was more auspicious. On the eve of the Carter administration the state department assessed the Persian ruler favorably, being "both an old-fashioned authoritarian ruler and an enlighten modernizer" who dominated every branch of the government "and makes the major political, economic and military decisions." State favorable assessed shah the man as "intelligent, personable, well educated and idealistic . . . and inclined to lecture Westerners on their permissive societies."[19] Marc J. O'Reilly goes even further: "The Shah stuck an omnipotent pose within Iran, an impression that lulled the Carter administration into complacency."[20] The shah was concerned about leaving the cozy comforts of the Nixon and Ford administrations, sending repeated signals to the incoming Carter administration. If the United States refused a "tiny" ten percent oil price increase, bad things were set to happen.

Decreasing oil revenues would force Iran to scale back its military development programs. Who then would guard Persian Gulf on behalf of the west? If the US was not forthcoming, Moscow was always an option. "He is concerned that the 'special relationship' between Iran and the US may not be as firm as he had assumed, and he is reacting characteristically by talking tough and taking every opportunity to stress the benefits of this relationship to us and the potential costs if it should be lost." This was the other weapon in the shah's arsenal in addition to the speech; realistically there were no other powers that could assume Iran's defense obligations. The Carter administration would therefore apply the appropriate stroking to calm the shah, signaling its strong commitment to the relationship.[21] Rattling the oil weapon and Iran's military and economic beneficial relationship to the west, was part of the shah's standard operating procedure. On July 1, 1976 he instructed the Iranian ambassador to London on how to deal with what the Persian monarch considered negative British press: "Do what you can to change the attitude of the [British] Press, but it might be useful to remind them once in a while that Iran can always diversify her sources of supply, but Britain can't very well do without Iran's market." While ill disposed to suffer criticism himself, the shah was not above lecturing others: "While it is true, for instance, that the British have grown lazy and lost their former discipline, for HIM [His Imperial Majesty] to say so on television will lose him the sympathy of his listeners."[22] This is where the shah miscalculated, for only two years later the Labour government let go of the lucrative Iranian market instead of interfering in favor of the shah when he was in trouble. The shah sang from the same song sheet to everyone, including the British prime minister James Callaghan. When Callaghan visited Tehran, the king of kings advised him: "He then placed his need for additional revenues in a broader context, saying that if Iran was to assume its proper role in the Gulf, the sub-continent and the Indian ocean, he must spend more on arms."[23]

While ostentatiously emphasizing human rights, it is clear that the Carter administration visualized much of the same in terms of policy towards Iran. Searching for a new ambassador to Tehran, Gary Sick opinioned: "It should be an individual with considerable managerial capabilities and experience due to the vide variety of programs which he must contend with in Iran," as well as "an individual who can speak with authority on technical issues such as intelligence and military equipment." The state department was well aware of the shah's omnipotent position in Iran: "To a considerable degree, the state of US relations with Iran are dependent on the personal relationship which the Ambassador is able to establish with the Shah, and this will be Ambassador [William] Sullivan's principal objective in his first few months in Tehran."[24] Carter himself told Sullivan prior to his departure for Iran, that the country was of vital strategic importance and that the shah was "a close friend and a trusted ally." Carter emphasized that Iran was a force for stability in the Persian Gulf.[25]

But for the shah, the Carter administration's official human rights policy was a cause for considerable concern. The Persian monarch was extremely sensitive to criticism from the West, whether government or press, and was 'stung' by the assault on the lack of human rights in Iran. Among other things he undertook in trying to remedy the situation, he publicly announced that torture was no longer practiced in Iran.[26] While pushing for human rights, the CIA was well aware of growing security concerns in Iran, as well as threats against American citizens in the country, but discounted the possibility that terrorist organizations could undermine the shah's rule.[27] And this, when the Carter administration at the same time was well aware that the 30,000-strong American community in Iran was 'a prime target' for Iranian terrorists.[28]

The first high-level encounter between the shah and the Carter administration was when secretary of state Cyrus Vance visited Tehran in May 1977. Vance came away deeply impressed with the king of kings: "The shah's interests are encyclopedic and his grasp of both concepts and details is impressive. He sees Iran as playing an increasingly important role in the world and the U.S.–Iranian relationship is a crucial factor in his policies." The imperial whining paid off, Vance brought the grand prize: a November invitation for the shah to visit Washington. However much he strutted on the world stage, and however much the Americans encouraged independence from its ally, in his hearts of hearts the *Aya Mehr* must have been painfully aware that Iran was an American client. And for him to play his enlarged role he required constant stroking from his western benefactors. Pleased with the invitation, the long rehearsed speech followed, the light of the Aryan's *tour d'horizon*; the central premise being the fusion of Russian expansionism and Soviet policy seeking to extend its influence into the Persian Gulf and elsewhere. "He sees Iran as the principal bastion against this threat." To fulfill his self-appointed role, the shah needed a continued flow of American military equipment – but always with the underlying threat that if not forthcoming Iran had to look elsewhere.[29] Incidentally, the speech was also the fare the shah presented to Sullivan when first meeting the new American ambassador.[30] Sullivan reported shortly after arriving Tehran that the shah was "anxious to establish personal ties" with the president.[31] But the relationship needed constant tending by Sullivan, the shah always being in need of assurance of the American connection.[32] And that was the underlying message until the November 1977 Iranian–American summit in Washington: while grousing about some American policies, the shah made clear he valued his relations with the United States.[33]

Still, on the eve of his first tête-á-tête the shah exuded public confidence, as John Campbell explains in an article in *Foreign Affairs*: "Iran, in the view of Shah Mohammed Reza Pahlavi, has a great imperial past and a greater imperial future. In the next few years it is to assert its dominant role in the Persian Gulf region and the nearby reaches of the Indian Ocean. By 1990 it will attain the status of a Britain or a France in the global hierarchy of powers. Seeing this dream in the future, the Shah is already acting as if it were reality."[34] But the regime was corrupt, not only in an economic sense, but also morally, beginning with the shah who far from being immune from the temptations of money and power claimed that without enjoying "this one little indulgence of mine I'd be an utter wreck." The *shahanshah* was heartily endorsed by his court confidant, Asadollah Alam; "I agreed, remarking that every man in a position of responsibility needs some sort of distraction, female company being in my opinion the one cure that really works." Alam ran, or oversaw, a steady stream of European women to Tehran "with promises of extremely generous remuneration." [35]

The American side was certainly not blind to the benefits of the relationship. This is also suggested in the arrival statement and toasts by the president to the imperial couple:

> "You are indeed a trusted friend.
> We in the United States have a special attachment to Iran.
> Today as a result of your energetic and wise leadership:
> – Iran is secure politically and militarily;
> – It plays an increasingly prominent and important role in world affairs.
> Our guests are extraordinary accomplished and energetic human beings, dedicated to advancing the lives of their people and the stature of Iran. They are widely honored, but I [Carter] want to pay them special honor for their steadfast devotion to the cause of Iran–American friendship and their unswerving commitment to the furtherance of world peace and understanding." [36]

Vance, too, stressed the importance of American–Iranian relations to the president; the US exported two billion dollars in civilian goods annually to Iran, US direct investments in the country exceeded 500 million dollars; 30,000 Americans lived in Iran, while the same number of Iranian students resided in the US. "In a major sense Iran has reached the position of a stable and moderate middle-level power which has been a goal of United States policy ever since World War II." But there were additional benefits to the United States for its relationship with Iran, as Vance explained the president:

> Iran quietly provides Israel most of its imported oil, and access to a secure source of oil is a critical factor in Israeli security. Iran also maintains excellent, but unpublished relations with Israel. [Israeli foreign minister Moshe] Dayan has secretly visited Tehran several times this year, and there is an active intelligence collaboration. At the same time, the Shah is bluntly outspoken about the need for Israeli moderation and flexibility in moving toward a Middle East peace, and he is willing to use his influence with both the Arabs and the Israelis as necessary to further the peace process. – On this issue, the Shah is cooperative, and we rely on him very heavily to maintain the oil flow to Israel. It is not an issue we can use for bargaining. [37]

The shah on his side attempted to squeeze as much American public support as possible from his United States visit. Carter, trying to keep down the ostentatious and ceremonial aspects of his presidency, had pledged himself to give a state dinner for the king of kings on November 15, but had declined a return dinner the day after. "The Shah, through his Embassy, is requesting that you host a luncheon for him on the 16th and that you attend his return dinner on the 16th." [38] The president, when meeting the shah, reassured him that the United States valued its relations with Iran under the leadership of the *Aryamehr*.[39]

Shortly after meeting the shah in Washington, the president was off to Tehran. The king of kings needed more stroking and reassurance:

> The real purpose of the visit is to symbolize Iran's emergence as a middle level power which plays an essential role in the stability of the region and, at the same time, is acquiring a larger role on the world stage trough oil politics, financial activities, and involvement in international affairs. Concretely, the visit will serve to continue and reinforce the dialogue which was so successfully established between the President and the Shah during the November visit to Washington.[40]

On New Year's Eve, the president toasted the "great leadership of the Shah" who had made Iran "an island of stability in one of the more troubled areas of the world; This is a great tribute to you, Your Majesty, and to your leadership and to the respect and the admiration and love which your people give to you." In a little more than a year afterwards, the respectful people had forced the shah into a loving exile. The huge American community in Iran worked, according to Carter, "in close harmony with the people of Iran." So much so that the successor regime to the shah felt the need to take Americans hostages to prevent their harmonic co-workers from leaving. For Carter, even the problematic Iranian human rights record was unproblematic: "The cause of human rights is one that is shared deeply by our people and by the leaders of our two nations." It all came down to the top-level friendship: "And there is no leader with whom I have a deeper sense of personal gratitude and personal friendship."[41] One must, perhaps, question the president's political *fingerspitzgefühl* when so fulsomely praising the shah and identifying the United States so closely with his regime. Brzezinski had warned the president on December 5, 1977, almost a month prior to Carter's New Year's Eve Tehran *tête-a-tête* with the shah: "[The] CIA believes that the tough measures used to suppress student disorders in the past few weeks suggest the Shah has reverted to his traditional intolerance of political dissent."[42] By travelling to Iran after the crackdown the president, implicitly at the very least, signaled American acceptance and support for the shah's authoritarian measures. After his Washington visit, and having successfully brought Carter to Tehran, the shah was quite full of himself boasting in early 1978 in an interview with *The Washington Post*: "Nobody can overthrow me, I have the support of 700,000 troops, all the workers, and most of the people, I have the power."[43]

All in all, then, 1977 had been good year for American–Iranian relations. And so the British thought for Anglo-Iranian relations. Filing his annual report for 1977, British ambassador to Tehran, Anthony Parsons, observed: "British interests have continued to prosper." Exports were up 25 per cent compared to 1976, totaling almost £650 million. The shah's position was secure: "He is in control, his armed forces must be presumed to be as loyal as ever, and the opposition is fragmented. The problems facing the Shah and his Government are troublesome rather than dangerous; the economy is basically healthy and the present spirit of realism is a sounder basis for progress than the arrogant overconfidence of the past."[44] Despite trying to convince themselves that all was well, there was a smattering of reports during the first half of 1978 indicating that the regime might be in serious trouble. Brzezinski warned the president on January 31, 1978 that the shah had seen the most serious incidents against his regime for a decade and that he seemed "uncertain how to handle the challenge."[45] On May 10, the shah vented his frustrations to Sullivan: "This was the first time he has expressed the view that something may be fundamentally wrong with his system."[46]

Although continuing to receive information that something was amiss, it was only in the fall of 1978 that the United States and Britain realized that the shah was strongly challenged by the Iranian opposition. On October 24 the president learned that the king of kings solicited the advice of Sullivan and Parsons on how to deal with the domestic unrest in his country. Actually, what the shah needed and wanted was Anglo-American guidance on how to deal with the situation. The ambassadors tried to downplay the crisis, arguing that "the outlook was not as dark as it seemed." Carter's response was to minute on the memorandum: "Give him whatever advice we can."[47] This is actually less than three months before the shah was forced to leave his country, but Carter here does not evidence any serious concerns or give any hint that he understood the depth of the crisis in Iran. While the shah was floundering and seeking guidance from his British and American patrons, he was at the same time, paradoxically, deeply suspicious of Britain in particular, repeatedly claiming to the British ambassador to the Peacock throne, Anthony Parsons: "If you lift up Khomeini's beard, you will find MADE IN ENGLAND written under his chin."[48] To many this is an example of the shah's paranoia, but he personally had ample experience of Britain's perfidy and omnipotence. Britain had deposed his father in 1941, and the shah's rival prime minister Mossadegh in 1953. The *Aryamehr* could have but little doubt that he reigned by Anglo-American sufferance. Later the shah had occasion to observe how Britain ruthlessly purged the sheikh of Abu Dhabi for refusing to follow the edicts of the political residents in 1966.[49] And similarly, how the Adeni sheiks were betrayed in the final days of the Aden protectorate. Leaving the Aden federation (Southwest Arabia) Britain callously abandoned their allies and clients of long standing. As Clive Jones has observed:

> the Labour government of Harold Wilson, despite assurances given to the Federal potentates that Britain would honour its commitments to safeguard the transition to independence and beyond: for those rulers and their followers who had thrown in their lot with the British, their sense of betrayal was profound. As the old Arab adage had it, 'it is better to be the enemy of the British than their friend: if you are

their friend: they will sell you whereas if at least you are their enemy they'll attempt to buy you'.[50]

The British had repeatedly assured the Persian Gulf sheiks on a continued British presence, only to leave abruptly. The old sultan of Oman was deposed for not toeing the British party line, while only a year afterwards Britain, in a miniature version of the Molotov–Ribbentrop Pact of 1939, singlehandedly redrew the map of the Gulf by handing the Abu Musa and Tunbs Islands belonging to Ras al Khameneih and Sharjah to the shah without being overly concerned about local Arab feelings or rights. After these demonstrations of ruthless, arbitrary and overwhelming British power local rulers, the shah included, were well conditioned to react appropriately to any signal emerging from London. Otherwise, as sultan Taimur learned to his cost in July 1970, failure to take guidance from the leaves in the British teacup earned you a one-way ticket to the Dorchester Hotel in London, courtesy of the British special force SAS regiment. British and American policy had since been to raise the shah from client status to an Anglo-American ally. But in his hearts of hearts, however much he strutted on the world stage, the *shahanshah* knew he was a client and when in trouble he expected to be saved by his patrons or at the very least receive instructions on how to handle the crisis. When neither was forthcoming, no wonder the Persian monarch was at loss of what to do. It did not help the shah that his western benefactors lost respect for him and his rule. The Bureau of Research and Intelligence of the state department observed in the aftermath of the Iranian revolution: "Iran became a 'theater-state' in which the Shah ruled from the stages of his glittering palaces and the people were the passive audience, with a great gap separating them."[51]

At the same time the Persian monarch also suspected that the CIA had turned against him, fearing that he was the sacrificial lamb in an US–Soviet scheme to partition Iran.[52] The shah's despondence triggered an American assurance of unconditional support to do whatever necessary to restore order, mildly admonishing the Persian monarch that after order was restored: "We hope he will restore prudent efforts to promote liberalization and eradicate corruption."[53] In his memoirs Brzezinski wrote: "My purpose in calling the shah was to make it clear to him that the President and the United States stood behind him and to encourage him to act forcefully before the situation got out of hand."[54] As the situation in Iran deteriorated, Brzezinski recommended, with the president's acceptance, that for Iran the main problem was restoring order: "This requires unequivocal support for the Shah, not diluted by conditional references to elections or liberalization." In the longer term, it required steering Iran's modernization without violent upheavals.[55] Carter's envoy, Arthur Callahan, transmitted assurances of unequivocal American support in Tehran, and requested feedback from the shah: "I told him that should he think of other ways in which we might be helpful he should not hesitate to let us know by any appropriate channel." There is no question at this stage of the game that the president fully supported the shah. But the shah was no longer a confident ruler: "I really could not get him to give any kind of broad balanced assessment of the situation and I had the impression that he finds it baffling, incomprehensible and almost overwhelming. In addition he seems to trust no one and his one-time confidence in his own judgment seems deeply shaken."[56] Towards the end of his reign, the shah was completely at a loss what to do, clinging to straws in the hope that the Americans and British would save him. His moods vacillated with the news coming from Washington, as this example shows from Carter's daily brief: "Ali Amini informed Ambassador Sullivan today that the Shah has reportedly plunged into a deep depression as a result of the President's remarks on Iran at the press breakfast yesterday. The Shah interpreted the remarks as calling for a popular referendum on the future of the monarchy."[57]

Stansfield Turner, director CIA, sent an alert memorandum to the National Security Council on November 29, 1978 warning: "The Shia Muslim holy month of Moharram that begins on 2 December 1978 is likely to bring an especially severe challenge to the Shah of Iran and to the military government installed by the Shah in early November." Commemorating the death of Hussein, grandson of the prophet Mohammed, would steadily increase religious intensity. "Even in calm times these observances emphasize the clerical challenge to secular authority that is integral to Shia Islam." Now, it could possibly threaten the Peacock throne at the hands of Ayatollah Khomeini.[58]

On the other side of the Gulf, the Arabs felt that the shah deserved what was coming to him, as the CIA noted on December 8, 1978: "We cannot help but believe that for Sheikh Zayid of Abu Dhabi and some of the other United Arab Emirates' leaders who chafed under Iran's military takeover of three Gulf islands- – Abu Musa and the two Tunbs – in 1972, that the shah's problems are considered his 'just deserts.' The Gulf Arab rulers, with their democratic Bedouin heritage, always sneered at the imperial pretentions of the Shah."[59]

For Britain, the fall of 1978 was a time to reassess British relations with Iran. One source, who prefers to remain anonymous, worked as junior civil servant on Iranian affairs until August 1975 observed: "It was a madhouse of greed on all sides, with seconded members of the armed forces, civil engineering project managers, and Iranian and other middle-men taking advantage from what at the time seemed an endless pot of dosh." Anthony Parsons confirms this; the principal task of the embassy in Tehran was to promote British exports. This went all the way up to the Foreign Office, who offered but little guidance when the shah began faltering. "The plain fact is that Pahlavi Iran was, in the short term, a valuable ally for Britain as well as a highly lucrative market." For many years, the British gamble of Iran was successful: "I have no regrets on this score."[60] To foreign minister, David Owen: "His Imperial Majesty the *Shahanshah* held himself like a preened peacock." When his power slipped away, the shah believed that Britain could save him: "The shah also became obsessive about the hidden hand of Britain, attributing to us a role and influence which we ourselves were never able to live up to." Furthermore, the shah's criticism and "ostentatious flaunting of wealth and power" were deeply resented by British politicians.[61] In early November 1978, the Cabinet considered the implications of the deteriorating political situation in Britain for Iran: Iran produced almost 12 percent of the world's non-Communist oil, this was for all practical purposes the totality of Iranian exports. Iran was Britain's 14th largest export market, but the largest market for British defense exports. In sum, the Iranian market created 100,000 jobs in Britain.[62] If the British economic involvement was extensive, the American was even more so. Iranian oil production had peaked around 6 million barrels per day; the quadrupling of oil prices after 1973 had dramatically increased revenues "much beyond the absorptive capacity of its economy." By 1978, Iran had become a major market for American goods and services. Almost 400 American companies had sales totaling $3.8 billion, total direct investment stood at $700 million. "Some 40,000 Americans were in the country working on construction, communications, and military project contracts." Commercial activities were sharply reduced after the shah's departure, but began picking up in the latter half of 1979, only to be brought to an abrupt standstill with the seizure of hostages on November 4, 1979. [63] Ironically, as we shall see below, Britain pledged to restrict commercial relations with Iran, but as Brzezinski informed the president on September 29, 1980: "British trade with Iran in the first seven months of 1980 was more than double the comparable period of 1979."[64] But being a major Anglo-American economic and not to forget strategic interest, it was evidently not of sufficient importance to warrant direct western involvement, not to mention use of military force in Iran. When the shah no longer served a useful purpose, neither Britain nor the United States had any difficulties in discarding him. The arrogance of power by the shah in his prime did little to endear him to the West.

When the leaders of the West met at Guadeloupe in early January 1979, there was but little sympathy and support for the shah. The president's wife, Rosalynn Carter observed that Helmut Schmidt exclaimed: "We all knew how weak he was, but I'm surprised he is going under before the Saudis," while British premier Callaghan chimed in: "Everybody is of the same opinion . . . very weak. Nobody has been willing to tell the shah the truth. We haven't told him the truth about the disintegrating situation in ten years."[65] In an official meeting between the four, Carter expressed optimism explaining: "that the chances of a stable outcome of the crisis were rather better than they had been a fortnight earlier."[66] After the shah had left Iran on January 16, 1979, Carter noted in his diary: "Khomeini sent his representative to pledge increased friendship and cooperation, and to make sure that we supported a stable government in Iran. We gave him that assurance."[67] The shah was promised sanctuary in the United States when departing Iran, but the president soon reversed himself. At a July 27, 1979 breakfast with his foreign policy team Carter said that "he did not wish the shah to be here playing tennis while Americans in Tehran were being kidnapped or killed." In fact, the Carter administration had long since decided to cast its lot with the Islamic Republic of Iran. Meeting the Iranian prime minister, foreign minister and minister of defense in Algiers on November 1, 1979, Brzezinski almost pleaded for better relations: "We are prepared for any relationship you want ... We have a basic community of interest but we do not know what you want us to do."[68] While Vance had assured the Iranian foreign minister in October that "the United States wanted a relationship with Iran based on mutual respect, equality and friendship."[69] Despite several American attempts to ingratiate itself with Khomeini's regime, Iran did not reciprocate.[70] Despite repeated American attempts under Carter and Reagan, the Iran/Contra scandal being the most notorious example, to improve relations in Iran there were no takers in Tehran. The clerical regime has been fundamentally hostile to the West. After hobnobbing with the great and powerful when on the Peacock throne, it was not only the United States that held the shah at arm's length. Informally inquiring if he could move to his private residence in Surrey, England he was rebuffed by Callaghan. Besides, there was a genuine concern about security, the Foreign and Commonwealth Office informed the American embassy in London: "It would be impossible to ensure the safety of the Shah and his entourage at his country house."[71] Margaret Thatcher upon taking office would follow the same policy on refusing the shah a British exile: "The Prime Minister made it clear that she was deeply unhappy about the Government's inability to offer sanctuary to a ruler who had, in her view, been a firm and helpful friend to the UK. The Prime Minister is nevertheless very conscious of the need to avoid any risk to those British subjects remaining in Iran or to our Embassy there."[72]

But before it came to this, and when realizing that the shah had go, it was a question of easing him out of power and salvaging as much of American influence as possible in Iran. Distrusting Sullivan, Carter dispatched general Huyser to Iran from January 4 to February 4, 1979. "General Huyser was instructed to keep senior officials in Washington informed of the morale and effectiveness of the Iranian military forces and to ensure that the Iranian military leaders maintained confidence in United States support. In addition, he sought Iranian military cooperation in safeguarding sensitive U.S. military equipment." With the shah in exile, it was important for the US to keep the Iranian military intact to ensure a 'responsible' government. But for all American good intentions: "General Huyser was in no position to affect the basic realities of the Iranian revolution." In other words, the Huyser mission was a complete failure.[73] Also, as the United States was forced to acknowledge, the Carter administration had been misguided in its reliance on the Iranian military. The intelligence and research unit of the state department observed on June 25, 1979: "By mid-1978, the Iranian armed forces had made impressive steps forward in the modernization programs initiated by the Shah. The military establishment gave the impression that it had reached new levels of strength in keeping with its progress toward modernization. Yet, only six months later, those forces were in a state of nearly complete collapse." Despite public perceptions of strength, the Iranian armed forces were plagued by serious problems. In reality, the armed forces, in contrast to for instance Turkey, "where the armed forces have been widely accepted for many years as the ultimate guarantors of the country's complex political system, the Iranian armed forces had been the chief support first for a family and finally for an individual." As supreme commander the shah controlled his military down to the smallest detail:

> He personally approved all promotions above the rank of major, selected most of the foreign equipment to be purchased, met every few days with senior commanders, fixed the special perquisites which kept the military happy, kept an excessively large number of loyal officers in senior positions long after retirement age, and carefully subverted all efforts to alter his system of personal command.

The shah kept the military compartmentalized, never meeting his senior commanders as for instance a general staff collectively, but individually, encouraging the officers to compete with each other for the favors of the king of kings. The shah kept all reins in his own hands: "There was no joint planning or mechanism for effective coordination. The Shah was not prepared to loosen his single, central hold on all the levers." The system rewarded loyalty and mediocrity before competence. The shah did not want independent thinkers and actors in his military. In fact, "the military was isolated from the population, was increasingly a distinct sub-culture, and had few functions of direct relevance or benefit to the people." But the Iranian national character was also at fault: "The Persian character trait of shunning responsibility was also a negative factor as the strength of the anti-Shah forces grew. In the military it was necessary to go to flag rank (or virtually so) to get even the most insignificant points decided." The shah himself was a major contributor to the collapse, by refusing to lead at critical junctures. By not ordering his army to take the necessary actions to back up his regime, resulted in undermining the officer corps loyalty to its supreme commander. But there are larger issues involved: to his credit the shah refused to engage in wholesale slaughter of the population. During the fall of 1978, "the Shah did not seem to be able to make decisions at all. The leader who could do no wrong [in the eyes of the army] was doing nothing."[74] Not only that, but Iranian forces rapidly lost operational capability with the loss of American technicians and spare parts.[75] The United States was willing, almost eager to establish relations with the new Iranian regime. Vance met the Iranian foreign minister Ibrahim Yazdi on October 3, 1979: "I told him we were prepared to deal with Iran in the future on the basis of friendship and mutual respect."[76]

The British had their own post-mortem on the fall of the shah. One Foreign and Commonwealth official had travelled in remote parts of Iran in the spring of 1977, and found the most backward of conditions making them even more intolerable by contrast to the opulent cities.[77] This at the time when the shah was full of his contributions to the country, boasting of his 'Great Civilization' and that Iran soon would join the ranks of the industrialized countries. Simultaneously, the *shahnashah* kept up a steady drumbeat for increased oil revenues; if they failed to materialize the West would lose valuable export markets. This was combined with a ruler becoming increasingly haughty, regarding himself immune from criticism and more and more remote from the life of ordinary Iranians. The last British ambassador to the shah explained the reasons for British policy and failure toward Iran: "After 150 years of gross British interference in Iran's internal affairs, all Persians, including the Shah, were obsessed by the hidden hand of the British. Our only hope of establishing a profitable working relationship with the Shah was to do everything possible to allay these suspicions and nothing to feed them. Hence the deliberate policy carried out by myself and my two predecessors of avoiding all contacts with the Mullahs and the old politicians, the two elements were our hidden hand had been most active in the past [sic]."[78]

Iran: Getting Stuck in the Rubble

Even after the shah was forced to leave Iran, the lingering effects of the twin-pillar strategy remained with both the Carter and the successor Reagan administrations. Iran was simply too important to ignore for American foreign policy makers, fearing Soviet penetration of this strategically located and oil-rich country. The Carter administration repeatedly sought good relations with Khomeini before the hostage crisis, but there were no takers in Tehran. President Carter applied force with great reluctance and his hostage rescue operation was almost purposely designed for failure and to calm the American domestic scene which was clamoring for forcible action. Significantly, the military option was never seriously considered again by the Carter administration after the failure of the rescue attempt. The Reagan administration's policy towards Iran was even more disgraceful: myopic, with a cold war focus and fear of the Soviets, the president and some of his advisors sought openings to the moderates in a post-Khomeini Iran. Unfortunately, for the Americans there was no such thing as a 'moderate bloc' in Iran, the Mullahs having killed most of the opposition and driven the rest into exile. Nevertheless, the policy pursued based on this flawed assumption ended in the Iran/Contra debacle and almost cost Reagan his presidency. The British, on the other hand, kept their distance from the ruling theocrats in Tehran, but not to a greater extent than that British trade with Iran continued to prosper and the Thatcher government effectively using the threat of a militant Iran to strengthen its ties and position on the Arab side of the Persian Gulf.

Following the departure of the shah, Brzezinski wrote the president on February 22, 1979:

> "The fall of the Shah's regime in Iran has added a new and dangerous dimension to the crisis in the Middle East. Immediately, we face a problem of perceptions and expectations. For all the countries, and especially those whom we have good relations, the future is uncertain and threatening. They lack confidence in the direction of U.S. policy and in the willingness of the U.S. to use power on behalf of their security. This political and psychological crisis can only be contained by forceful and

purposeful U.S. action. (. . .) At the same time, the voracious appetite of the West for oil makes it difficult to manage the economic development of the oil-producing states, especially Saudi Arabia, in an orderly manner. This set of conditions makes it highly desirable that U.S. steps to enhance Middle East security be coupled with new steps to reduce U.S. dependence on Middle East oil and to coordinate policy initiatives with the Europeans and the Japanese. (. . .) Our ultimate objective in the Middle East must be to cultivate an awareness of common security problems that will lead to cooperative actions."

For the Persian Gulf this meant an increased American military presence. Interestingly, as we see here, the United States began moving with full force into the Gulf long before the enunciation of the Carter doctrine in response to the Soviet invasion of Afghanistan. Furthermore the US was considering overt and covert cooperation with Egypt against Libya and with Saudi Arabia against the PDRY: "In collaboration with the Saudis and, perhaps, the Egyptians, a comprehensive plan for the security of Oman should be implemented. This should include military and internal security support, joint exercises and planning, and occasional demonstrations of presence."[1]

Shortly after arrival, Khomeini began setting his imprint on the Iranian body politic. On February 12, 1979 he issued the following proclamation: anyone who did not support the Iranian revolution "will be considered as opposed to God Almighty and a traitor to the country and the Islamic movement."[2] When the US finally relented to have the shah admitted for medical reasons in October 1979, the Carter administration took care to inform the Iranian regime. "The Iranian leadership indicated that the Shah's travel to the United States would produce a sharp reaction in Iran, but assured the charge that protection for the Embassy would be provided. Based on that assurance, the improved physical security of the Embassy, and the increased security precautions taken by the Embassy staff, the United States decided to admit the shah for medical treatment."[3] Paul B. Ryan is of a different opinion: "No one seemed disturbed that the Iranian government took no steps to place an armed guard around the embassy. And Washington did not direct the virtually unprotected embassy staff to destroy all classified documents in its files."[4] Soon thereafter, on November 4, Iranian students attacked the Embassy taking 61 Americans hostage. Khomeini's role on November 4 is unclear, but he soon tried to take advantage of the situation to strengthen his position domestically. Carter laid down two principles to solve the crisis: "protection of the honor and vital interests of the United States," and, "protection of the well-being of the hostages and their safe release at the earliest possible moment." This was to be done by diplomatic means; Carter did not at the early stages of the hostage crisis seriously consider military measures.[5]

When prime minister Margaret Thatcher met with French president Valery Giscard on November 19, 1979, president Carter called: "We are having a difficult time. You have been very helpful to us so far. I called to ask you and Valery to talk over between ourselves what you might do to express your condemnation publicly of the potential trials of hostages in Iran and to take the strongest possible protestation to Khomeini that you can and to consider anything else you might do to help." The president was concerned about the prospective trial of American hostages and requested British and French support. The prime minister promised condemnation by the entire EU. When asked by Giscard what the United States intended to do, Carter replied: "What can we do?" The president wanted moral support for the American position, and at this stage there is no hint of military measures.[6] Thatcher explained British policy in detail to American legislators on December 17, 1979: "The Americans had recognised the efforts of our Embassy in Tehran, which had been very considerable. We had done everything possible despite the fact that our own Embassy had been sacked earlier in the year and briefly held hostage at the time of the takeover of the American Embassy. Britain was giving the United States all the help she could; we had sent no military equipment to Iran since the taking of the hostages; our trade was down," and furthermore the prime minister had pledged to the president to support the US in the United Nations. "The special relationship was indefinable, but it existed and gave the Americans the right to expect to be able to count on Britain."[7] Cleverly, the prime minister clearly implies that Britain should also expect to count on American support in a crisis. But the president was not above a little threats of his own, after the blocking of Iranian assets in US banks domestically and abroad, the move was challenged in British courts. Carter urged Thatcher to use her government's influence "to stay any judgment in that case on the grounds that this is sovereign matter between two governments." American patience was growing thin, and failure to respond positively could have an adverse effect on Anglo-American relations: "The plans that you and I have for more intensive cooperation in the defense area, including the modernization of the British strategic deterrent, would not be understood in the United States should Britain be seen as taking actions to undermine our peaceful bargaining leverage in this crisis."[8]

In response to the occupation of the Mecca mosque (more on this in the chapter on Saudi Arabia) in November 1979, Khomeini engaged in some truly tested Stalinist verbal gymnastics:

> This act is contrary to Islamic principles and, in addition to the fact that the blessed Mosque is a Muslim sanctuary, the great Mecca itself is likewise a sanctuary. It is clear that certain criminal hands are trying to split the Muslims and make Islamic revolutions look ugly. *It is not farfetched to assume that this act has been perpetrated by criminal American imperialism so that it can infiltrate the solid ranks of Muslims by such intrigues.*

For good measure, the ayatollah tossed in the specter of Zionism that were in cahoots with American imperialism: "It would not be farfetched to assume that, as it has often indicated, Zionism intends to make the house of God (Mecca) vulnerable and create riots."[9] The great irony, of course, was that while fundamentalist in nature the occupation of the mosque was a domestic reaction to the modernizations policies of the Saudi regime as well as rooted in Saudi tribal politics, many of the occupiers being descendants from opponents of king Saud when he forcibly united the kingdom under his house.

The hostage situation made the United States appear weak, but it was not all bleak. Early in the new year the United States registered a small but welcome victory. On January 29, six Americans who had hid in the Canadian Embassy "departed through the Tehran airport using assumed identities. Canada then closed its Embassy and withdrew all personnel." While their homecoming was a cause for celebration in the US, "Iranians reacted sharply, complaining of a 'violation of international law.'"[10] Carter, with the possible exception of the rescue mission, was basically conciliatory toward revolutionary Iran. But even the rescue operation fits the conciliatory pattern, the president only giving a green light when all venues for a peaceful solution had broken down. The operation was almost designed for failure (to be discussed below), but afterwards the Carter administration never seemed to have seriously considered the military option again. The Carter administration instead assiduously worked to find a peaceful solution to the crisis, outside the traditional diplomatic channels. With the president's permission, White House chief of staff, Hamilton Jordan, negotiated with intermediaries to the Iranian official leadership president Bani-Sadr and foreign minister Ghotzbzadeh. On February 15, 1980, Carter instructed Jordan to transmit the following assurance to the Iranian leaders: "If, at any time, the Government of Iran desires to release hostages at an earlier date than called for in the mutually agreed plan, the Government of Iran has my personal assurance that the United States will abide by all terms of that plan."[11] This was not the first time and would not be the last time the United States did its utmost to assure Iran about its good intentions.

The reward was that Iran constantly broke its agreements, as it did on the UN commission of inquiry, an agreement between Iran, the US, and UN general secretary Kurt Waldheim, which was created for two purposes: "to hear the grievances of the Iranians and to allow a resolution of the crisis." As part of the agreement, the commission was to visit all the American hostages, a deal the Iranians negated after two weeks of discussions in Tehran. Carter then advised Thatcher, on March 13, 1980, that the failure of the commission "will be a severe setback for any early progress through negotiations." The president appealed again for British support: "I would appreciate it very much if you could review those measures which you instituted during the winter, such as informal financial measures, the restraint on buying Iranian oil at prices sharply different from other OPEC producers, and the ban on supply of military equipment, to ensure that they are being enforced. I need your help in impressing on Iranian authorities the gravity of their continuing disregard of international law and human rights."[12] It must have been a quite interesting and peculiar experience for the prime minister experiencing an American president in the role of supplicant. The parallel to the situation under the Vietnam war is almost uncanny. The deeper the American involvement in the jungles of South East Asia, the greater the need for British support.[13] Thatcher assured the president of British support: "The British Government and people have the deepest sympathy with you over the tragic predicament of the hostages. We want to do everything we can to help." Every time the occasion permitted, the prime minister would repeat the mantra of Britain being the most faithful and reliable American ally. But this, of course, came with a price; the implicit message being that when Britain was in need of American support it was expected to be forthcoming.

Responding to Carter's March 13, letter, despite being supportive, Thatcher urged restraint, as she promised to write Bani-Sadr, encouraging other governments to do the same, to ensure an early release of the hostages: "Precipitate action at the present juncture could well have effects contrary to those which we are all seeking." But if all efforts of a peaceful solution failed, Thatcher pledged, "then my government will of course give you its support." The nature of the support remained deliciously imprecise, but would require close coordination and cooperation with the British government. In this way, Thatcher while giving cost free (for Britain) assurances of support, it ensured that the United Kingdom would have an influence on American policy towards Iran.[14]

It is fair to say that the president had exhausted almost all other means to find a solution over the hostage crisis, before breaking relations with Iran on April 7, 1980. Carter also announced at the same press conference that all exports to Iran were prohibited, and no new visas to the US would be issued to Iranian citizens. "In order to minimize injury to the hostages, the United States has acted at all times with exceptional patience and restraint in this crisis."[15] With the imposition of sanctions, further appeals reached London for British support. But Britain had, in fact, previously given considerable practical support to the Americans. Britain had stopped giving new official export credits to Iran; informally informed British banks to restrict Iran from operating freely in the British financial market; would no longer buy Iranian oil on non-OPEC terms; and would "not ship military equipment and spare parts to Iran." The US wanted Britain to tighten the embargo of exports to Iran, with the exception of food, medicine and medical supplies; for Britain, with the other American allies, to withdraw its ambassadors from Iran, and eventually, to break diplomatic relations with Iran.[16] The crisis was taking its toll, sufficiently so, that the 'iron lady' expressed her concern to the president during a phone conversation on April 19, 1980, to which Carter assured her, that he was "Just fine". Thatcher was still concerned: "You sound a little bit – well, it is not surprising that you sound a bit worried."[17] Incidentally, the president had approved the rescue plan on April 11, eight days before his conversation with the British and the French leader.[18]

The material in the Carter Library strongly suggests an administration intent on going it alone, albeit seeking allied support. While informing the allies, they were rarely consulted. It was also an administration that eschewed military force. The hostage rescue mission was the exception proving the

President Jimmy Carter hosts a state dinner at the White House for Prime Minister James Callaghan, 10 March 1977.

President Jimmy Carter and Prime Minister Margaret Thatcher, 13 September 1977.

The Shah of Iran, Empress Farah, President Jimmy Carter and First Lady Rosalynn Carter, on a podium, 15 November 1977.

President Jimmy Carter's infamous New Year's Eve toast to the Shah of Iran, 31 December 1977.

President Jimmy Carter hosts a luncheon for king Khalid of Saudi Arabia, 27 October 1978.

Chancellor Helmut Schmidt, Prime Minister James Callaghan, President Jimmy Carter and President Giscard d'Estaing in Guadeloupe, 5 January 1979.

President Reagan walking his dog Lucy with Margaret Thatcher, 20 February 1985.

First Lady Nancy Reagan and Sigourney Weaver at a White House state dinner for King Fahd of Saudi Arabia, 11 February 1985.

President Ronald Reagan and Queen Elizabeth horseback riding at Windsor castle, 8 June 1982.

Photograph of President Reagan motioning to Ed Meese during a press briefing on the Iran/Contra issue, 25 November 1986.

rule. The mission was complicatedly planned and executed: "The mission began with 8 helicopters flying toward the staging point in the [Iranian] eastern desert. Two helicopters were lost en route. The failure of the third helicopter at the staging point necessitated a decision to terminate the mission. In the attempt eight airmen lost their lives and five others were seriously injured."[19] The rescue mission, was almost designed for failure. There was almost no reserve capacity, a view shared by Richard Thornton: "If no one thought of repairing the helicopter [hydraulic pump failure], it simply testifies to the inadequacy of the Carter leadership under pressure." Thornton argues that Carter never intended "to do more than carry out a show of force in the first place." This to shore up his own image of "ineptitude, and in an attempt to intimidate the Iranian leadership and to demonstrate his ability to take action."[20]

Thatcher was informed in a terse note of the failure of the rescue mission.[21] The United Kingdom was not informed of the rescue operation in advance, as Carrington was forced publicly to admit.[22] After the failed rescue attempt of hostages on April 24, the Carter administration did not seem to engage in further military efforts. Secretary of state, Cyrus Vance, resigned in protest over the rescue attempt. The new secretary of state, Edmund Muskie, minuted the president on July 31, 1980: "The rescue attempt has, I believe, made it less likely that you would be criticized for not taking further action to free the hostages." This was also Carter's sentiment; there is nothing in the president's annotated comments suggesting he contemplated armed force against Iran.[23] In fact, I have found no evidence in the declassified record that the United States considered any military measures after the botched rescue attempt.

The US policy in the hostage crisis rested on three principles: first to ensure the safe release of all hostages held in Iran, secondly to "preserve the United States' reputation in terms of Prestige and Power", and finally uphold the respect for International Law and diplomatic immunity in particular.[24] As time passed, and with the added burden of an opportunistic Iraq invading Iran, the hostages began losing its value for the Islamic state. Khomeini issued the following statement on September 12, 1980:

> You, the Moslems who are praying beside the House of God, pray for those who are resisting the United States and other superpowers, know that we do not want to fight against Iraq and that the people of Iraq support the Islamic revolution, we are fighting the United States which is today acting through the Iraqi government.
> . . .
> You in the nonaligned countries know that the U.S. wants to destroy us, so help us in our objectives . . .
> I have repeatedly said that taking hostages by our Moslem, militant, and responsible students was the natural reaction of our nation against the damage that the U.S. inflicted on our country.
> They will be released by giving back the property of the defunct Shah, cancella-

tion of all American claims against Iran, guaranteeing U.S. political and military non-intervention in Iran, and freeing all over assets.[25]

As part of the package deal solving the hostage crisis Jimmy Carter issued a *Formal Declaration of the President of the United States of America* entitled <u>*Non-intervention in Iran*</u> [emphasis in original]. "The Government of the United States of America hereby declares that it is the policy of the United States to accept the Government of the Iranian Revolution and the freedom of choice of the people of Iran; to accept the Government of the Islamic Republic as presently constituted; and not to intervene, directly or indirectly, politically or militarily, in Iran's internal affairs."[26] Significantly, the United States saw no need for reciprocity from Iran. When the hostages were finally released, the Iranians as a final insult took care to wait after Carter's term had expired. President Ronald Reagan appointed Carter his envoy to meet the returning hostages in Germany. Carter reported his meeting with the liberated hostages to Reagan on January 21, 1981:

> They have been abused more than I had previously known. The Iranians have – even up to the last moment – acted like savages. Even going from their last bus ride in Iran to the plane the Americans were forced individually to walk a gauntlet – Through a human corridor receiving verbal & physical abuse from both sides.
>
> This long, official criminal act of terrorism should never be accepted nor forgotten nor forgiven by the civilized world.[27]

Iranian abuse of the hostages was well known to the American public at the time their release. *Newsweek* reported on February 2, 1981: "Some of the hostages endured dark threats, beatings and mock executions: A few spent long periods in solitary confinement. All of them put up with boredom, rancid food and theft of their belongings." Although American officials denied it, there were reports that some of the male prisoners were abused sexually.[28]

As we have seen, the Carter administration and Brzezinski in particular, saw Iran to a large extent through the lenses of the cold war. This in part may explain why the United States shelved any further military rescue operations under Carter. It has been argued that the Iranians feared the responses of a more militant United States after Ronald Reagan became president.[29] This as we also have seen was somewhat removed from the practice of the new president and his administration, who was rather long on rhetoric but considerable less willing to put his verbal gymnastics into political practice. While Thatcher clearly was boosting British influence, the Reagan administration did the best it could to reduce American prestige and influence by the Iran/Contra scandal. As Ann Wroe wryly notes: "Two illusions lay at the heart of Iran/Contra. The first was that the Iran of Ayatollah Khomeini could, in some sort, be reasonably dealt with; the second was that a band of rag-tag guerillas, the Nicaraguan contras, could save the West from Communism. Both illusions were shattered in ways that underlined how fragile and ramshackle the policies were, and they were shattered within a month of each other."[30] Even more devastating was the final Congressional Report on the Iran/Contra affair: "The lesson to Iran was unmistakable. (. . .) All U.S. positions and principles were negotiable, and breaches by Iran went unpunished. Whatever Iran did, the U.S. could be brought back to the arms bargaining table by the promise of another hostage."[31]

The Iran/Contra scandal has been analyzed elsewhere in this work, but if the Carter administration's vision on Iran was rather blurred by cold war focals, this was probably the case to even larger extent for the Reagan administration. Many have excused Reagan's reckless handling of the Iran/Contra affair, being saved from impeachment by the memory of Watergate, because he was so concerned about the welfare of the hostages during his administration, particularly American nationals captured mostly in Lebanon. Indeed, he was very concerned, but it also served as a convenient excuse for engineering a new American approach to Iran. But the hostages as a Trojan mouse for changing American policy was not very well thought through. As soon the Iranians learned that the value of the hostages increased, they did what all sensible entrepreneurs do, they got more of the valuable commodity, that is they kidnapped more Americans and other westerners in the Middle East as they released some of the earlier hostages.

Peter Kornbluh and Malcolm Byrne in their edition of declassified documents on Iran/Contra write: "In the end, the Americans and Israelis provided Iran 2,004 TOW and eighteen HAWK missiles (. . .), 240 HAWK spare parts, and a variety of sensitive intelligence on Iraq. They were willing to provide much more, including more HAWKs, radar equipment, and other materiel. In return, only Benjamin Weir, Lawrence Jenco, and, on November 2, 1986, David Jacobsen was freed – a partial accomplishment that was offset by later kidnappings. Ironically this sequence of events supported President Reagan's public stance – ignored in practice – that dealing with terrorists only contributes more terrorism."[32]

Rapprochement with Iran was not something that suddenly occurred to the president while riding on his ranch.[33] It had its gestations from deep in the American bureaucracy. On March 23, 1982 deputy undersecretary of state Lawrence Eagleburger received a memorandum warning that the situation in the Persian Gulf was dire and could soon blow up. "Various reports suggest that the threat has recently become more acute owing to increasing Soviet and proxy penetration of Iran and Iranian moves against the Gulf States." The memo argued that even after the recent successful Iranian offensive against Iraq, American policy should be more than just tilting toward the latter. Besides Iran's size, location and resources was too important to be left alone to Soviet penetration. But behind every problem there is usually an opportunity; the renewed Iranian threat gave the United States a chance to actively demonstrate its commitment to Gulf state security. This policy whould be combined with a more active and forthcoming policy towards Iran in order to increase western influence in the country.[34]

Almost simultaneously, Henry S. Rowen, chairman of the National Intelligence Council, warned about the possible dire consequences of an Iranian victory in the war against Iraq. Iran aimed at replacing Saddam Hussein and his Baathist regime by a fundamentalist Islamic regime, or at the very least controlling Iraq's Shia population as well as other Shia areas in the Gulf region. "The importance of the Gulf region to the US resides largely in its oil: It contains 35% of known world oil reserves, 35% of the non-Communist world's production capacity and 25% of current output. The power to interrupt the supply of this flow entails the power to wreak havoc on the economies of the West." Actually, Iranian success could potentially destabilize most of the region: "Although President Assad's, like Saddam Hussein's, hold on power is sustained through tight internal controls and brutal repression, Assad's power has been threatened by Sunni fundamentalists (the Moslem Brotherhood). Despite the recent brutal crushing of their revolt in Hama, if Saddam Hussein were to fall, and, especially if the Baathist regime in Baghdad were to be thrown out, the example could give heart to those who fervently want to end Assad's and the Syrian Baathist hold on power." This give credence to Peter Hahn's argument that in the Middle East the United States preferred stability over democracy. Rowen argued furthermore that for the Saudis: "the memory of the attack on Mecca is no doubt refreshed by the challenge from Khomeini". In short, assuming Iranian success (and perhaps even without it) the next months or several years may see a general overturning of regimes in the Gulf region and beyond, both "radical " and "moderate".[35] Implicitly, an even greater reason to contain the Iranian ogre.

Undersecretary of state William Clarke briefed the president of the expected consequences for the US of a successful Iranian invasion of Iraq. Some 100,000 Iranian troops massed against Basra. If successful of occupying Iraqi territory and destroying the Iraqi army, Clarke feared there would be important ramifications for the US, especially if Iran also was able to foment unrest among Iraq's Kurds and Shias, resulting in toppling Saddam Hussein's regime: "In these circumstances, Iranian forces will sit astride Kuwait, leaving the Kuwaitis vulnerable to direct or indirect Iranian threats. The Saudis, Jordanians, and Gulf states will be extremely alarmed, and can be expected to turn to us for protection." For the US, maintaining influence was a delicate balancing act, because the Reagan administration had to address often contradictory concerns: "To deny Iran to the Soviet Union and keep open the possibility of US rapprochement with Iran." The initiative ending with the Iran/Contra scandal had been, as we can see from the above, long in gestation before Reagan's ill-advised swap of arms for hostages. The United States wanted, furthermore, to protect the moderate Arab states from Iranian aggression and keep the area oil safe for the West. In addition: "To prevent a strengthening of Iraqi ties with the Soviet Union or the 'capture' of Baghdad by Tehran or Damascus." But with every crisis or problem there is an opportunity: "We should use this situation as an opportunity to foster enhanced strategic cooperation with key states." In this, Reagan and Thatcher pursued similar policies, using perceived local crises to strengthen their position in the region – Britain as we have seen in the United Arab Emirates, but also in Oman. Clarke's remedy for the situation outlined above was a presidential letter by special emissary to Saudi king Fahd outlining American concerns and readiness "to cooperate in the defense of the kingdom." This cooperation was to be combined with visual joint military exercises with Oman and Saudi Arabia.[36] The British, on the other hand, did not believe that Iran could win, and wisely kept their distance from both belligerents.[37]

On Reagan's instructions National security Advisor Robert McFarlane requested the feedback of Weinberger and Shultz on a National Security Decision Draft Directive titled, "U.S. Policy toward Iran." The NSC feared that the unstable internal situation in Iran could redound to the benefit of the Soviets: "While we pursue a number of broad long-term goals, our primary short-term challenge must be to block Moscow's efforts to increase Soviet influence. (. . .) This will require an active and sustained program to build our leverage and our understanding of the internal situation so as to enable us to exert a greater and more constructive influence over Iranian politics." Concretely this meant preventing Iran's disintegration, "and preserving it as an independent strategic buffer which separates the Soviet Union from the Persian Gulf." In addition to the other usual suspect, access to the Persian Gulf oil, it also would be nice if Iran stopped supporting international terrorism. Furthermore, the NSC wanted in the long run for Iran to turn into "a moderate and constructive role" in the "the non-communist political community, of its region, and of the world political economy." The Americans would also certainly appreciate if Iran eliminated its "flagrant abuses of human rights". This was a pretty tall order given that the National Security Council had only a limited idea who would win the post-Khomeini power struggle.[38] Besides, as events would show all too clearly, there were no moderate pro-western or pro-American forces in Iran. The theocrats in Tehran were fundamentally hostile to the United States, even after Khomeini. It seems that anti-Americanism was a prerequisite to be part of Iran's governing elite.

The Iran/Contra initiative failed miserably on almost all accounts, as the Congressional investigation of the affair concluded: "The United States armed Iran, including its most radical elements, but attained neither a new relationship with that hostile regime nor a reduction in the number of American hostages." There were no Iranian moderates emerging in Iran as a result of American policies, and Iran continued its promotion of international terrorism. Even more importantly, the United States seriously weakened its position in the Persian Gulf by having one official policy but at the same time conducting a clandestine policy towards Iraq and Iran. "The public policy was to improve relations with Iraq. At the same time, the United States secretly shared military intelligence on Iraq with Iran and [colonel Oliver] North told the Iranians in contradiction to United States policy that the United States would help promote the overthrow of the Iraqi head of government."[39] American policy was even more Machiavellian than that. According to Bruce W. Jentleson, when Iran was slow to release hostages even after several American shipments of arms, CIA director William Casey thought if the Iranians were placed in a situation where they "needed to need American arms a little more", urging Saddam Hussein through several channels such as vice president Bush, President Mubarek of Egypt and king Hussein of Jordan, to step up Iraqi bombing of Iran. "To help the effort, Casey provided Saddam with additional military intelligence including satellite photographs of bombing sites. Sure enough, in just two days following Bush's meeting with Mubarek, the Iraqi air force flew 359 missions, many of which struck more deeply into Iranian territory than ever before. Now, maybe, Iran would want U.S. arms enough to release all hostages." At the same time, Robert McFarlane, in Iran, pledged American assistance in ridding Iraq of Saddam Hussein.[40] British and American cynicism and ruthlessness seem to be without any bounds and often with a very limited moral restraint.

Everything about Reagan's initiative to Iran, as the Congressional investigation concluded flew in the face of established American policy: "Since November 14, 1979, first in response to the hostage crisis and then because of the Iran–Iraq war, the United States had embargoed the sale of arms to Iran. Moreover, it had been the policy of the United States since December 1983 to pressure other governments, through 'Operation Staunch,' to stop the sale of arms to Iran in order to bring an early end to the Iran–Iraq war." In addition, Iran's support of terrorist activities was an added inducement to continue the arms embargo. Reagan Administration policy on terrorism was well known and was clearly stated by the President: "We make no concessions. We make no deals." [41] Reagan addressed the nation on November 13, 1986 explaining his initiative towards Iran: "It's because of Iran's strategic importance and its influence in the Islamic world that we chose to probe for a better relationship between our two countries." The president sought to justify the policy by seeking legitimacy from Nixon's opening to China: "There is ample precedent in our history for this kind of secret diplomacy. In 1971, then-President Nixon sent his national security adviser on a secret mission to China."[42] Reagan also sang from the same song sheet when briefing members of Congress: the purpose with the dealings with Iran was "to improve our strategic position in the Middle East. [This was] important because of Iranian oil and [the] USSR. We also wanted to get [the] hostages released."[43] Clearly the president's alleged tendered hearted concern for the hostages was secondary to America's strategic imperatives. The impression from the archival record is of a president vacillating, not to mention being defensive, being driven from position to position and, unfortunately, often being economical with the truth. Being an eager letter writer, Reagan tried to keep in touch with his political base, but not always in a convincing way, as this letter to a supporter suggests. The president claimed that they had been approached by the opposition to the Irani theocrats, concerned with what would happen in their country following the ayatollah's death: "As for the hostages, they were not ransomed. Their captors have a relationship with Iran. We had been asked by those who contacted us to prove our sincerity by arranging a military sale. We, in turn, told them they could prove their sincerity about being anti-terrorist by using their influence to free our hostages. They did so, and we would have gotten all of them if the story hadn't broken in the press."[44]

In the Carter/Reagan era Iran went from being a pillar of the American defense system, far exceeding the importance of Saudi Arabia, to becoming an open self-inflicted wound for the Americans. The chief consequences for the Americans was almost bringing president Reagan down. Fortunately, the Republicans had learned a lesson or two in crisis management, and saved Reagan from suffering another Watergate. For western strategic concerns, apart from the harebrained thinking behind a potential opening to Iran, the former Persian monarchy was written off with relative ease and had little bearing on the conduct of the cold war. The Soviet Union imploded regardless of Iran pursuing and anti-American policy. For the United Kingdom, despite having had a major economic interest in Iran, it wisely stayed out of Iranian affairs. The departure of the shah and the fall of the Persian monarchy do not seem to have had long-term effect on British policy. This was also the final delusion of the shah, lamenting as he does in his memoirs that he thought he was part of a joint Iranian effort with its western allies, the United States and Great Britain in maintaining regional security. From his exile, the former monarch learned how little his persona and his policies had mattered for the West. The fall of the Iranian pillar led the United States and Britain to pursue alternative strategic positions in the area, their attention now turned to the Arab side of the Persian Gulf. Much Anglo-American attention was showered on Saudi Arabia, but as this analysis will show Oman was the key, and would remain so possibly up to the present time, for this renewed British and American direction of policy. British prime minister Anthony Eden requested president Eisenhower during the run up to the Suez crisis that the Americans took care of the bear (Russians), while Britain handled Egyptian dictator Gamal Abdul Nasser. As we know, this ended with dismal failure for Britain. But in Oman after 1979, it worked. The Americans took care of the bear via the Carter doctrine, the American presence in the sultanate increased considerably, still under the umbrella of the Carter doctrine, and the Thatcher government was able to expand and deepen British influence in Oman.

VII

Saudi Arabia: The Myth of Independence

The Saudis want us to play the lead role in protection of the Persian Gulf region. They want to give us quiet backing but not be associated with us publicly – which might hurt them with their Muslim brothers.[1]

Every American president from Truman to Reagan had guaranteed the security of Saudi Arabia. If there is possible of talking of any kind of Saudi policy, let alone foreign policy in this period, it is the overriding concern Saudi leaders envisioned about the security of regime and the Saudi royal family. For the Saudi royals their own survival and the government's survival was more or less the same thing. Living as they were in a dangerous neighborhood they must have been acutely aware of that political survival ensured personal survival. That is they feared not only losing their power but also their lives. As we have seen from the above, it is hard to discern any independent Saudi foreign policy or strategy even in what may be considered the near abroad for the Saudis. There was a strand, it probably cannot be dignified with the name foreign policy, and that was in addition to craving and demanding and expecting security from their western benefactors, the United States and Great Britain, the Saudis in addition expected the Anglo-Americans to bring the results and policies the royal house was clamoring for. For Britain, Saudi Arabia and king Faisal expected and demanded satisfaction on the issue of the Buraimi oasis.[2] In fact whether as king or crown prince Faisal repeatedly pushed Britain for a solution on the oasis to his benefit. If satisfaction was not forthcoming, he consistently would 'punish' Britain by withholding, cancelling or refusing to sign arms contracts. In the period under consideration here, 1977–85, after Faisal's murder in 1975 and Buraimi more or less solved as a contentious Anglo-Saudi issue, the Saudis would, as we shall see, expend much time and energy over the showing on British TV of the drama *Death of a Princess*, depicting in a quasi-documentary form the execution of a Saudi royal princess for adultery. As with the shah, the Saudis were acutely sensitive about how they were portrayed in the western, particularly British and American media. Again, the British would be punished with the stalling of arms contracts, and the banishment of the British ambassador to Saudi Arabia for a four month period. But even during this low point in Anglo-Saudi relations, the regime took care never to jeopardize the all important security relationship with Britain. This is also the key to Saudi relations with Great Britain and the United States. In times of lesser troubles, the Saudis felt free to strut on the world stage and demand British and American action and accommodation to their point of view, but they were also acutely aware about how far they could go. In contrast to the shah, in his flight of delusions and grandeur, who began play the role of a co-equal of the West, the Saudis whatever their public pronouncements and posturings were well aware that they still were Anglo-American clients.

For the Americans, the repeatedly reiterated demand was that the United States should pressure Israel into an acceptable peace for the Arabs with the Palestinians. While Palestinian rights resonated heavily and emotionally with the Saudi leadership, it was also extremely useful for the regime in brandishing its Arab credentials in not being seen as an American stooge in the Middle East. But when the regime felt its very foundation threatened by Islamic fundamentalists occupying the Grand Mosque in Mecca in November 1979, all concerns for the Palestinians went out of the window for receiving tangible security guarantees from the Carter administration. The price for western security assistance was a small one to pay for the Saudis: buying suitable weapons systems from the Anglo-Americans, systems the Saudis neither had the infrastructure or educational level to operate, and which required large numbers of British and Americans to run their military machinery – a classic example of structural dependency. In addition, it was easy to request from both the Carter and Reagan administration funding from Saudi Arabia for financing their pet projects. Dishing out very small percentage of their huge pile of petrodollars to please their patrons was not something that required great sacrifices for Saudi Arabia. Among the American requests were the contras in Nicaragua when Reagan was president, and from his predecessor to build and maintain president Carter's library in Atlanta, Georgia and Reagan's Library in Simi Valley. Incidentally, when Bill Clinton was president, the University of Arkansas, Little Rock, was the beneficiary of much Saudi munificence.[3]

When the Iranian ambassador to Whitehall, Paris C. Radji, met Saudi king Khaled in London on April 14, 1977 the Saudi royal observed: "Talk is about Islamic unity, the ideological impeccability of the tenets of Islam, and as the King sees it, the twin dangers of Zionism and Communism."[4] In this Khaled followed in the footsteps of his predecessor king Faisal who toward the end of his reign would constantly drag up the same bogeymen, often much to the embarrassment of his western interlocutors. The Saudi leadership believed in a Zionism world conspiracy of the most lurid kind.[5] The British had long been frustrated by the passive Saudi foreign policy. As the British political resident in Bahrain, G. G. Arthur, observed in 1971, venting his frustration on the ambiguity of Saudi foreign policy: "and behind them all would be the Great King [Faisal] with his reputation for infinite wisdom, which (as far as foreign affairs were concerned, at any rate) was probably founded on the fact that he almost never said or did anything."[6] These phobias combined with oft-repeated Saudi demands on Britain and the United States to promote policies in their favor constitute in sum what might pass for a Saudi foreign policy.

The incoming Carter administration was met with a favorable assessment of Saudi Arabia from the departing administration of president Gerald Ford, who was personally optimistic about the Saudis' new-found confidence and assertiveness internationally. Saudi Arabia was believed to be a nation with increased influence in the Middle East, viewing the US as an ally and the monarchy as no longer a client of the Americans. Thus, for the Americans the relationship was now the fulfillment of a longstanding aim, but in reality it was wishful thinking that Saudi Arabia would take the role as a full-fledged ally. Apart from its anti-Israeli rhetoric and sending money to all and sundry it is difficult to discern an independent Saudi foreign policy in the period. Also in the Saudi calculation was the belief that the United States was the only power capable of forcing the necessary concessions out of Israel in order to achieve what the Arabs believed could be peace at acceptable terms; equally important was the perceived US role in preventing the emergence of radical Arab regimes particularly in and around the Arabian Peninsula. The partnership was based on the usual suspects: Saudi oil and American technology. The Ford administration's assessment noted the important role played by the Arabian American Oil Company (ARAMCO) in Saudi Arabia: "Aramco came close to playing the role of a benevolent colonial authority in the new country [since its first explorations for oil in the 1930s]; it gave advice on the structure of government departments and took a hand in foreign policy. Unlike most such relationships, the experience was seen as mutually rewarding by both parties, and the Saudis came away with considerable respect for US technical abilities."[7] But while underpinning Saudi Arabia, ARAMCO had by this time long ceased to play an independent role. Because of its support and encouragement of Saudi irredentism, particularly during the conflict over Buraimi in the early 1950s, successive US administrations had long since reined in ARAMCO's possibilities of conducting policies independent of official American policy.

The CIA viewed the regime as stable, but: "In the longer term, however, enormous wealth, rapid economic development, and the resulting changes could erode the monarchy's traditional underpinnings." Despite its rickety construction and long-term American fears and suspicions that the monarchy was on the verge of collapse, the basic structure of Saudi Arabia has remained remarkably sturdy. This strand of thought emerged in particular during the Kennedy administration, where the United States kept the conservative monarchies in the Middle East (Saudi Arabia and Jordan) at arm's length, believing them to be brittle constructions, out of touch with their own masses and with only the dimmest prospects of survival.[8] The American economic stake in Saudi Arabia was large, exports worth 1.5 billion dollars in 1975, furthermore: "In 1976 alone, US firms secured contracts worth an estimated $27 billion, to be spread over five to ten years." As in Iran, a large number of Americans worked in Saudi Arabia at the time of the CIA assessment: 28,000, a number expected to be increased to 50,000 in 1978. For Saudi Arabia in this era of great oil wealth most political and social problems could be overcome by tossing money at them: "The Saudis are determined not to follow the example of Kuwait, where the National Assembly – until its recent suspension – gave free expression to radical and antiregime ideas. Rather than toy with similar democratic experiments, the Saudis will try to grease social frictions with money, already a key factor in ensuring Saudi stability."[9] But as always, the United States overestimated the modernization of Saudi Arabia and its ability to play a vital role in support of American policy in the Middle East. Saudi foreign policy under Carter would remain essentially passive, waiting and demanding that the United States would deliver policy results to the regime's satisfaction. Even more importantly, as we shall see, as in Iran the threat to the regime did not come from the left, as feared in Washington, but from the right – from religious fundamentalists that intensely disliked and opposed the very cautious modernization of the monarchy. King Faisal was murdered in 1975, in part because he had allowed TV in Saudi Arabia.

From early on the Carter administration sought to signal the importance it attached to Saudi Arabia. [10] Carter tried his best as feudal overlord. After visiting Iran on New Year's Eve 1977, the president went to Saudi Arabia in early January 1978, to demonstrate the importance of Saudi Arabia to the US. Also noteworthy from the perspective of Anglo-American relations, the Carter administration anticipated discussion "of Saudi interest in purchasing an advanced fighter, preferably the F-15, to replace their aging British Lightnings."[11] In so doing, Carter continued the Nixon policy of taking back what had been given with the Anglo-American air deal with Saudi Arabia of 1965.[12] The Saudi Arabian Air Defence Assistance Programme (SADAP) was 'inaugurated' in 1964, extended for five years in 1978 and in this period expected to earn £800 million in foreign exchange for Great Britain. After the United States had taken over the aircraft business, the United Kingdom earned its keep less from military hardware but from training and technical services to the Saudi Airforce and airdefense systems like radar and anti-aircraft missile bases. In total, 2,000 British nationals serviced Saudi Arabia in these respects. In addition, Britain was still heavily involved in the Saudi National Guard, with a British military mission signed to it as well as teams from the Ministry of Defence to establish a nationwide communications network for the Guard. On top of that, Britain played a key part in the National Guard military hospital project.[13] British exports to Saudi Arabia rose sharply in 1978, up £200 million to £800 million, in the process strengthening the pound.[14]

The US Senate was decidedly unenthusiastic about selling the F-15 to Saudi Arabia – "the most advanced fighter bomber in the world" – for fear of upsetting the Arab–Israeli balance of power, and the limited absorptive capacity of the Saudi Air Force. It fell to US secretary of defense Harold Brown to calm Congressional concerns.[15] *Newsweek* assessed US–Saudi relations on March 6, 1978: "The cornerstone of Saudi Arabia's foreign policy is its close – and mutually beneficial – relationship with the U.S. The Saudis enjoy a spot under the American military umbrella, get a steady influx of technical assistance and receive priority treatment in trade matters. In return, the U.S. gets a fat share of the Saudi's investment dollars – at least $35 billion in fixed Treasury bonds alone, and countless other dollar holdings totaling billions – and a healthy measure of security regarding its future oil demands."[16]

President Carter wrote His Majesty Khalid ibn Abd al-Aziz Al-Saud on April 14, 1978: "It is clear to me that the interests of Saudi Arabia and the United States are closely intertwined and will continue to be so. (. . .) Because of the longstanding relationship with which we are both familiar and because the common interest that we share, the United States feels a deep concern for the security of Saudi Arabia, and you may be assured of full U.S. support for the maintenance of Saudi Arabia's integrity." For good measure, the president included his personal support for the security of the Saudi regime.[17] Here Carter continued in the tradition of a long line of American presidents that previously had also guaranteed the security of Saudi Arabia. Truman assured king Saud in October 1950 "that aggression or threat of aggression against Saudi Arabia would be a matter of 'immediate concern' to the United States"; while Eisenhower in May 1956 wrote King Saud that "the United States continued to be deeply interested in the territorial integrity of Saudi Arabia." Kennedy and his secretary of defense Robert McNamara assured the then crown prince Faisal about the same in October 1962. And in March 1963 Kennedy would repeat the assurances, and again in May and October of that year, adding for good measure American support of Faisal's leadership. President Johnson and his administration repeated American assurances several times, as did president Nixon thereafter. As did Ford upon taking office August 9, 1974 in a message to Faisal, the president "affirms everything said to you on this by President Nixon and Secretary Kissinger."[18] President Reagan, too, would also give an American guarantee to the security of Saudi Arabia.[19]

The president became rather adept in his role as patron. On September 26, 1978 he wrote Khalid who was in the US for surgery: "My son Chip is available to help you in every possible way, and I would personally appreciate your letting me know how we might be of service to you during your visit to our country. Our prayers are with you for an early and complete recovery after your operation."[20] Still, the Saudis, like the shah, needed constant American assurance. US ambassador to Jeddah, John West, reported home on what appeared to a fundamental Saudi insecurity: "It is abundantly clear to West that [foreign minister] Saudis probing limits of our commitments to Saudi Arabian security and will not be satisfied with anything less than specific answers." What the Saudis really wanted was a relationship with the US as Israel had: "There is no treaty, but you always respond to Israeli needs . . . that is the kind of understanding we want and need here in Saudi Arabia."[21] Indeed, US defense secretary Harold Brown gave the Saudis such a commitment when visiting the country in early February 1979, but when offering to put it into writing the Saudis declined.[22] United States guarantees were needed and appreciated as long as the Americans remained discreet about them. The Carter administration was but little concerned about Saudi Arabia as long as relations remained fairly calm. London, in fact, believed that there was but little knowledge and contact between top foreign policy makers in the US and the Saudi leadership.[23] For the Carter administration it was a revelation to learn of Saudi reluctance to use their military forces outside their own territory: "This demonstration of lack of confidence in their own military capability, combined with less than effective confrontation with Arab radicals in recent political fora, may have gone some way toward undermining the perception in the area that Saudi Arabia is a significant force for stability on the Peninsula. At some point, this lack of Saudi confidence in its own military may provoke resentment at the inability of the US, after years of providing training and expensive weapons, to produce an effective fighting force in Saudi Arabia."[24]

As with the United States, for Britain the early years of the Carter administration had seen Saudi Arabia and the Persian Gulf as fairly tranquil. But with the fall of the shah, concerns increased. What were the nature of British policy and interests in the region? The Foreign and Commonwealth Office pointed to the usual suspects: access to oil at a reasonable price; to prevent the region's large accumulated wealth be used to the detriment of the West; to prevent the destabilization of the area; and, finally, "while recognizing the limitations of our present position, to honor as far as possible any moral obligation we have acquired towards some of the Rulers and peoples of the area through our long years of tutelage over them by trying to encourage peaceful evolution rather than violent change."[25] For both powers there was no sense of urgency to their relations with Saudi Arabia, while they did not always see eye to eye the western relationship with Saudi Arabia seemed to be percolating on a fairly low level, with the occasional hick-up – for Britain the controversy over the movie *The Death of a Princess* and for Saudi–US relations a Saudi unhappiness over the Camp David accord, where Saudi Arabia because of its exposed position had to follow the Arab mainstream and not support the agreement. Discussion over Saudi oil production levels was always ongoing. But on the whole relations were sound, and the Saudis understood all too well that there were limits to which they should not go beyond, being utterly depended on the United States, and to a lesser degree the United Kingdom for their security. But with the exception of the shah, even at the inception of the Carter administration, there was little need for Britain and the United States to be overly concerned with the Arabian Peninsula and the Persian Gulf. However, things were to change. The departure of the shah increased British and American concerns for regional instability, which worsened considerably when, despite major efforts, the Carter administration failed to establish a working relationship with revolutionary Iran. But worse was to come, beginning with the taking of hostages of the American embassy in Tehran in November 1979, followed by the occupation of the Holy Mosque in Mecca and burning of the American embassies in Tripoli and Islamabad – carried out by Islamic fundamentalists. Suddenly the Anglo-Americans were confronted by an entirely new strategic situation: radical Islam was in full force for the first time. This was toppled by the Soviet invasion of Afghanistan in December, rendering the American strategic equation almost null and void.

The Saudis pondered their own lessons from the fall of the shah, as John West advised the state department on July 15, 1979: "The Shah, with the best trained, best equipped armed forces in the area, fell to a group of untrained and ill-equipped urban revolutionaries. His U.S. arms together with the friendship they implied were useless to sustain him in power. Friendship with the U.S., in fact, was one of the Shah's most vulnerable points, as it became a rallying cry for Khomeini and the masses as they toppled the Peacock Throne." The ruling family dynasty sought to increase internal stability to prevent the second act of a downfall of monarchy from taking place in Saudi Arabia. Furthermore, while distrusting their radical Arab brothers – South Yemen, Libya, Iraq and the PLO – the Saudi Arabians made a point to remain in the fold of Arab brotherhood. "The Saudis realize more than ever that the political leadership of a traditional Muslim society must not get too far ahead of its people's religious traditions. They will go to extreme lengths to avoid any major altercation with religious leaders and will be particularly careful in the application of Islamic laws and principles." The Saudis, while still needing and wanting American protection, could be expected to downgrade the American connection for public consumption. Also since "U.S. needs favorable Saudi oil policies more than Saudi Arabia needs the U.S. for security," or so the Saudis thought, it ought to give Saudi Arabia more leverage over American policy; that is a larger say in the Arab–Israeli peace talks, more forthcoming on part of the US in regards to military equipment and lesser restrictions on Saudi investments in the US.[26]

On November 28, 1979 Vance reported to Carter on the occupation of the Grand Mosque in Mecca. At the request of the Saudi authorities the United States had airlifted riot control equipment to the country. At the same time, the Carter administration worried about the security for the more than 35,000 strong American community in Saudi Arabia. A large and sudden draw down of American personnel could potentially have an unsettling effect locally. John West was therefore instructed "to consult with Prince Fahd about our concerns for the security of US citizens in Saudi Arabia and [determine] what further appropriate steps should be taken to ensure their safety." Carter noted tersely on the memorandum: "No precipitous withdrawal."[27] Crown prince Fahd had sent Carter a pretty chilling and bloodthirsty message when the Mosque was occupied: "Fahd ordered that maybe 1,500 people occupying the mosque be shot and killed, and has privately told our people that this is a good way to get rid of these militants."[28] For a president concerned with human rights this announced abuse of the same did not elicit much comment and concern from Carter. This may be caused by the fact that in his involuntary role as feudal overlord, which was not always successful, the president (as for most liberal Americans) had little use for the Arab kings, sheiks, amirs and pashas. Hiding behind a remark by Spanish prime minister Adolfo Suárez Gonzáles the president noted in his diary on January 14, 1980: "He described some of the Islamic nations as 'Allah above, oil below, nothing in between.'"[29] Carter's lack of reaction also hints that he may not had become too upset if the shah had cracked down with equal vigour against the domestic Iranian opposition. Brzezinski feared the occupation was a counter-reaction to modernization of Saudi Arabia. Speaking to the British ambassador, Henderson, the national security advisor opined: "This raised the question of the form that the Islamic revival was going to take. Brzezinski thought there was a serious danger that the whole of the Muslim world would seek revival on the basis of anti-western xenophobia. As he saw it, this was one of the most important subjects for the future and he implied that it might usefully be touched on when the Prime Minister talked to the President."[30]

After the Saudis had finally cleared out the occupiers from the Grand Mosque, Carter wrote crown prince Fahd on December 5, 1979: "I share your sense of relief and satisfaction that the government of Saudi Arabia has restored the Holy Mosque in Mecca to worshippers and ended the abhorrent seizure. I know that people throughout the world were repelled by this act of sacrilege and are impressed as I am with the restrained and effective manner in which the government of Saudi Arabia has dealt with this tragic situation."[31] Fahd showed his effectiveness, restraint and humanity by allowing the prisoners to be tortured, thereafter publicly beheading 63 captives on January 9, 1980.[32] All of this without a whiff of protest from the great humanist in the White House; 10 Downing Street did not bother to protest, either.[33]

In fact, even before the occupation of the Holy Mosque, the Saudi royal house kept a tight rein on society, as the British ambassador John Wilton reported to Carrington on September 12, 1979: "Saudi Arabia is not a comfortable place for foreigners to work and it is becoming less so as Saudi determination to defend their traditional values and their own way of life increases with the growing foreign presence. Much of what is called the present 'revival of Islam' is in fact a reaction against the widespread and sudden impact of an alien culture." For the foreigner, Saudi Arabia must seem like a police state, "inspired by the certainty that it is God's will that the infidel should confirm to Saudi standards of modesty and sobriety; and that in any argument or dispute the foreigner must be wrong."[34] The occupation of the Holy Mosque did not produce more openness in Saudi society, as Rachel Bronson has observed: "The Saudi regime squelched the Grand Mosque uprising but proceeded to adopt much of the religious radicals' agenda."[35]

The issues facing American–Saudi relations prior to the occupation of the Grand Mosque were at best surface cruising. The Carter administration, as in the case of Iran, really did not have any clue what was going on in the country. Vance cabled West on December 26, 1979: "We believe, however, that the Dept [State Department] and embassy need to be in closest possible touch on the question of the Saudi regime, what further information we need to assist our ongoing analysis of the situation, what Saudi reactions may be, and what actions we might take to strenghen [sic] Saudi Arabia internally." The US believed the Saudi monarchy to have wide domestic acceptance, "there are few unemployed disaffected 'coffee house' intellectuals, around whom discontent might coalesce," and had feared that the greatest danger would come from a coup of "Arab nationalist type like Nasser in Egypt." But for the Americans this seemed like a remote possibility given the absence of discontent in the army "which is in any event balanced by a well armed national guard drawn from tribes close to the Royal family." The United States had not so far believed the Saudi regime could be challenged from the right, as evidenced by the Mosque occupation. Furthermore, the Carter administration did not know almost anything of the temper of the tribes. Vance continued: "The fact that such a plot could go undetected or ignored and that the perpetrators could have access to a significant store of weapons and the training to use them effectively indicates serious Saudi intelligence and security failures." For the US, then, the crisis translated into an urgent need for more information on the Saudi internal security situation.[36] Like the shah, Saudi royals had kept the Americans in the dark about the internal situation in their country. It is also a clear indication that as in Iran, Carter as well as his predecessors did not feel any great urge to obtain a greater knowledge of the desert kingdom. The situation in Saudi Arabia was thus dangerously parallel to Iran under the shah, perhaps luck more than anything prevented a Khomeini-type revolution in the kingdom. One reason was, perhaps, that Saudi royals veered sharply to the right doing much to accommodate the conservative religious forces, with what seems American benign acceptance.

The United Kingdom noted, with some concern, the current unrest in Saudi Arabia; in addition to the Mosque occupation there had been rioting at the end of November 1979 by the Shia minority in the eastern province of Saudi Arabia. The response of the Saudi government left much to be desired; its intelligence service had been aware of the group behind the occupation, but had failed to prevent the attack, while the Saudi armed forces were slow to respond and had suffered heavy casualties when retaking the Mosque. For Britain, the Islamists were not the main threat: "There is a danger that the Saudi government may over-react and adopt yet more Islamic social policies, thus increasing the restiveness among the middle-class/army officers whom we still regard as the greatest threat to the monarchy." But the crisis in Saudi Arabia was potentially good for British business; more military hardware could be hawked on the Saudis under the guise of preserving the security of the regime. First of all Britain sought to extend the Saudi Arabian Air Defense Assistance Project (SADAP) beyond its expiry date in 1982: "In the meantime, SADAP has much political and economic significance and its continued success and extension is therefore important for good relations in the future." But there was more: the Saudis were close to signing a deal worth £95 million in artillery and engineer equipment for the army. "The [National] Guard, who performed poorly in the Mecca incident, represent a particularly fruitful market for defence sales." For the guard Britain was setting up "a nation-wide communication network the first phase of which is worth £230 m." All of this, in a brief for foreign minister Lord Carrington for his upcoming Saudi Arabian visit. While there, Carrington was urged to sooth Saudi feelings. Regarding the recent Soviet invasion of Afghanistan, Carrington was urged to explain: "Invasion typically ruthless, devious and opportunist. Essential to make Russians pay in political terms, to discourage further adventures, Western response must be measured, coherent and concerted. Wide range of retaliatory measures under consideration: grain, technology, credit, exchanges etc." The Saudis were urged to support the western position in the UN and use their influence to make their fellow Muslims see the light.[37]

It was not until August 1981 that the United Kingdom was reasonably certain what had taken place during the seizure of the Grand Mosque. The occupiers of the Mosque belonged to a group that believed "the Saudi leadership had diverged from the path of the true Islam, that the modernization process had led true believers to forget the precept of their religion and that there must be a return to the 'original' Islam – if need be, by force." The initial Saudi reaction was slow and confused to the occupation; first the ulama, the religious leaders, had to be consulted to give religious sanctions for military operations in the Mosque. From the Saudi royal perspective the ulama came through magnificently, quoting the Koran in its justification for military operation: "But fight them not at the Holy Mosque unless they fight you there. But if they fight you, slay them. Such is the reward of those who suppress faith." The occupiers were able to hold out until December 4, two weeks after the takeover on November 20. Saudi forces captured 102 of the occupiers and executed 63 of them. The research department of the Middle East section of the Foreign and Commonwealth office noted "that although a small French military advisory team was asked by the Saudi Government during the early stages of the incident, they were neither used nor consulted, and do not appear to have moved beyond the point of disembarkation."[38]

Confronted by domestic upheaval, compounding the problem seen from Riyadh for the Saudi royals, their borders seemed far from secure. In the West, the Saudis feared communist penetration in Northern Yemen: "The spectre of Cubans and East Germans roaming about North Yemen (possibly in American equipment) will profoundly frighten the Saudis, threaten Oman and alter the balance of power in the Arabian Peninsula." To counter this Brzezinski advised the president: "We have begun contingency planning of our own and offered immediate and intense consultations with the Saudis to preclude this development."[39] One tool of the Saudi arsenal was to bribe off friends and foe alike, but old difficulties died hard: "While Saudi Arabia recognizes common security interests with Oman, it has not been an enthusiastic supporter of the Sultan. Levels of Saudi assistance fluctuate with the immediacy of threats to Oman and peaked during the Dhofar insurgency."[40] Hailing from South Yemen, a marxist-leninist guerilla movement had tried to topple the sultan of Oman. The guerillas were finally defeated, after years of struggle, with British assistance. Needless to say, the rebellion brought urgently home to the sultan of Oman that his personal and political survival depended on British assistance.

The occupation of the Mecca mosque and concomitant loss of face for the Saudi royals rankled. So much so that crown prince Fahd had an evening session at his residence with ambassador West on March 13, 1980. The crown prince was deeply worried about reports that the Administration Carter and his associates "had lost confidence in the Saud Family's capacity to govern, were predicting an early downfall of the present regime, and had lost confidence in his (Fahd's) ability to run the country. He said he was reluctant to raise such a sensitive subject, but because of the persistence of the reports, it had become a source of worry and concern to him and he felt he should tell us frankly of his concerns. He wanted to know directly from the President whether these reports were accurate." West tried to assure the crown prince: "I was certain that these reports were completely erroneous," but pledged to convey Fahd's concerns to Carter and solicit a reply from the president. "Our government recognizes the fact that our mutual interests are so interdependent that we are virtually brothers as well as allies in today's world; that any change in the government of Saudi Arabia would not be in the interests of either party." While pleading for American support, Fahd also conveyed an underlying threat that, if not forthcoming, the crown prince would consider de- aligning Saudi policies with the US: "Please ask President Carter to ponder this point, especially at this sensitive juncture in our bilateral relations and your own interests in this region."[41]

Carter replied in a private handwritten letter to West on March 20, 1980, and expressed great "concern that the Crown Prince has any doubt about my commitment to or confidence in him or the government of S.A. In all of my public and private statements, even among my closest advisers, my position has never changed. We value the friendship and cooperation and mutuality of purpose with the SAG [Saudi Arabian Government] as highly as with any other nation. Also, the severe testing of the royal family during the past year has proven their original strength and, in my opinion, has enhanced it." But as Carter pointed out, the American – Saudi relationship was not a one-sided affair. Even in this atmosphere of crisis, neither side could resist negotiating. American support would be forthcoming, but with a price tag. The United States would "need help" in solving the Palestinian problem, help "in strengthening the security of the entire Middle East/Persian Gulf region", help to maintain the strength of the dollar and world economic stability, help to heal the split between Egypt and Saudi Arabia.

"Also, although I am no military expert I am concerned about security and the state of readiness of SAG military forces. We have demonstrated our willingness to supply advanced weapons, including the F-15s. However, the more mundane and conventional forces may need more attention."

West was instructed to relay the president's opinions to crown prince Fahd. "I will do what I can do to express public confidence in the SAG, to expedite delivery of weapons, to conclude the Mid East peace effort successfully, and to urge a cessation of verbal criticisms from Egypt. S.A. can help to marshal maximum concerted opposition to Soviet expansionism, and help us as much as possible not to permit Arabs to block progress toward Mid East peace."[42]

The National Security Council concluded its evaluation of the occupation of the Grand Mosque on March 21, 1980: "The raid on the Grand Mosque in Mecca was primarily Saudi and fundamentalist Moslem. Outside elements played no major role. Like Islam itself, it was an organic union of politics and religion. Its members came largely from tribes in central Arabia who have traditionally been enemies of the Saudi royal family – indeed, it included some of the grandsons of those who fought Abd al-Aziz." The royal family was the target for being corrupt and lackluster in its role as guardians of Islam.[43] For Britain the incident was evaluated by the British defence attaché to Jeddah: "The Mecca incident threw a depressing light on the ability of the Saudi armed forces to combat internal stability. The response of the services to the incident revealed poor intelligence, an inability to coordinate actions between the various commands and the superiority of the Army to the National Guard in most aspects of military activity." The British defense attaché concluded that Saudi armed forces could not defend its territory against almost any potential foreign attack, "let alone conduct any military activities outside the borders of the Kingdom", not even in the near abroad like for instance the north or south Yemen. Saudi Arabia was therefore in a military sense utterly dependent on its western benefactors, most importantly the United States. Britain's interest in Saudi armed forces had two aspects: First, could they ensure the stability of the Kingdom? The conclusion was dismal against any external threat, while the defense attaché believed the forces sufficed against potential domestic unrest. The second aspect was as a market for British military equipment, a much brighter scenario from the British point of view.[44]

It did not escape the Carter administration that Britain had a substantial but low key presence in the kingdom. Brzezinski noted that: "British personnel, largely civilians on contract, are heavily involved in the Saudi Arabian Air Force and air defense system. In 1978, for example, the Royal Saudi Air Force renewed its contract with the UK for support of the RSAF's Lightning aircraft, the King Faisal Air Academy, and operation of the Technical Institute in Dharan through 1982. The British Aircraft Corporation [BAC] maintains and services Saudi planes and is also installing the Saudi missile defense system. Almost 2,000 BAC personnel are currently in Saudi Arabia."[45] With the fall of the shah the United States and Great Britain quietly shifted its focus to the Arabian side of the Persian Gulf and would thereafter systematically strengthen its presence there. Saudi military ineptness was not such a cause for alarm but to pilfer more military hardware on the kingdom, an ever more sophisticated military machine that required an increasing presence of western experts to run it. This became a classical example of the Nixonian policy of structural dependence. Whatever Saudi Arabia did, however frustrated the Saudi royals were at their western benefactors, they took care never to jeopardize their all important security relationship with Great Britain and the United States.

But Brzezinski underestimated the British presence in Saudi Arabia. Britain's stake was of a similar size as the US, almost 30,000 United Kingdom nationals working in Saudi Arabia, sales of almost 900 million pounds, while importing oil worth over one billion pounds annually. In early 1980, relations were soured because Britain had not prevented airing of the program *Death of a Princess* on ATV (a television channel) regarding the execution of princess Misha for adultery. Still, the Foreign Office was well aware that there were limits to which the Saudis would express their displeasure: "Nevertheless, we would not expect the wide-ranging and close relations in defense, and security cooperation with Saudi Arabia to be adversely affected."[46] But the controversy, for the Saudis, over the movie *Death of a Princess*, continued to bedevil Anglo-Saudi relations. The British Cabinet discussed as late as April 25, 1980, problems associated with the movie. The Saudis, when wanting to show their displeasure to the British, retaliated in the only way they knew how by cancelling contracts, this time for turbine generators. Thatcher was concerned enough to consider personally intervening with the Saudi leadership to smooth things over.[47] Interestingly, with a keen eye to their own self-interest and security, the punishment did not extend to British forces serving in Saudi Arabia. In fact, a British SAS team provided training assistance to Saudi forces at the height of the crisis when the Grand Mosque was occupied.[48]

Thatcher wrote crown prince Fahd on April 25, 1980. "I am distressed and saddened by the unfortunate consequences which the recent television film has had for relations between Britain and Saudi Arabia. I understand and sympathise with the feelings of deep injury which are felt by the Royal Family and the people of Saudi Arabia. (. . . .) You will have seen from reports of exchanges in Parliament on April 24 that the British Government's concern and regret is shared by Members of Parliament from all sides of the House. (. . .) Both the Independent Broadcasting Authority and the British Broadcasting Corporation will have taken note of the adverse comments and unfortunate consequences which followed this film. The growing tensions in the Middle East and the latest very serious turn of events in Iran underline the necessity for our two countries to keep in the closest touch. There is an urgent need to restore relations to their normal friendly basis as soon as possible."[49] Long after the crisis had blown over, Lord Carrington would write in his memoirs: "I remember the television programme 'Death of a Princess' which was regarded by the Saudis as intolerably and inaccurately unfriendly – indeed they asked the British Ambassador to quit Riyadh. The incident demonstrated the sad irresponsibility of some entertainment media in a free society, with programmes made regardless of their impact on British interests."[50] But the movie soured relations from Saudi point of view, demanding recall of UK ambassador Craig to London. Only in July the same year was the relationship repaired and Craig allowed to return to Jeddah.[51] Adding to potentially problematic Anglo-Saudi relations was the death of the British nurse Helen Smith in May 1979; while her death was ruled an accident there are strong indications that Helen was murdered, leading her father, Ron Smith, to embark on a decades long quest for justice for his daughter. There are strong indications that the Foreign and Commonwealth Office tried to downplay the incident to avoid disturbing already much ruffled Saudi feathers on *The Death of a Princess*. In any case, the Foreign Office mandarins' response was less than adequate, to put it charitably, to meet the needs of the grieving father Ron Smith. Paul Foot observes: "Foreign Office officials at every level strove mightily to deflect Ron Smith from his justified anxiety about his daughter's death. They refused him even documents and telegrams which reflected their own doubts and suspicions. In one interview at the Foreign Office, Mr. Patrick McDermott, who was introduced to the case late in the day, begged me to understand that all mistakes and mistranslations which emerged from the Jeddah embassy were coincidental – just a catalogue of unfortunate error. I shall be surprised if anyone reading the record shares that view."[52] Typically, lord Carrington, who gets himself quite worked up on *The Death of a Princess*, as we have seen above, does not deign to mention the Helen Smith story in his memoirs, neither does Margaret Thatcher.[53] The prime minister's response to Helen's brother Graham was cool and rather callous: "The Prime Minister fully understands and sympathises with the grief and concern which Helen's death must have caused your family. The matter has been looked into carefully and the Prime Minister is satisfied that officials in the Foreign and Commonwealth Office in London and the embassy in Jedda have done everything they can to help your family."[54] Douglas Hurd blames everybody but the politicians, and himself in particular, above all Ron Smith, an irresponsible press and his legal advisors: "We were not sufficiently robust in our rebuttals of nonsense, because I listened to attentively to the caution of our legal advisors."[55]

The Anglo-Saudi process of reconciliation started with British minister of state for Foreign and Commonwealth affairs Douglas Hurd's Saudi Arabian visit in July, while foreign minister Lord Carrington visited Saudi Arabia on August 25 to 27, 1980. Hurd began his meeting with the Saudi minister of foreign affairs, prince Saud al-Faisal, by once again apologizing for the film *Death of a Princess*. "The British Government had felt real distress at the wretched film. We quite understood and deeply regretted the offence which it had caused. He had seen it himself so he could understand the offence which had been taken; it was full of bad taste." The abject apology came with a price, Hurd wanted that Britain no longer lost out on commercial opportunities in Saudi Arabia. And could the Saudis please stop maltreating and beating British nationals imprisoned in their country? The Helen Smith case did not warrant discussion on this august level.[56]

Carrington's visit had additional purposes than Hurd's: "to reopen opportunities for us to win business in Saudi Arabia, and to establish a relationship of confidence with the Saudi Government in which it will be possible to discuss the problems of regional security, energy policy, the Middle East question etc. in a spirit of mutual trust." And the prospects were good, the Saudis promised Carrington the red carpet treatment: "It may be possible to exploit this mood to obtain preferential consideration for British firms or projects and thus for us to bounce back into a better position than we were before." The price to pay for an increased British market share was small: "A further statement (if the Saudis still want this) of HMG's regret at the consequences of the film for Anglo-Saudi relations, and a reaffirmation that the Secretary of State found it deeply offensive." At this point British apologies seem to have become more than fairly ritualistic. Britain had even during the height of Saudi displeasure sent a training team of SAS between April and July 1980 to the kingdom. As already noted, the main concerns of the Saudis were the security of their domain, and the political and physical survival of the royal family. Helen Smith was as expected, of no concern of Carrington.[57] Restored to his position, James Craig reported home on September 3 that lord Carrington's visit "was a marked success. He was received by the King and four royal Ministers." But on the Saudi side, anger over the film simmered. Nevertheless Carrington succeeded from the British side to calm Saudi angers, smoothing the way for British business, which was the main reason behind the foreign minister's sojourn. [58] A little meaningless genuflection, on the part of Hurd and Carrington, was a small price to pay for increased business opportunities. With regard to Saudi Arabia, Britain followed largely the same policies as towards the shah, the main point of the official British establishment in the kingdom was to sell as many British products as possible. The Thatcher government, as the Labour government preceding, could live very well without having any formal obligations towards Saudi Arabia.

VIII

Saudi Foreign Policy: What Foreign Policy?

Saudi doom and gloom did not last too long in the aftermath of the Mecca inci-dent. By May they were back to true form complaining and blaming the Americans. The Saudis were displeased with the American delivery schedule of military equipment, while Saudi forthcomingness on oil production and pricing was rewarded by the withholding of arms and snickering against the regime in the American press. West, who at this point, seemed to be infected by localities, warned "that without addressing the equipment issue to Saudi Arabia's satisfaction, our already strained relationship will be further affected and we will not be able to induce the Saudis into a dialogue concerning wider security concerns and regional defense objectives."[1]

While the Saudis felt they were too accommodating on the oil question, it was not enough for the Americans. The president wrote prince Fahd on May 30 1980 warning against further price increases of oil, to prevent inflation from escalating: "Saudi Arabia plays a vital role in determining whether we will be able to dampen inflation, adjust to a world less dependent on oil, and still main-tain satisfactory economic growth. This is a grave responsibility. Under your leadership, Saudi Arabia has carried out that responsibility in a farsighted, consistent, and statesmanlike way." The American counterpart to Saudi oil policies was Carter's energy conservation programs, the president pointing out that American consumption of oil had declined beginning in 1979. The US encouraged its allies to adopt a similar conservation policy. But previous year's increases in the price of oil threatened escalating inflation and "pose[d] a substantial threat to my personal effort to restore economic stability in the United States, while avoiding a deep recession – a difficult task at all times, but especially in an election year." Rampant inflation could possibly threaten the necessary level of US defense spending to deter the Soviet menace. Therefore the president lauded the Saudi decision not to increase the price of oil, and urged them to keep prices and production steady for the remainder of the year. Implicit in the whole message was that the American guarantee of Saudi secu-rity hinged on cooperation on other areas of concern to the United States. In case Fahd had missed the point, Carter spelled it out to him at the end of the letter: "The health of the world economy and the common security are interests our two countries share to an extraordinary degree."[2]

West followed up with a long memorandum on June 1, 1980, warning: "A major crisis is coming in U.S.–Saudi relations. Indeed, it has probably already begun, and is simply now increasing in intensity and severity." The Saudis were displeased for getting little in return for their restraint on oil prices, and the American priority of Israel. The onesidedness of the American–Saudi relationship is typically demonstrated by the Saudis rattling the question of oil production to the hilt; there was little else they could threaten the Americans with. "Why do we continue to produce twice as much oil as we need to accommodate the U.S.?" The use of force to rescue American hostages in Tehran was condemned by the Saudi government. "With typical Bedouin frankness, Prince Abdullah, the third ranking member of the royal family, told me on June 1, 'Arabs all over the Mideast are now convinced that your policies are set in Tel Aviv and Jerusalem. Can't you give your friends in Saudi Arabia a basis to deny that charge?'" The Saudis were also frustrated that they did not get the same easy access to the American military arsenal as Israel. The sum of frustration had already led the Saudi government to begin backing away from its moderate role when it came to oil pricing. Thus, while they resented American demands, they were not above a little blackmail themselves. In addition to brandishing the oil weapon, Saudi Arabia ostentatiously sought other suppliers of arms; France was believed by the Saudis to supply any arms the regime might want. And of course there was the option of "forming an alliance with other Islamic countries to pursue a non-aligned course." West concluded by urging the Carter administration to take positive steps to restore American–Saudi relations.[3]

Ayatollah Khomeini was not the only one to use the occupation by Muslims of the Grand Mosque to fan the flames of Muslim rage against the West. Blaming the West for the sacrilege caused by the occupation of the Holy Mosque, on November 21, 1979, hundreds of Pakistanis stormed and burned the American embassy in Islamabad, killing marine guard Steven J. Crowley "and trapping 100 persons for five hours in a vault." In addition, crowds attacked the American consulate in Karachi, the American Library in Lahore and the British cultural center in Rawalpindi. Less than two weeks later the American embassy in Tripoli was forcefully entered and the furniture set on fire, making it the third American embassy in a Moslem country invaded in less than a month.[4] The attack in Islamabad could easily have gone much worse: "The embassy was burning around them. Outside, a mob of Pakistanis pillaged the building, howling, 'Kill the American dogs!' and trying to shoot through the air vents of final refuge: Inside, 100 U.S. staffers and embassy employees choked in the smoke and tear- gas fumes, watching the vinyl floor tiles blister and melt from the fire below, listening to the gunfire and the mob, and waiting desperately for Pakistani troops to come to the rescue." But the rescue was slow in coming in a military dictatorship under martial law; the embassy staffers "barely escaped being roasted alive."[5] The American reaction was largely to absolve the Pakistani government from blame, in return requesting Pakistani strong man Muhammed Zia-ul-Haq to intercede in Tehran to facilitate the release of the American hostages.[6]

Tripoli was more difficult for the Americans, Libya's erratic leader Mohammer Qaddafy having caused many headaches for the United States. After the attack on the embassy, the Libyan News Agency blamed the Americans, claiming that many of the Libyans students participating in the attack were injured "because of the poisonous gas that members of the American Embassy used against them."[7] Soon, Libya pleaded for better relations with the US, accepted responsibility for "the security of the US personnel and Embassy Tripoli", and offered to pay compensation for damages to the embassy.[8] But Libyan policy remained unpredictable: "Qadhafi's soothing words can quickly change to vehement invective and his explosive and changeable nature must be constantly taken into account." The State department concluded on February 1, 1980 that the Qaddafy had authorized the attack on the embassy to prove his revolutionary credentials against Iran. "Even so, there are still several good reasons, such as our dependence on Libyan oil and our large American community in Libya, for trying to maintain at least a minimal relationship with Tripoli."[9] For being a great power, a superpower, with abilities hitherto unmatched in history, the United States is surprisingly tolerant and even lenient in more or less passively accepting the destruction of American property and the taking of American lives abroad. But this is not a confined to the Carter administration, Ronald Reagan followed the same line despite heavily ratcheting up the rhetoric against terrorism.

The Carter administration from its beginning was well aware of the problematic American relations to Qaddafy's regime. Vance briefed Carter on February 14, 1977: "Between 1969 and 1974 the Libyans ejected us from Wheelus Air base, attacked an unarmed American C-130 plane in international airspace, partially or totally nationalized U.S. oil interests in Libya, expelled American missionaries and confiscated their properties without compensation, and, during the 1973 Arab–Israel conflict, applied an embargo on the sale of petroleum to the U.S. which lasted until 1975." Qaddafy was committed to the total destruction of Israel as well as supporting international terrorism. Still, the United States maintained relations with the regime: "Despite our political problems with Libya, we maintain active commercial relations; nearly 10 percent of our crude oil is imported from Libya." This amounted to 30 percent of the total Libyan oil production. There were 2,000 Americans residing in Libya and 2,000 Libyan nationals in the US.[10] American relations with Libya remained more or less sour for the remainder of the Carter administration and despite the political problems business as usual. It is clear for Carter that Qaddafy was more of a nuisance than a problem.

For the United States, Qaddafy's Libya served many useful purposes. In the Nixon administration it had been a useful entering wedge to break the power of big oil. In the Nixon era, the British believed Qaddafy to be mentally unstable and the Libyan leadership amoral, having no sense of obligation to or consideration for other people. Still, the British preferred to continue relations, the British ambassador to Tripoli, Peter Tripp, citing the usual suspects of oil, trade and investment.[11] The Americans believed Qaddafy to be sane and his regime firmly in control, having the same concerns as Britain, but, in addition, made great efforts to improve relations with the regime.[12] For the Reaganites Qaddafy was a useful whipping boy for all that the Americans believed was wrong in the Middle East, and being basically a nuisance, a gnat against an elephant, useful to display American military might with little fear to risk a full-scale war for the US. Still, there was a lot of huffing and puffing in the new regime. Early in the new administration Haig warned Reagan: "Libya under Qadhafi is a significant threat to U.S. interests throughout the Middle East/African region, and in the broadest sense to our concept of an international order. (. . .)Libya poses a serious threat to the long Mediterranean lifeline of our capability to project power into the Persian Gulf area as well as directly threatening the survival of friendly regimes in the area. This endangers our entire strategy in that region. The urgency of dealing with the Libyan problem is increased by the fact that the West may be even more vulnerable to Libyan oil blackmail in three to five years than at present. Our ultimate objective must be no less than a basic reorientation of those Libyan policies and attitudes which are now harmful to our interests." To remedy this Haig suggested the US should in concert with its European allies "begin mobilizing an international consensus isolating Qadhafi." The United States would assist nations threatened by Libya, and also mobilize international opinion against the country. The United States should conduct military exercises in the Gulf of Sidra, despite Qadaffy claiming it to be Libyan waters, but Libya should be warned that any use of force would be met by strong American countermeasures. Furthermore, American oil companies operating in Libya were to be encouraged to reduce their staff to prevent them being held as future hostages. Haig warned that this was only the first of steps, "they are still only interim measures, and, as such, not commensurate with the truly serious threat Libya poses. Accordingly, we will be developing more serious, concerted programs in the near future."[13]

Libya was the perfect country for American punitive measures, run by an unpopular dictator with rhetorical flights of fancy. When the Soviet Union wrote off the regime the United States could tangle with Qaddafy with relative impunity.[14] For instance, when it was reported that Libyan hit squads were coming to the United States targeting senior officials and even the president himself, the Reagan administration made the most of the political benefits that could be extracted from something that in reality was overblown. Besides, seven billion dollars worth of oil imports and 2,000 Americans residing in Libya being potential hostages to the regimes severely limited the Reagan administration options in dealing with the 'mad dog of the Middle East'.[15] When the US finally did act, shooting down two Libyan planes on August 18, 1981, the Reagan administration sought to reap maximum propaganda and political benefit from the affair, as Reagan's secretary of defense Caspar

Weinberger explained afterwards in his memoirs: "We had demonstrated not only a greatly increased American resolve, but also a greatly increased capability for dealing with the enemy quickly and decisively. That alone did more to reassure our allies than any budget amounts we were committed to spend, or any amount of rhetoric, no matter how well delivered."[16] Weinberger was not the only tough talker in the Reagan administration, the president himself fully joined the act: "We'd sent Qaddafi a message: We weren't going to let him claim squatters' rights over a huge area of the Mediterranean in defiance of international law. I also wanted to send a message to others in the world that there was new management in the White House, and that the United States wasn't going to hesitate any longer to act when its legitimate interests were at stake."[17] Empire management, Weinberger and Reagan style, required comparatively little effort.

Robert McFarlane, then in his position in the state department, noted in a memorandum of November 16, 1981: "Qadhafi and the *power* that he could command by virtue of Libya's small population of 2.5 million would pose a relatively small threat were it not for *Libya's huge oil income*," estimated at $25 billion annually. "Before the discovery of oil, Libya was one of the world's poorest countries." Still, McFarlane considered Qaddafy as "an international outlaw."[18] Paul Wolfowitz advised Judge Clark on the broader implications of Libya on November 25, 1981: "The litany of American failures in the Middle East is by now familiar to all. Our unwillingness to provide support for Iran when such support might have made a difference, our surprise in the face of the Afghanistan invasion, and our supineness during the hostage crisis caused others to question both or will and our comprehension of regional events. Less well publicized , but equally damaging, was our reluctance to take Libya and the Soviet proxy problem seriously. This both bewildered and demoralized our friends." The Reagan administration, Wolfowitz claimed, was doing better, but the results had failed to materialize, despite 'serious private consultations and public rhetoric' but this was caused by "resource constraints (. . .) and other bureaucratic difficulties, we are seriously lagging in the realm of concrete action. (. . .) Over time and with effort we should be able to close the gap between rhetoric and action. At the moment, however, our position in this regard is serious. In the short term, it was important for the United States to increase international awareness of the seriousness of the threats coming from Qaddafy, "unfortunately, to many in the West, Qadhafi appears as a volatile eccentric rather than a concrete menace."[19] Ronald Bruce St. John observes: "The despicable Qaddafi was a perfect target, a cartoon character Americans love to hate . . . Libya was neither strategically nor militarily formidable. Taking Qaddafi on was the counterterrorism equivalent of invading Grenada – popular, relatively safe, and theatrically satisfying."[20] Despite all the bureaucratic nonsense of trying to build up a Libyan menace, Qaddafy, almost in spite of himself, served as a useful idiot for the US under Nixon to use as an entering wedge to break up the cooperation between western governments and their oil companies; it was a punching bag scenario to demonstrate American power.[21]

The Reagan administration matched its tough rhetoric with easy targets, where the Reagan administration could demonstrate American power with little risk and even less cost.

While Libya was and remained for all realistic purposes on the periphery of the American global interest, Saudi Arabia was on top because of its strategic location; oil was of much greater importance for the United States. On October 27, 1980, West again penned one of his regular (and long-winded) assessments of Saudi Arabia, this time on the recent outbreak of the Iran–Iraq war: "One of the more frustrating parts of the problem is our inability to predict and control the present series of events." The war most certainly meant increased oil prices, and an increased American military commitment to Saudi Arabia, and also to contain a possible expansion of Soviet influence in the region. But the war was also to the American benefit; Saudi Arabia calmed down its criticism of American policies, being so obviously in need of American protection. After the almost mandatory discourse on how American support of Israel upset the Saudis, West concluded: "The quick and effective response by the United States when the Saudis felt themselves threatened by the Iraq-Iran hostilities has caused the immediate crisis over Camp David to be postponed." When things quieted down, West expected the Saudis to brandish the oil weapon again. "On the other hand, the Saudis are by instinct and heredity traders and survivors. The experience of 3,000 years of swapping camels, trading horses and selling carpets seems to be in their genes."[22] Saudi foreign policy was dormant as ever, as James Craig reported in his annual review for 1980, while opposing the Soviet occupation of Afghanistan the Saudi Arabian government was loath to take any action. "But when it came to military and financial action, they were as reluctant as ever to take difficult decisions." The same applied to the Saudi role on the Iran–Iraq war: "In public they told the western powers to keep out of the Gulf. In private they made it clear that if the war spread they would welcome British help in keeping the sea lanes open." After the contretemps over the *Death of a Princess* and Craig's four-month banishment from the kingdom, Anglo-Saudi relations had been restored; British exports exceed £1,000 for the first time.[23] Whatever one may call Saudi actions, whether dignified with the term foreign policy or not, the Saudi royals were consistent; when Anglo-Saudi relations improved so did the prospects for British business in the kingdom.

As with the Americans, there was an extensive British presence in Saudi Arabia. In November 1980 there were three British service teams present, a total of 80 UK personnel. "As part of the SADAP arrangement, BAE provide qualified flying instructors for training pilots for the RSAF (Royal Saudi Air Force)." Furthermore: "The SAS trained Saudi Special Forces (SSF) in counterterrorism from May to August 1979, and the SSF were used in the Grand Mosque incident." Since the British trained forces had acquitted themselves well when reoccupying the Mosque, Saudi Arabia requested the aid of another SAS team, this during the height of the controversy caused by the film *Death of a Princess*. "The SAS team was sent in at short notice, when Anglo-Saudi relations were at their lowest."[24] After calming the Saudis, the main British concern in Anglo-Saudi relations was to sell as much military hardware as possible to the Kingdom.[25] On the Saudi side, they not only needed western technology but also western manpower to have their civilian and military equipment running, all of which, of course, mitigated against any long-term breach in relations.[26] Later, when visiting Saudi Arabia, the prime minister pushed the sale of British military equipment and for renewal of the air training contract, otherwise due to expire in 1982. Thatcher assured the Saudis that she personally would follow up any contracts. Never shy about her own importance, she used her personal touch: "She took personal interest in major contracts, and if any particular problems came up, she would look into them. Her intervention, in matters of this kind could sometimes have a miraculous effect."[27] The prime minister had a very utilitarian attitude towards state visits: "Visits whose objective is mainly to generate good will achieve, in the Prime Minister's view, little if anything. It is firm agreements on policy issues and, above all, contracts that we should be pursuing." Contracts involving the British government required careful preparation months in advance of the visit.[28] But even when having done the necessary kowtowing to the Saudi leadership there were often difficulties in recruiting British personnel to the kingdom. The Ministry of Defence warned Thatcher of the problems which were a serious impediments to the recruitment of British personnel: " With regard to civil law in Saudi Arabia, the local arrangements are often arbitrary, harsh and nasty, and it is possible for quite innocent team members or their wives to find themselves apprehended, unable to communicate with their guards or their friends and incarcerated under the most unpleasant conditions."[29]

Pressure for sales from the UK did not let up. On June 10, 1981 British defense secretary John Nott urged his Saudi counterpart Sultan to join in on a long-term matter – development of a new combat aircraft for the 1990s.[30] This is possibly an early antecedent of the 1985 *Al-Yamaniheh* deal between Saudi Arabia and Britain. Anglo-Saudi relations were solidly back on track when king Khaled visited London 9–12 June 1981. Apart from improving relations it was too a great an opportunity to be missed in pilfering arms on the Saudi. UK ambassador to Riyadh observed to Carrington after the royal visit: "It was hard to imagine, as the King rode down the Mall in the Irish State Coach between cheering crowds, or circumnavigated the great dining room at the Guildhall, manifestly moved by the applause of 700 guests, that only a year before he had been deeply upset by a British television film, had sent me packing from his Kingdom and had imposed a boycott on British firms. That episode is now happily behind us, and the King's visit was the final seal on a reconciliation which has not only restored our relations but made them probably warmer than ever before." And, Craig should have added, more profitable than ever before. The price as always for British friendship was buying British. As Carrington himself told the Saudis: "it is time the warmth of our reconciliation was marked by some more tangible success – a large contract or some new field of cooperation." [31] The French king Henri the fourth once famously said, 'Paris is worth a mass' when converting to Catholicism and renouncing Protestantism to gain entry to the great city; similarly, for British leaders some reflexive genuflection towards Saudi sensibilities was well worth the effort for Saudi contracts and cash.

While Anglo-Saudi relations and business improved there was always a lingering suspicion in Britain about what the Americans were up to. The Foreign and Commonwealth Office complained about intense US competition and that the Americans were trying to edge the British out; "they have used most of the tricks in the book to capture business from us." Still, the British had a substantial share of the Saudi arms market, particularly of the Saudi airforce, which included maintenance and support of 31 Lightning and 40 Strikemaster aircraft, training of Saudi pilots and ground crews in Saudi Arabia, and organizational support for most of the enterprise. More than 2,000 British nationals were required for this effort.[32] British suspicions were not entirely without foundation. Briefing the president on July 24, 1981 on the importance of selling AWACS to Saudi Arabia, secretary of state Alexander Haig noted: "The Saudis probably would react to a denial of AWACS by expanding their military ties with West European states to the detriment of U.S. strategic, economic, and intelligence interests. Equally important, prospects for cooperation with the Saudis on prepositioning, joint planning, and regional air defense could suffer a heavy blow, as would our effort to have them finance our arms sales to Pakistan and other countries where our strategic interests are large. (. . .) The U.S. would also meet difficulties in the Arab world generally. The Gulf States have already expressed reservations that our regional security objectives serve only U.S. interests. They are watching the AWACS decision as an indication of the Administration's attitude and intentions toward them. Moreover, they would feel a loss to their own security because the Saudis have proposed to share AWACS-derived data with them. The reaction in Oman is likely to be especially significant. Oman feels vulnerable because it has been criticized by other Gulf Arabs for cooperating militarily with the U.S. and depends on tacit Saudi acceptance of cooperation with Washington to offset Arab criticism."[33]

But Reagan's success in subduing the Senate and defying the Israel lobby also had international ramifications, enhancing the president's stature and power. Thatcher lauded the president on October 31, 1981: "First may I congratulate you most warmly on the outcome of the vote on AWACS in the Senate. This is good news for all the West's friends in Saudi Arabia and the Gulf. And I am sure they will all appreciate your fantastic personal efforts which led to this result."[34] Reagan replied on December 1: "It was good to have your congratulations on the AWACS outcome. I am convinced that the sale will directly contribute to greater stability in the Middle East and to broadening the basis on which a genuinely even-handed resolution of the problems there can be found. (. . .) There is no doubt that much remains to be done in the Middle East and that time is pressing upon us. Nevertheless, I feel confident that we are on the right track and that your invaluable assistance has greatly improved our prospects for eventual success."[35] Jason H. Campbell argues that AWACS was of major importance in US–Saudi relations; "the sale paved the way for greater bilateral cooperation on a host of issues of mutual concern and increased American military access in the strategically vital Persian Gulf region."[36] AWACS was in many ways the confirmation of the institutionalizing of American control over large segments of Saudi armed forces. In a brief found in the Edwin Meese papers for Senate hearings on AWACS the Reagan administration also argued the Saudi side of the deal: "The Saudis have run heavy risks in being as responsible as they have been. Let me emphasize this is not simply a matter of national pride on their part. It is a matter of sustaining credible and constructive Saudi leadership in the world of Arab politics, and the sometimes deadly world of Arab radicalism."[37] This key point is often forgotten, Saudi Arabia needed 'cover' particularly against its radical opponents. This goes way back to the hostility between Saudi Arabia and Nasser's Egypt from the late 1950s to the 1967 war and beyond.

Christopher Van Hollen assessed the new Reagan administration approach to the Persian Gulf in the summer of 1981: "Saudi Arabia, the world's largest oil reservoir, is an extraordinary weak state. With a native-born population of only about five million, and a small 35,000-man army which has never been tested, the Kingdom must rely on outside manpower to run its economy and on outside help for its security. Concerned about the Soviet threat, and about dangers from Iran and South Yemen, the Saudis view the United States as their ultimate protector. (. . .) Moreover, with still recent memories of the November 1979 Grand Mosque occupation, Saudi Leaders also worry about internal dissidence from those who believe the regime is sacrificing Wahabi orthodoxy for force-draft Western modernization" [sic]. The American presence in the kingdom had ballooned to 45,000. "This is a small number when compared with more than a million Yemenis and other foreigners but, relative to the size of the Saudi population, it is about seven times as large as the American presence in Iran during the heyday of the Shah."[38] Reagan himself pointed to the usual suspects when explaining American policy towards Saudi Arabia: "Even though Saudi Arabia had opposed the Camp David accords, I thought it was important to strengthen ties with this relatively moderate Arab country, not only because its oil exports were essential to our economy, but because, like Israel, it wanted to resist Soviet expansionism in the region. In some ways, our interests in the Middle East and those of Saudi Arabia coincided. Its oilfields were among the richest in the world, coveted by the Communist world and neighboring Iran, but protected by a relatively small Saudi military establishment. The Saudis needed the friendship and, if necessary, the help of a great power in defending their oilfields."[39] Early in his office, the president reaffirmed American security guarantees to Saudi Arabia. Reagan's letter to king Khalid encapsulated American policy towards the desert kingdom: "For over thirty years our presidents have affirmed the importance which the United States attaches to the security and territorial integrity of the Kingdom. In reaffirming this, I pledge my dedication to building on the strength of the many which our governments share." The president was well aware that the Saudis needed constant stroking, whatever his private reservations, if any, Reagan as Carter easily adopted the role of feudal overlord. The assurances were repeated in April combined with the dispatch of Haig which "will aim at showing Saudi Arabia that the United States intends to be a consistent and reliable friend."[40] In their own way the Saudis reciprocated: "In a gesture to the new administration and on the occasion of [US ambassador] West's impending departure, [crown prince] Fahd said he had ordered the release and amnesty of 21 Americans held for offenses against the kingdom."[41] The British also faced the questions and problems of UK nationals detained in the kingdom for real or alleged offenses; taking the larger view it is tempting to see the detainees as potential hostages for acceptable Anglo-American policies as the Saudi defined them. What is striking is how little concern, at least what is reflected in the official correspondence and papers, both the United Kingdom and the United States evidenced about their nationals in Saudi captivity. Apart from Hurd's comment, cited in the previous chapter, on July 27, 1980, that he would appreciate the Saudis to stop maltreating and beating up British nationals, I have found little official concern on these points. But as with the Carter administration, the Saudis were not above rattling the oil weapon, claiming excess oil revenue to its budgetary requirements and wanting political favors from the West for its 'generous' oil policy. But as Clark dryly noted to Reagan this was essentially a Saudi fiction, as the kingdom wanted to sell as much oil as possible because they needed the revenue and not for doing the Americans any favors.[42]

While successfully ramming through AWACS in the Senate, it also had implications for British arms sales, having held up NIMROD (a British surveillance plane) as an alternative to the Saudis. Meeting king Khaled on November 4, 1981, Carrington suggested to the king: "Perhaps the Saudis would buy NIMRODS when the AWACS were worn out. Following the US decision they did not need NIMRODS now: but they did need political support from Britain." The underlining in the text was by the prime minister herself, showing that both parties had a clear grasp of each side of the equation; buying arms from Britain also potentially bought security.[43] Not buying British was also a virtual guarantee that no security or assistance would be forthcoming from the United Kingdom, or so the government thought. Historically, the British had never been shy to apply military power in the Middle East, particularly the Persian Gulf and Arabian Peninsula, when it suited their purposes.

Restored Saudi goodwill soon translated into British military contracts; the Saudi National Guard ordered communication facilities worth £200 million, to be supervised by the Ministry of Defence, which in addition secured a government to government contract at £370 million for training and support for the Saudi Airforce to be operated by a British aerospace company. Negotiations had been difficult "but now it has been completed it could clear the way for us to pursue other military aircraft and equipment sales to the Saudi Defence Ministry."[44] The Saudis blew hot and cold in their relations with

Britain; pulling out all the stops as when later foreign minister Francis Pym visited the kingdom, then back to true form complaining about, from their point of view, an unacceptable item on the BBC, producing the usual and standard genuflections from Thatcher as well as continued reassurance of the importance Britain attached to Saudi Arabia.[45] Lest the Saudis forget, the prime minister took care to underline the connection between the regime's security, even survival, and the purchase of military hardware from its western benefactors. Writing king Fahd on December 23, 1983, the prime minister pointed to the volatile situation in the region generally and the heightened tensions caused by the current unrest in Lebanon: "In such difficult and dangerous times I think it is of the highest importance that like-minded countries should meet frequently and take counsel together so that we may be better able to defend and further those things in which we believe." This, after the prime minister had strongly pushed Rolls-Royce engines on the Saudis to be used in their planned purchase of Boeing aircraft.[46] The efforts paid off handsomely. British defense contracts with Saudi Arabia increased by 38 percent in 1982, and each successfully signed deal was used as a staging post to gain ever more sales.[47] In 1983 sales were up by 20 percent compared to 1982, totaling £2,255 million. Britain was also winning out against one of its main competitors, France, whose sales declined by 25 per cent in 1983.[48] All of which clearly paved the way for the historic *Al-Yamamah* deal.

When Reagan met Saudi king Fahd in Washington in February 1985, Peter Schweizer describes the encounter in glowing terms. "The two leaders had mutual admiration, each believing the other to be quite a courageous figure. To the president, Fahd was standing by the United States in an increasingly hostile and turbulent region. He was also providing tens of millions a year to the mujahedin in Afghanistan and the contras in Nicaragua, two of the president's favorite foreign policy projects. Fahd saw in Reagan someone who had fought hard for Saudi interests on a number of occasions. (. . .) At one point Reagan looked the Saudi king straight in the eye and gave his absolute assurance that he would do whatever necessary to ensure the integrity of Saudi Arabia." Schweizer has a flair for the dramatic here, but whatever the theatrics what Reagan did was only a reaffirmation of traditional American policy towards Saudi Arabia. Reagan continued: "A strong America was in the Saudi interest. Saudi Arabia's chief enemies – Libya, Iran, the Soviet Union – benefitted from high oil prices. The United States hoped for a cooperative relationship with the royal family." Here is the key: security guarantees not only for the territorial integrity of Saudi Arabia but for the personal and political survival of the Saudi royal house.[49] A good thing cannot be repeated too often, especially with the Saudis. When meeting king Fahd's personal envoy, prince Bandar, on June 25, 1985, Reagan again repeated American assurances: "There can be no doubt about the strength of the friendship between our two countries and the fundamental importance we attach to that relationship. The security and well-being of Saudi Arabia are matters of vital interest for the United States." For good measure the president added his personal guarantees: "Our security cooperation is a central element of our relationship, and I am determined to maintain that tie."[50] Despite all insistence to the contrary both from the Saudis and the Americans, the Saudi royals fully realized that they were essentially American clients, not allies. When Reagan solicited Fahd for money to keep the Nicaraguan Contras in operation, despite Congress having turned off the spigot, the king willingly complied, forking out over more than a million dollars monthly to the president's favorite guerilla outfit.[51] Saudi Arabia, of course, had no interest or strategic concern whatsoever in Central America, but they happily paid up to keep their American patrons happy. There was no end to the need of American assurances. When vice president Bush was dispatched to the Persian Gulf in April 1986: "The purpose of your trip is to reaffirm continuing US support for Arab friends in the region. (. . .) Of primary importance are the bilateral meetings. Arab leaders put much stock in measuring the man, and indirectly his country, by his personal presence and attitudes. Your head-to-head-sessions should emphasize personalism, concern and project warmth. Much of the substantive success of this trip depends on the enduring personal relationship developed with these leaders."[52]

In the early Thatcher/Reagan period both the United States and Great Britain had a common interest in maintaining the territorial integrity of Saudi Arabia and the survival and power of the Saudi royal family. Carter, Thatcher and Reagan took easily to their roles as feudal overlords and overlady in their relationship with the Saudi monarchy. Britain continued to enjoy the benefits of access to the Saudi arms market; competition with American companies was much muted and mostly expressed locally. At the top level, the United States and Britain were in basic agreement on what policy to follow. With the close American identification with Israel and the power of the Israeli lobby in the US, it was also in the interest of American foreign policy that the United Kingdom publicly supplied key arms components to Saudi Arabia. Oman, however, was the key in the new Anglo-American relationship in the lower Gulf after the fall of the shah. Up until then, the sultanate had been an exclusive British enclave. Now with the enunciation of the Carter doctrine the United States moved in not only with a full force, but an overwhelming force; suddenly there were rumblings over old Anglo-American rivalry which had clouded relations for much of the 1950s in to emerging competition for influence in Oman. For Britain, the key was how to maintain and possibly expand influence under the umbrella of the Carter doctrine.

CHAPTER
IX

Oman: Discretion Required

When Carter took office Oman was an exclusive British enclave. The United States had but a small presence there and there was no hint in the early Carter years that the president would wish it differently. But with the dramatic events in Iran, Saudi Arabia and Afghanistan all taking place within the two last months of 1979, it is the central argument of this book that Oman became the key to a continued Anglo-American presence in the Persian Gulf and has to a large extent remained so ever since. I am not suggesting that the occupation of the Grand Mosque is on a par with events in Iran and Afghanistan, but for the Saudi ruling family it was THE traumatic event of the year. The whole elaborate foreign policy planning apparatus of the Carter administration were now put in gear to expand the American role and presence in Oman. Before that, few, if any, of the central players in the Carter administration had given much thought to Oman. But the foreign policy machinery was recalibrated to exploit the opportunities presenting themselves there. The whole process gives a strong indication that the Carter administration was more reactive to events, than anything else. For Oman, new vistas opened up – the country was suddenly vied by two important suitors. Despite having an embassy opened in Oman since 1972, the total American impact and presence on the sultanate until 1979 was distinctly limited. The British role and presence in Oman, however, was substantial. For all the public rhetoric of divesting itself of overseas responsibilities and remnants of empire, for all practical purposes, even after 1971 Persian Gulf UK military withdrawal, Britain ran Oman. British officers controlled all branches of the Omani military establishment, all the way up to the chief of the general staff. This was shadowed on the civilian side, where British nationals held commanding positions in the Omani civil service and in the private enterprise sector. Labour, after the 1968 Persian Gulf withdrawal announcement, had a change of heart of sorts and prepared the ground for the coup against the old sultan Taymur, which took place only a month after the new British Conservative government took office in July 1970. The Heath government, for all the talk about being concerned about the UK joining the Common Market, would deepen British ties with the lower Gulf and Oman in particular. When Labour returned to power in 1976, they were, rhetorically and publically at least, concerned about reducing and cutting British ties with Oman. The slogan of the day was Omanization; replacing British Loan Service Personnel (LSP), the term used for British military officers and troops serving in Oman's armed forces. The process of Omanization was slow and anything but a straightforward process. Sultan Qaboos had neither wished for it nor asked for it; besides, it turned out to be a problem to find qualified Omani replacement for departing British officers. Interestingly, even in this process of attempted withdrawal all roads towards a negotiating solution went through London, enabling Labour to remain in control even when pursuing disengagement. Omanization was soon given up by the Thatcher government, reversing Labour's policies and deepening Britain's commitment to a much greater extent than before. At the same time, while welcoming the new American interest in Oman, particularly Washington policy makers themselves, the Thatcherites sought to contain and channel the American presence to their own benefit and simultaneously worked to strengthen their own influence.

Oman was engaged in 1978 with Ras Al-Khaiman (one of the sheikhdoms in United Arab Emirates) in a border dispute on the Musandam peninsula. The American embassy advised following standard United States operating procedure in such matters; to stay neutral, and if able let the British sort matters out. The American ambassador acknowledged Britain's dominant stature in Oman, being for practical purposes in control of Oman: "Regular UK military officers command the services, British expatriates dominate defense ministry ranks. (. . .) This British orientation serves overall U.S. interests, although we may wish it to phase out sooner than London intends."[1] For Britain the dispute represented a potential problem in their Imperial micromanagement because both Oman and Ras Al-Khaiman had British military Loan Service Personnel (LSP) in their employ. Oman had 160 LSPs, while the United Arab Emirates had 20 LSPs in their employ. UK ambassador to Oman, Ivor Lucas, agonized over the situation: "Both sides also employ British contract officers. A conflict between them would therefore be acutely embarrassing to the British Government and could call into question future British military assistance to both countries." A secret directive instructed local British commanders to consult with the ambassador if faced with a potential conflict of his loyalties toward his local employer or the British government. British officers commanding opposite sides in a military confrontation had to be avoided at all costs.[2] All roads on the southeastern Arabian Peninsula ran through London, giving the British large influence with a little presence. Whatever the public perception promoted in the United Kingdom, it is clear that Britain controlled and ran the Omani military.[3] When it came to the selection of a new British commander of the Sultan's Armed Forces (SAF), one official remarked: "I do not think there can be any question of giving [Omani head state, sultan] Qaboos a choice but I agree with you that it would be good tactics to let him feel he had one."[4] So spoke a true imperial civil servant long after the seemingly demise of the British empire.

The fall of the shah changed everything. So much so that the sultan sought added protection from an even more powerful benefactor, the United States.[5] The Carter administration, after having had a minimum of interest in the sultanate prior to the Iranian revolution, began upgrading its relations with Oman.[6] In response to Qaboos expressing concern about area security, president Carter replied on January 19, 1979: "You can be certain of our resolve to help our friends to preserve the independence of your region."[7] As American interest in Oman increased, Qaboos informed the Carter administration of the nature of the relationship he envisaged. The American ambassador to Muscat reported: "The Omanis do not want separately identifiable U.S. military bases with a large number of U.S. military personnel, but are willing to permit an expanded use by U.S. forces of Omani owned and controlled facilities. The Sultan believes a formal defense treaty would have too many adverse political consequences in the regional context, and instead prefers a 'gentleman's agreement' backed by an exchange of letters." American military personnel ought to be kept to a minimum and the military bases in service of the American armed forces maintained by civilian contractors.[8] Still, the increased American activity in Oman from the Carter administration came with a price. Both the Carter administration and Oman hastened to assure the Thatcher government that there was no intention of replacing the British behind this new foreign policy orientation. Lucas thought an increased American presence was not necessarily to Britain's detriment, but there was every reason to keep a watchful eye on developments.[9] Clearly, in response to the United States establishing itself in Oman, British interest increased. The queen paid a visit in in the spring of 1979 and as Lucas argued in his annual review for 1979 British attention deepened further after the Conservatives took office in May 1979: "More flexible arrangements were agreed on the future of British Loan Service Personnel in the Sultan's Armed Forces."[10]

Britain,too, was well aware of the heightened security concerns in the region after the shah. Oman was of great importance for western and UK oil supplies, for straddling key sea and airlines of communication, and for promising great opportunities for the sale of British products. The question was how to defend this. The Defense Ministry (MoD) explained: "that it would be inappropriate to raise the UK military presence to any significant extent, especially as this would imply some commitment to the defense of the host country. Furthermore a high profile could easily provoke the very instability we are seeking to avoid." The last sentence is, of course, the key to modern management of empire and also a strong justification to avoid formal commitments, thus preserving empire on the cheap. Also to avoid a large foreign presence that would only produce local resentment. But withdrawal from present positions was also ruled out "because of the instability and vacuum which this would cause." To get around these obstacles, the MoD suggested beefing up training in Oman and of Omani forces in Britain, combined with increased defense sales. It also had the added advantage of prolonging the British presence in order to give Omani forces sufficient skills to operate sophisticated weaponry.[11] Needless to say, Lord Carrington was in full agreement.[12] This was also in line with what the sultan wanted.[13]

Because of the events outside Oman, 1980 saw a deepening of Anglo-American engagement in the sultanate. Briefing Carrington for his near eastern tour, H.D.A.C. Miers of the Foreign and Commonwealth Office advised on January 7, 1980, that the foreign minister should inquire how Oman was able "to preserve traditional social structures and religious values which contribute so much to stability," while at the same time being responsive to social change. Carrington was advised to reaffirm British support for Oman. "I know that your Majesty feels that the expatriate presence in the armed forces causes no embarrassment internally nor calls for any apologies externally." As always, Carrington and other British leaders carried a strong pitch for further UK arms sales to Oman. The connection between arms sales and oil prices was made explicit: "We regret we cannot in present economic circumstances see our way to reducing the cost of LSP. But your own revenue prospects resulting from actual increases in the price of oil should surely be able to take care of this." Britain sought to reduce the presence of its officers in commanding position in Oman, but progress was slow especially in the navy and air force, "where the latest assessments show that Omanis will not be able to take overall command before 1983 and 1990 respectively." This was not a policy sultan Qaboos wished for, he preferred British officers commanding his forces.[14] When the Americans began taking a closer look at Oman, they found a substantial British presence in the Sultan's Armed Forces: "140 seconded and 610 contract military personnel (as well as 100 Royal Engineers). In addition, the Sultan's air force, which has been likened to a miniature RAF, is supported by approximately 847 civilian contractor personnel. The commanding officers of the land and air forces are British, and British officers occupy every leadership position in the air force, while all military specialists in all the services are British loan-service, contract officers, or NCOs. It might also be noted that the armed forces include some 1226 Pakistanis, 117 Indians, and 19 Jordanians." Britain, had because of recent events, slowed down the process of 'Omanization'. "The British decision to slow down their withdrawal process, with its negative implications for "Omanization", insures the availability of a competent and dependable officer and technician corps in the SOAF should hostilities break out. (. . .) At the present time, the armed forces are still best characterized as command, controlled, administrated, and maintained by the British." After the first Omani–American honeymoon of the blossoming of the relationship, David Newsom and Hal Saunders argued "for a moratorium on further overt measures involving U.S.–Omani military cooperation for the foreseeable future." There was a need to consolidate the relationship before moving ahead.[15]

While the United States sought ways to increase its presence in Oman, the United Kingdom continued, early on in the Thatcher government, to decrease its role in the sultanate. On February 11, 1980, Omani minister of state for foreign affairs, Qais Al-Zawawi, informed Lucas on the lowering of the number of British Loan Service Personnel (LSP) from 157 officers and NCOs in August 1977 to 90 in August 1979: "This reduction has in the main been [made] possible by the rapid and wholly satisfactory Omanisation programme. However, in the increase of maintaining the efficiency of the Land Forces while our Omanisation programme continues we consider it necessary to retain a Loan Service presence, in reduced form, for some time to come."[16]

But whatever mouthing of the mantra, that the US was not out to replace Britain in Oman, the Carter administration held out the prospect of massive American aid and assistance. In addition to improving Omani facilities, it could "handle emergency deployments of air and sea forces which might involve up to 10,000 personnel." Furthermore, the Carter administration planned large-scale American military exercises in Oman, and permanent placement of American technicians at Masirah and Thumrait and Seeb. To gain the sultan's acceptance, the plans were sweetened by a large credit to Oman to purchase American military equipment; $100 million annually in aid for five years, and finally, "Offer the Omanis 'a guarantee in any form they wanted' of help against aggression." From the rather stingy American presence in Iran in the times of the revolution and taking of American hostages, this is a dramatic reversal of policy and a stunningly open-ended commitment to the sultanate. American involvement on this scale was, of course, by its very nature a challenge to the British dominant position in Oman. Alyson Bailes at MoD explained to D. E. Tatham on February 22, 1980: "The US have stressed that they mean to keep us fully informed of their activities in Oman, that they see our role as complementing not supplementing our own and that they have no wish to disrupt plans for Omanisation." But there was no question for Britain in giving up 'Omanization' in favor of 'Americanization'. There was no way Britain simply would give up its special relationship with Oman to the Americans.[17] In reality, there was little danger that this would happen; the Omani leadership was well aware that if its relations with America overshadowed the British role in the country, British commitments could diminish. Qaboos preferred a strong and continued British presence.

The British were extraordinarily inventive in finding ways to maintain influence in Oman. The British Chiefs of Staff noted on April 2, 1980 that while the overall state of training in the Sultan's Armed forces were good: "the limited ability of Omani officers to plan and conduct realistic training creates the need for a British training and advisory team, which is planned to replace LSP." A presence would therefore be sustained even while the main goal was achieved: "The aim of the UK in providing LSP for Oman has been the safe and orderly Omanisation of the Sultan's Armed Forces (SAF) in order to ensure that, when military assistance is finally withdrawn, the Omanis are left with fully capable armed forces." The increased American presence in the Gulf was a direct consequence of the fall of the shah and the Soviet invasion of Afghanistan. "President Carter has stated publicly that any outside attempt to gain control of the Gulf and its resources will be seen as a threat to US vital interests and repelled by force if need be." This, of course, is the Carter doctrine as enunciated by the president after the Soviet invasion of Afghanistan. MoD officials foresaw different US and UK roles in Oman: "The US can provide equipment, financial aid, and visible assurances of military support, whereas the UK provides LSP, advice, training support, and some defence equipment." The new relationship was not necessary disadvantageous to Britain: "The UK's continued presence can, indeed, be seen as a balancing factor, giving the UK a position of influence and channel of advice, and avoiding an all-out US take-over which apart from its political implications may not increase the effectiveness of Omani forces." Britain should be sufficiently flexible to continue Omanization of the Sultan's Armed Forces, to avoid local and Arab resentment that the military establishment was run by white faces, but at such a pace as not to diminish the effectiveness of the same forces.[18] It is interesting to note that even with the process of Omanization in the best of times going full speed ahead, there were always ways to maintain British influence. Zawawi was therefore at pains to assure the British ambassador, Lucas, that their relationship with Britain was Oman's number one priority.[19]

Having lost its Iranian 'pillar' the Americans found a substitute in the lower Gulf and in Oman in particular. Under the auspices of the Carter doctrine the contemplated American involvement was massive. Here we see an example of one of the key problems in terms of the application of American power. For instance, in Iran, just prior to the occupation of the American embassy in November 1979, despite the regime's claim that the embassy was a nest of spies, there were only three CIA agents in Tehran.[20] The United States had, after the Iranian revolution, formerly a key American interest, for very valid reasons, a very limited presence. Furthermore, the United States, in spite of the shah practically begging for instructions and assistance, offered neither, and made the most feeble attempts to either prevent Khomeini's power grab or to establish relations with him. Having said that, it might not have mattered much whatever the US did given the scale of the cleric's suspicions and hatred against America. In Oman, a country where the United States had evidenced but little interest previously, it wanted a presence that could potentially completely overwhelm both the British and the sultanate itself. Ironically, after investing so many resources in its newfound ally, accepting the tenets of a low-key presence and respecting Omani sovereignty, the Carter administration in one of its first acts in the newly established alliance, violated the Sultan's trust by mounting the rescue operation for American hostages in Tehran from Oman. The United States signed an access agreement with Oman on April 9, 1980. In addition to a low key American presence, the Omanis requested no publicity about the agreement, and were dead set against any use of Omani facilities against Iran.[21] The feebleness of the rescue attempt stands out in stark contrast to the reality of American might as applied in Oman.

But with a long line of Anglo-American 'friction' in the Middle East, the Americans also had a well developed suspicion about British motives and actions in the region. In the Carter administration key officials believed that

British loan officers were "stirring the Sultan's suspicions" so that the US feared that Qaboos would back out of his agreement with the Americans. But in reality this was only an excuse used internally in the Carter administration for the Omani–US problems following the rescue operation. Carter's officials urged the president to assure Qaboos that no states in the region had been consulted about the American attempt to free the hostages. When the president received this he instructed Brzezinski: "Draft a good, strong, quick letter offer in it to send a personal representative."[22]

As always, when poaching on British turf, the American justification was the larger strategic picture, concern about the ramifications of the Soviet invasion of Afghanistan, and Carter's pronunciation of the doctrine carrying his name: the US would oppose any Soviet attempt at the Persian Gulf, with any means necessary, including force. The British, of course, were well aware that American policy in this regard was driven by reasons of grand strategy. "They would hope to demonstrate that Soviet intervention, e.g. against Iranian and Gulf oil fields, could only be contemplated if the Russians were prepared use very powerful forces indeed and to accept that such an incident was unlikely to remain localized." This was followed by the usual caveat that the United States had no intention of replacing Britain in Oman, but was at the same time working for a closer relationship with Oman. "There was no treaty or security commitment, but US intentions were rooted in President Carter's recent statement on the security of the Persian Gulf." At this stage, the consensus within the Foreign and Commonwealth Office was that Britain could maintain its position in Oman even with an increased American presence; the Americans were the only ones able to counter the Soviet threat, while Britain should continue the process of Omanization and assist Qaboos with his internal security needs.[23]

Despite American assurances of gently moving into Oman and keeping a low profile, something both Saudi Arabia and Oman deemed necessary to avoid giving their radical neighbors and competitors additional arguments against them, the United States violated the trust Qaboos had bestowed upon them. The hostage rescue operation was mounted from Oman without informing or consulting Oman or Britain. Carter wrote Qaboos on May 1, 1980, starting with reiterating American security assurances to Oman: "We will work with you and other friendly leaders in the region to help blunt any political attacks against Oman inspired by Iran and encouraged by the Soviet Union." Carter claimed the rescue mission, if successful, "would have allowed Iranians and other peoples in the region to focus more clearly on the serious threat to region created by the projection of Soviet power and influence. (. . .) Because the mission did not succeed, however, we must work together to limit the adverse consequences and to persevere toward our larger common objective." In other words, Carter left it to Oman to pick up the pieces of the American failure. The president explained that the lack of consultation prior to the rescue mission was necessary in order to maintain operation security. Again, the implication being that the Omanis were not to be trusted. "If you believe it would be useful, I am prepared to send a personal emissary to elaborate further my commitment to our relationship, to consult you on steps to advance it, and to explain the details of the rescue mission." Having just violated Omani trust and confidence, Carter concluded the letter: "A relationship of trust and the closest cooperation between us continue to be of the highest importance to me."[24]

Lucas, in Muscat, was uncomfortable with the increased American presence in Oman, wondering whether all implications, despite positive noises from London, "have been fully thought through on a Whitehall-wide basis." While the Americans claimed to be cognizant of Omani susceptibilities, it did "not stop them from mounting the hostage rescue operation which had obvious implications for just those susceptibilities." Besides, the situation in Oman had uncomfortable similarities with the situation in Iran during the last years of the shah's rule; "there were valid reasons why the Shah's military might should be built up – the proximity to the Soviet Union; the policing of the Gulf; the preservation of Iran's trade routes to the East etc. But with the wisdom of hindsight one can see that this build-up, together with the enormous responsibility which it imposed on the Shah, was more than even he could sustain, and at least contributed to his eventual downfall. The parallel with Oman is not exact, but it is far too close for comfort – and the Sultan's shoulders are much less broad than the Shah's. Have these things really been thought through?"[25] Adrian Fortescue in the British Embassy Washington wanted to believe American assurances, but thought they looked "pretty suspect in the light of the Iran rescue attempt." Furthermore, there was a real concern that American business might elbow out British firms in Oman. "It would surely be unrealistic to expect the Americans actively to discourage any interest which the presence of their personnel and equipment might excite the Omanis; and they might well go further than that if the US military sales juggernaut finds it impossible to resist the temptation. But I do not believe that to be a major motivation behind the facilities idea. We will just have to work harder at holding our market."[26] Carrington writing Lucas on May 11 noted: "We hope this episode will be a reminder to the Americans of the need to maintain a low profile in Oman and not to ignore local sensitivities." Carrington intended to press this point home when visiting Washington the week after. "We shall be in a good position to monitor the development of the Omani–US relationship and to counsel both sides."[27] Britain, by luck, continued in its favored post-imperial position, whatever the realities of British power and influence; the roads towards working acceptable positions for all parties ran through London.

In the meantime, the British did a little stroking of their own; on May 15, 1980 Lucas informed Al-Zawawi, who was minister of state for foreign affairs in Oman, on a continued British LSP presence, but also: "Her Majesty's Government will give sympathetic consideration to any requests for further adjustments to loan service personnel, subject to constraints on availability."[28] When Zawawi met his British counterpart, Francis Pym, on May 29, 1980, he welcomed "the increased numbers of UK training deployments. He felt that these were useful and demonstrated the close ties between Britain and Oman. A number of Nimrod aircraft had been deployed to Seeb in Oman and his Government were looking forward to the forthcoming deployment of RAF Jaguar aircraft and Victor tankers." Zawawi was pleased that this presence was augmented by the deployment of British infantry and Royal Engineers, which he expected to assist in "development programmes in remote parts of the country." There was never any doubt who depended on who: "Concluding, His Excellency said that he had spoken frankly but honestly to the Secretary of State [Pym] and hoped he had not given any offense; he believed, though, that the very old and close relationship between Oman and Great Britain allowed him to express himself so."[29]

Tatham wrote Lucas on July 14, 1980 explaining the rationale behind the current American build-up in the Persian Gulf; with the Soviet invasion of Afghanistan, further Soviet expansion into Iran or Pakistan remained a distinct possibility. "A year ago, we should have thought a Soviet occupation of Afghanistan most improbable. As the US was the only country which could challenge a further Soviet push, their aim was to build up a capability to do this. They might not be able to repell [sic] a Soviet attack at such distance but at least the Russians would have to reckon with a conflict of say Korean proportions. The Gulf was so essential to the West's security that the Americans must have the capability to defend it." The scale of the threat necessitated a large American presence in Oman, and while the Foreign and Commonwealth Office shared Lucas' concern about the American intrusion into the Sultanate, it had become convinced the United States was sincere in wanting to complement Britain and not replace it.[30] Still, the Foreign and Commonwealth Office was deeply conscious of the implications of the increased American presence: "Our task is now to ensure as far as possible that our own and American interests remain complementary rather than conflicting."[31] Senior British officials from the Foreign and Commonwealth Office, the Ministry of Defense and from the Defence Policy Staff discussed Oman on December 11, 1980 and concluded: "Our principal objective remains to maintain the security and stability of Oman under a Western-orientated government in the interests of preserving Oman's willingness to provide facilities in support of the wider Western position in the Arabian Peninsula and the Gulf area and of avoiding the serious repercussions to be expected elsewhere in the area from the collapse of the present Sultanate régime." The United Kingdom, "in support of wider Western interests in the area as a whole, [have] welcomed the US plans for a Rapid Deployment Force with the necessary facilities in the region to enable it to be moved to the area without delay." While encouraging Qaboos to grant the Americans the necessary facilities, the British wanted at the same time the American presence to be as unobtrusive as possible unless their very presence encouraged instability where the intention was increased stability. Despite an increased American presence, the British wanted to maintain their own forces in the lower Gulf, arguing that their forces were often more acceptable locally than American personnel. For all the sentiments and concerns for Oman's stability business was an equally important British concern, courting Oman was necessary "to preserve our favorable trading and defence sales interests." All in all, the bureaucrats were rather pleased with the current state of affairs in Oman: "There was no real contradiction between the present policy of Omanisation designed to lower the Western military profile in the country and the development of American facilities for the RDF, since the Americans were well aware of the need to keep a strict limit on the number of US personnel permanently in Oman." Furthermore, the UK influence in the Armed Forces "would not disappear with the departure of the Loan Service Commanders since it was intended that they would be followed by a sizeable training team for an indefinite period in the future. As advisors, however, they would be less likely to be seen in the region as detracting from Oman's credentials as a fully independent Arab country." The document gives an important clue about client management: "we must continue to give the Omanis the impression that we are taking them broadly into our confidence, even if at times this would be more a matter of cosmetics than real substance."[32]

These issues remained more or less a constant to the end of the Carter administration. Upon leaving office, the president sent a farewell note to the many heads of state he had engaged with during his tenure. To Qaboos Carter wrote: "As I leave the Presidency of the United States after an eventful Administration, I look upon the close relationship established between Oman and the United States as one of the outstanding accomplishments of the past four years."[33]

The Soviet invasion of Afghanistan and increased American presence in the Persian Gulf changed British perceptions on future planning for the region. On the British side: "Complementary to the US effort, scope exists for a modest increase, carefully judged and phased, in the UK peacetime military involvement in the Middle East." Oman remained key to the British effort, "but every opportunity should be taken to encourage co-operation with and between other states in the area." Most of the effort would be conducted "in the form of military training assistance and Loan Service Personnel will remain of great importance as offering low profile and inexpensive help." As a consequence of the new situation, "The British Military presence in Oman should be continued throughout the 1980s by formation of advisory teams to replace the gradual phasing out of LSP."[34]

Complicating the picture further in the Persian Gulf, war broke out between Iran and Iraq in September 1980. On September 27, Zawawi startled the British by announcing that Qaboos at the request of an Iraqi delegation, had offered Iraq facilities to mount operations against Abu Musa and the Tunbs and against Iranian naval units. "Oman had come to the conclusion that, such was the degree of instability in the Gulf area caused by the Khomeini regime that they felt obliged to give assistance to the Iraqis." The action might also potentially involve Britain directly, because in the event of retaliation Qaboos expected British Loan Service Personnel to take part in operations on Omani territory.[35] Qaboos had earlier in the summer tried to improve his Arab credentials by seeking closer relations with Saddam Hussein's Iraq; when the two leaders met in June 1980 they wanted the Soviet penetration of the Persian Gulf checked. To show his good will, Hussein offered Iraqi troops to Qaboos in the event of a South Yemeni attack on Oman.[36] This, of course, was a highly ironic turn of events as Iraq had previously been the chief outside instigator and supporter of unrest on the Arabian Peninsula aimed at destabilizing Saudi Arabia and Oman.

Thatcher spent the weekend at the Prime Minister's country resort Chequers, but was sufficiently worried to call Carrington on Saturday afternoon on September 27. Carrington's immediate response was: "The consequences for us are really gruesome beyond words." Carrington had already sent a telegram to Muscat urging the Sultan to withdraw assistance to Iraq, since if the thing blew up the Persian Gulf might be closed to international shipping. The British government had not before these last developments been overly concerned about the outbreak of the Iran – Iraq war. Thatcher remarked: "The whole strategy, Peter, was to isolate it [the war]. And I thought we'd succeeded."[37]

Tunnell at the British embassy, in Muscat met Zawawi again after receiving instructions from Carrington: "I said that the reaction of the British Government was one of horror that the Omanis should contemplate participation in the proposed operation. The Secretary of State had personally requested me to urge the utmost restraint. (. . .) More ominously Zawawi suggested in strict confidence that the Iraqis in their gratitude might cede the island to Oman instead of the states of UAE should the operation be successful. I said that I could see no possible benefit to Oman from such a solution, which would set them against not only Iran but their closest neighbours also."[38] Washington weighed in urging caution on the Omanis, wanting to limit the Iran–Iraq war from spreading. But for the United States far more than international issues were at stake: "We are also concerned over two other dangers from prolonged or widened conflict; (1) if such a conflict leads to a greatly weakened Iran, the opportunities for enhanced Soviet influence or direct intervention in Iran increase proportionally; (2) the safety of American hostages in Iran could be seriously threatened, especially if states Iran consider close to the US become involved in the conflict." On the other hand, if Oman was a victim of Iranian aggression, secretary of state Edmund Muskie pledged immediate consultation about possible countermeasures.[39] There is, perhaps, shades of the geo-strategist Brzezinski here; whatever the nature of the Iranian regime it was important to avoid an Iranian weakening or collapse in order to prevent the Soviets from exploiting a potential political vacuum. Once dominant in Iran, the entire oil rich Persian Gulf would have been within Russian reach. The hostages played a second role to Brzezinski's great game of empire.

Carrington, while seeking to restrain the Omanis, warned: "there is no guarantee that the Americans would feel committed to coming to Oman's defence against retaliatory attack from Iran, particularly given the problem with the hostages." But if push came to shove, British LSPs would assist Oman in a crisis.[40] Fortunately for Qaboos, Iraq was late in putting its forces forward and proved unable to mount an operation from Oman. Lucas observed in his annual review for 1980: "Qaboos gained kudos in Baghdad for having agreed in principle without having to pay the price. The cost could have been Iranian retaliation against vital economic installations whose almost total vulnerability would have been plain for all to see, and which would have virtually set at naught much that has been achieved over the past ten years."[41]

Like almost all crises, the Iran–Iraq war also came with opportunities, as Brzezinski noted to Carter on October 3, 1980: "The threat to the security of the Gulf gives us a unique opportunity to consolidate our security position in a manner which even a few weeks ago would have been impossible. The Saudis and the other Gulf states are much more inclined to seek U.S. military presence since they have become very anxious about their longer term security. While we should not appear over-eager in proffering military assistance, we would miss a major strategic opportunity if we fail to exploit this." Brzezinski even advocated 'subtle' and more 'covert initiatives' toward Iran: "we should actively seek new contacts with Iran to explore the possibility of helping it just enough to put sufficient pressure on Iraq to pull back from most, if not all, of its current acquisitions." This in order to "safeguard Iran from Soviet penetration or internal disintegration." For Brzezinski, at this stage, the American hostages in Iran were obviously a secondary concern. Carter wrote on the memo: "You, Ed[mund Muskie, Carter's secretary of state] should advise me on how to pursue this."[42] This thinking was by no means clear to the British ambassador to Washington, who sarcastically wrote home on the consequences of the Iran–Iraq war for American policy: "You know from last weekend how difficult it is to perceive any pattern of US policy on the Iraq/Iran crisis, but certain strands seem to be emerging that I shall try to describe though, being as they are without design or intent, too much shape should not be attached to them."[43]

In discussions with the Department of Defence and Francis Pym, Carrington of course was well aware of the potential threats coming from the Iran–Iraq war. But Carrington and Pym adhered to the dictum of former prime minister Edward Heath: maintain maximum political influence at minimum cost. Also a little effort could go a long way: "Our willingness and ability to make a speedy and practical response to the UAE's enquiries has put us in a favorable light and should have laid to rest any lingering doubts the Rulers may have had that we had lost interest in them."[44] Whatever else, economic prospects for Oman were bright, the economy was expanding rapidly, thanks in large part to increased oil revenues. Anglo-Omani relations were good at the end of 1980, a year on which a long line of British dignitaries had visited the sultanate, testifying to the importance of Oman to Britain. Even after these short-term successes, Lucas feared for the British position in the future: "Yet the solid content of the relationship is dwindling by comparison with the new and greater involvement of the United States."[45] Lucas was perhaps too pessimistic, as officials from the Foreign and Commonwealth Office and the

Ministry of Defence concluded on December 30, 1980: "We have a position in Oman which we should not allow to be significantly eroded, because (a) we can expect to be in a better position than the Americans to help the Sultan balance his need on the one hand not to give openings for internal or external subversion with, on the other, the requirements of external defence of Oman and of Oman's playing a role in the wider Western defence effort in the region; and (b) to preserve favorable trading and defence sales interest."[46]

Margaret Thatcher comes across as a very forceful prime minister, often interfering in and instructing government departments to pursue a more active policy. Following her April 1981 visit to Oman, she instructed through her private secretary Michael Alexander, the Foreign and Commonwealth Office. She wanted current British policy on costs of Loan Service Personnel to be reevaluated. "The Prime Minister would like our policy on this issue to be reconsidered. She wholly disagrees with the proposition that we should assess charges for Loan Service Personnel on a full cost basis. She believes that this approach does very great harm. She considers that we are unnecessarily upsetting friendly countries by raising 'trifling matters' such as this. The Prime Minister also regards the proposition that bills should be raised from the beginning of the financial year with adjustments being subsequently to reflect actual charges as 'most unsatisfactory'."[47]

Newsweek announced on March 23, 1981 that Qaboos had reached agreement with the Americans that the United States could use the old British base at Masirah Island. "The Reagan plan includes $75 million for new oil tanks, an upgraded airstrip and a water desalination plant. Other funds will go to improve another airfield at Seeb, which lies near the entrance of the Strait of Hormuz."[48] The Reagan administration planned to spend 300 million dollars in the period 1981 to 1983 to improve key parts of Oman's military infrastructure for American use. This came with American assurances that only "a few dozen US personnel would be permanently stationed in Oman"; the Americans in the country would keep a low profile, and the Reagan administration would regard its presence as 'complementary' to British efforts in the country. [49] In this respect, Reagan was singing from the same song sheet as Carter. Rhetoric apart, in the lower Gulf, then, there was not much difference in the policies pursued by Carter and Reagan.

The advent of the Reagan administration in no way diminished the British role in Oman. In fact the declassified record from the British National Archives for 1981 shows a Thatcher government being close to micromanaging almost all aspects of Omani affairs and also in the process significantly upgrading the British interest and presence in the sultanate. Miers advised Lucas in Oman on February 5, 1981 on the present stage of British policy towards the sultanate after extensive discussions in London. British interests remained constant; a stable and secure western orientated regime that willingly gave access to facilities on its soil to the western powers and as a market for British civilian and military industries. The Americans were to keep their heads down to avoid provoking the unrest their presence might engender. A continued British presence was, therefore, essential, which "is in some ways acceptable to other States in the Gulf [whereas] an American would not be, and also provides much of our locus standi for monitoring and advising on Omani policies generally." The vehicle for maintaining British influence was as always the Loan Personnel Scheme, but with a gradual scaling down as circumstances warranted to avoid provoking international resentment. While British loan service personnel were in the Sultan's employ, there were no doubt where their real loyalty lay: "It is important that they should feel that they have the confidence of HMG when they give unpalatable advice to the Sultan." But it was also to some extent a difficult balancing act, defense procurement ought to be basically from British sources. "This is not wholly self interest, since it is more efficient and economical for Oman to build on its existing defence structure and experience which is mainly British-inspired." While in agreement with the Americans of the overall goals in Oman, Lucas was advised to keep a certain distance from the Americans and maintain, as far as possible, work for an exclusive British sphere in Oman.[50]

Carrington advised the prime minister in November 1981: "During this year and particularly since your visit to Oman in April, the FCO and MOD have been giving continuing thought to our relationship with the Sultanate and in particular to the assistance we give in the military field. (. . .) Our defence cooperation with Oman has for many years included the provision of loan service personnel, contract officers, joint exercises and training. But the formal position lags behind that which characterises our relations with Bahrain, Qatar, and the UAE where under the 1971 Treaties of Friendship, we undertook to 'consult together on matters of mutual interest in time of need'. This difference is something of an anomaly." Douglas Hurd on his forthcoming December visit to Oman would give oral undertakings of a similar nature as Britain had with the other Gulf sheikdoms.[51] Thatcher thought the proposed statement to be inadequate: "It is hardly reassuring. Indeed quite the opposite."[52] The new line to take was, while it was difficult to foresee all contingencies: "we cannot therefore promise any particular response. However, we have come to your aid in the past; officers and men of all three Service serve with your Armed Forces; we have [an] RN patrol in the Gulf of Oman at present. I can assure you that HMG intends therefore to maintain its close defence relationship with Oman in the future."[53] It is fairly obvious here that Britain is reversing its policy in the Gulf, being much more assertive after a decade of withdrawal. This change is also interesting in light of the Carter doctrine and current historiography of Reagan overriding Thatcher. It is obvious where matters for British interests are expanding regardless of the Americans. Thatcher, in other words, used Reagan's cold war focus (and taking care of the bear), as the umbrella under which to extend British influence in the lower Gulf.

The reversal of British policy had, in fact, happened much earlier, as seen by Miers telling the Americans during Anglo-American talks on Oman July 9, 1981: "It was deliberate UK policy to promote the sale of our defence equipment in the Gulf since this would reduce unit costs to our forces and also provide employment in the UK. This in turn would increase the size of the effort we could make in the Gulf, and also make it easier for the Government to carry out a policy in the area which was not without its critics, since it was to some extent at variance with the 1971 philosophy of 'withdrawal.' "[54]

Oman was well worth Britain's attention, being a major market for British exports and imports. Although facing competition from the Japanese and the United States, there were plenty of opportunities left for British companies. "The large number of British expatriates in positions of influence and the Sultan's reported policy of 'buy British' should give us an edge over our competitors and with few locally produced goods, import demand."[55] With his 'buy British' policy, Qaboos, of course, clearly signaled he understood how the Thatcher government expected the relationship to play out. When meeting Qaboos in December, Hurd duly conveyed the assurances worked out previously. "Qaboos said he was very grateful for this encouraging reassurance. He hoped that the eventuality never happened, but one could never be sure. He agreed that these details should remain an entirely private exchange. It was essential to remain discreet in such matters. He did not (not) ask for further clarification or for a piece of paper."[56] Hurd did not want to inform the United States about the nature of British assurances given the sultan.[57] There was always a lingering concern about American intentions in Oman, particularly after Henderson reported from Washington on January 23, 1982 that while the American focus was both on Saudi Arabia and Oman, American foreign policy makers considered Saudi Arabia 'inadequate' for its strategic needs and purposes, hence a greater emphasis on Oman.[58] While suspicious, there was probably an element of exaggeration to British fears. Ambassador Lucas noted in his valedictory dispatch on December 3, 1981, that Qaboos had instructed his government officials to buy British whenever possible; "and has given earnest of his feelings in this connection by placing lucrative orders with us for the design and construction of Qaboos University, and for the supply of Chieftain tanks for his army, Vosper Thorneycroft ships for his navy, and Jaguar Aircraft for his airforce."[59]

On July 15, 1982 Thatcher wrote Qaboos signifying a strong British commitment to Oman. The letter is of considerable importance and deserves to be quoted extensively, as the prime minister accedes to the major Omani requests: "I can confirm that we agree to increase in numbers of British Loan Service Personnel until Omani replacements are available. We hope to be able to meet the current bid for an increase of 82 posts in 1982/83." This is of course a complete reversal of fading out the British military presence in Oman, and on the face of it an open-ended commitment, where the end of the British presence seemingly is no longer even a distant goal. Furthermore, the prime minister pledged the availability of UK specialty personnel: "we will endeavor to be as helpful as possible, particularly where new skills are required (for example, in operating mine countermeasures vessels, armoured personnel carriers or air defence systems)." Thatcher pointed out that Britain had already reduced charges for LSPs as well selective reductions in training charges "and there could be more where the provision of training is connected to the sale of British equipment." Needless to say, the prime minister again stresses the connection between security and buying British. Omani military students in the UK "will be given preferential treatment." Formally, Britain had kept its LSP personnel on a tight leash, while ostentatiously serving the sultan and Oman Britain had ultimate control of their dispositions. Thatcher now reversed this, in a stunning change of British policy: "On the question of the position of British Loan Service personnel in time of either internal or regional conflict, I can assure Your Majesty that we are fully committed to the security of Oman. While we would wish to be consulted before British personnel were used in circumstances which could prove embarrassing to either of our two Governments, we recognize that the urgency of a military response in the event of a direct threat to Oman might not allow time for consultation. In these circumstances, we would be content that British personnel should play their full part in Oman's defence. It is well understood between us that British Loan Service Personnel can only follow orders which are consistent with UK military law." For military operations outside Omani territory, Thatcher only requested consultations before LSPs were operationally committed. The prime minister further pledged specialists in bomb disposal to Oman as well as training Omani military servicemen in the same. Finally, in case of war after providing for Britain's own military needs: "I can assure Your Majesty that we would do our best to ensure the continued supply and delivery of such items if an emergency arose in Oman."[60] Thatcher's letter is a significant new British policy towards Oman. On April 28, 1981 the defense department issued *Directives to the Chief of the Defence Staff (Oman) and to the British LSP Service Commanders in Oman*: "Members of the United Kingdom and Armed Forces under your command have been made available to Oman on the understanding that the role of the Sultan's Armed Forces is the defence of Oman and its protection against external and internal threats. You are however to ensure that neither you nor any British Service personnel under your command are employed directly on active operations beyond the frontiers and territorial limits of Oman, without prior approval of Her Majesty's Government." In case of an urgent situation where there was no time to obtain prior approval: "These circumstances might include operations close to an undefined or disputed border, possibly involving emergency reaction to direct aggression which demanding immediate response by the local commander. In an emergency you are therefore empowered to authorize the employment of Loan Service personnel on such specific operations, provided you inform Her Majesty's Ambassador at the earliest opportunity." Control at all times rested in London: "If at any time in the execution of your duties you should be faced with a situation where it appears that the employment of British seconded personnel under your command, as directed by the Omani Government, could be against the interests of Her Majesty's Government, or involve you in a conflict of loyalties, you are to report the situation to Her

Majesty's Ambassador, in advance of taking any action." All this while being seen to be loyal to the sultan. But as we have seen, the source of ultimate loyalty was in London.[61]

The Americans showed their interest in and the importance of Oman when president Reagan received Qaboos on a state visit with full military honors on April 12, 1983.[62] Oman remained a continuing American interest. President Reagan wrote Qaboos on March 27, 1986, prior to vice president George Bush's visit to Oman. "The visit of Vice President Bush will further highlight the importance the United States attaches to the area as a whole. In particular, his time in Oman will allow us to continue the close consultations which have played so important a part in our special relationship"[63] British interest in Oman continued well beyond the Thatcher era, for instance conducting Operation Swift Sword II with Omani forces in October 2001 with 24,000 British troops – the largest taskforce assembled after the Falklands War.[64] For Saudi Arabia and Oman, the early years of the Thatcher premiership was anything but a withdrawal, but saw a deepening British interest and influence in this region of the Middle East.

Epilogue

When Reagan met the returning American hostages from Iran, he ratcheted up the rhetoric against the terrorists. Unfortunately, he did not have much success in preventing terrorists acts against American citizens. During the first five years of his presidency violent incidents increased dramatically: 660 American civilians and military personnel were killed or wounded by terrorists.[1] The president was unwilling or unable to devise strategies to prevent American citizens falling prey to terrorists. But this was not a 'policy' that started with Reagan. In fact, American officials seem to have been remarkably little concerned by the loss of American lives by foreigners. This is exemplified by the USS *Liberty* in 1967 and USS *Stark* in 1987 incidents. During the Six Day War, an Israeli plane deliberately and without provocation attacked the US spy ship *Liberty* in international waters, killing 34 and wounding 171 of the crew. Egyptian dictator Gamal Abdul Nasser, for his part, broke off diplomatic relations with the United States and Britain, claiming falsely, but in a desperate face-saving effort, that their planes were responsible for Israel's stunning success in wiping out the Egyptian air force. Nasser did so, despite being the recipient of substantial US food aid for most of the 1960s. American farmers at one point fed 40 per cent of the Egyptian population.

There was little doubt among key figures in the Lyndon Johnson administration that the Israeli government was behind the attack; the chair of Johnson's intelligence advisory board, Clark Clifford noted: "The unprovoked attack on the *Liberty* constitutes a flagrant act of gross negligence for which the Israeli Government should be held completely responsible, and [the] Israeli military personnel involved should be punished".[2] Secretary of state Dean Rusk "was never satisfied with the Israeli explanation. Their sustained attack to disable and sink *Liberty* precluded an assault by accident or by some triggerhappy local commander: Through diplomatic channels we refused to accept their explanations. I didn't believe it then, and I don't believe them to this day. The attack was outrageous".[3] Johnson's one-time under-secretary of state, George Ball, claims that "the *Liberty*'s presence and function was known to Israel's leaders". For Ball, the costs to the United States of the episode were much higher than the injury to the crew: "Israel's leaders concluded that nothing they might do would offend the Americans to the point of reprisal: If America's leaders did not have the courage to punish Israel for the blatant murder of American citizens, it seemed clear that their American friends would let them get away with almost anything".[4]

There is little doubt that ever since engineering a reestablishment of relations with Iraq in 1983, US relations with Saddam Hussein's regime were convoluted. I strongly suspect, if and when the archival record of the 1991 Gulf War is released, historians will learn that there is much more to the story than we hitherto know. The Iraqi dictator was much incensed when he learned about American double dealing towards Iraq, a crooked policy that came to light with the revelations following in the wake of Congressional investigations of the Iran/Contra scandal. With his well developed suspicion and paranoia, it is safe to assume that he did not take lightly or kindly to American offers to Iran to assist in deposing the Iraqi leader. Saddam Hussein wrote president Reagan on November 18, 1986: "Iraq, Mr. President, understands in principle your endeavour to establish normal relations with Iran. Now or in the future, regardless of whether we agree with your justifications and goals or not. What concerns Iraq, in these matters, is that such relations do not involve a threat to its security, sovereignty and legitimate interests. (. . .) What has shocked and caused our great surprise – and, frankly, even aroused our suspicions – is that the process of your rapprochement with Iran has involved supplying that country with quantities of U.S. military equipment, and that the contacts have been undertaken in the manner uncovered recently." Hussein further pointed out that he believed there was an American–Iraqi agreement based on several years of exchanges at the foreign minister level, that in order to make Iran desist in its war against Iraq was to embargo arms to Iran. "You informed us through official channels that you were continuing with an extensive world-wide campaign in this direction." The Iraqi dictator reminded Reagan that Iraq had, with other Arab states, cooperated fully with the American initiative. "I and my colleagues in the Iraqi government have rightly found that what has taken place involves a direct and grave threat to the security and safety of our country and a direct contribution to the prolongation of the war."[5] When receiving the letter US assistant secretary of state Richard Murphy assured the Iraqi ambassador to Washington that the US would continue to pursue the regional arms embargo 'vigorously'. But also noted "that the recent revelations will require special U.S. efforts to re-establish full credibility for Staunch [Operation Staunch,' to stop the sale of arms to Iran in order to bring an early end to the Iran–Iraq war] with all parties."[6]

The United States's willingness to sacrifice its own servicemen in the Middle East at the altar of the ally of the day is not just the case of typical Democratic spinelessness as the Johnson administration's feeble attempt to castigate Israel may suggest. When Iraq attacked its 'ally's' ship, the USS *Stark* in May 1987, killing 37 American sailors, Ronald Reagan, meekly accepted the loss, eager not to lose an ally against the Iranian ogre during the Iraq-Iran war. He dismissed the incident as trivial: "The months following the Reykjavik summit were very busy: (. . .) and then there was the tragic attack by Iraqi planes on the USS *Stark*". While the secretary of state George Shultz doubted whether the attack was an accident, he accepted Saddam Hussein's admission of error and apology. For Colin Powell "the U.S.S. *Stark* was accidentally attacked by an Iraqi Exocet missile".[7] The incident has caused far less controversy than the attack on the *Liberty*. Defense secretary Caspar Weinberger followed the official line while in office, but stated in a later interview that he believed the attack to be premeditated, believing Iraq "wanted to demonstrate that they could attack America and deal with a superpower and they should be the leading power in the Gulf."[8] Given the dramatic revelations from the investigations of the Iran/Contra affair, Saddam's implicitly threatening letter and Murphy's weak apologies, it is reasonable to assume that the Iraqi dictator reverted to his standard operational modus, purposefully ordered the attack on USS *Stark* to show he was not to be trifled with, and of course, to test American resolve. To his satisfaction he must have found that there was not any resolve; the American response was meek indeed. One can only speculate, but Saddam having killed off large numbers of Americans with impunity with the bombing of the USS *Stark* may well had reasoned that he could invade Kuwait with little to fear from the Americans. Particularly, since the American government had turned the blind eye, perhaps only with the most mild slapping of the Iraqi wrist when Hussein used poison gas against the invading Iranians and his own Kurdish population. Certainly, American sanctions or punishment whatever they may have been did little to modify the behaviour of the Iraqi dictator.

In spite of the Soviet Union being on the verge of collapse, there was little that was new with the American approach to the Persian Gulf under Reagan. Assistant secretary of state Richard W. Murphy testified before the Senate Foreign relations Committee on May 29, 1987 that the United States had three overriding objectives in the Gulf: "to galvanize the international community to press for a just end to the Iran–Iraq war; to motivate the Iranian leadership to cease its aggressive posture and rejoin the ranks of peaceful nations; and to prevent a strategic gain by the Soviet Union in the region." To explain American interests in the region Murphy rounded up the usual suspects: continued supply of oil; prevent Soviet influence and maintain the major American political interest in the in the non bellingerent Gulf states. On the USS *Stark* and US–Iraqi relations Murphy noted: "Our ability to communicate frankly with each other kept the tragedy of the U.S.S. *Stark* attack in context, so as to preserve our larger relationship."[9] One would have to look long and hard to find a clearer example of how little the Reagan administration was concerned about the loss of American lives, downplaying their loss to preserve a relationship with one of the worst dictators the world has ever seen, a dictator that had Joseph Stalin as his idol. The administration did much to downplay the *Stark* incident. Assistant secretary for international security affairs, Richard Armitage, observed to Congress following Murphy's testimony: "I want to say that no matter how terrible and heart-rendering the tragedy of the *Stark*, the May 17 tragedy, that terrible event, in end of itself, did not signal a new level of danger in the Gulf."[10]

There are, however, strong indications that the United Kingdom met this multitude of challenges in the region by strengthening its ties to the traditional rules in the Persian Gulf and Arabian Peninsula. Margaret Thatcher was arms sales woman supreme, the clear implication being that Britain's continued support depended on the regimes buying British arms and equipment. This went hand in hand with a strengthening of British military and political ties with the area. Among other things, in 1982 the prime minister giving the sultan of Oman a free hand to deploy British troops under his command without prior consultation with the UK in an emergency. Thatcher's reign thus saw a substantial increase in British influence and power in the Gulf, culminating with the *Al-Yamamah* with Saudi Arabia, the largest arms deals in the world to date. Later, under the premiership of Tony Blair, the *Al-Yamamah* deal became awash in scandal, with charges of high-level corruption among other things, but it is probably wrong to blame Thatcher for the failures of her successors. The Americans, on the other hand, floundered. Seeking accommodation with Iran after 1982, the Reagan administration even offered to depose Iraqi strongman Saddam Hussein as an inducement to Iranian mullahs, only for this policy to end in the ignominy of the Iran/Contra affair. With the publication of the Tower report, the offer to depose Hussein became public. It is therefore more than likely, even if the US meekly accepted Iraqi apologies, that the Iraqi bombing of USS *Stark*, killing 34 American sailors was payback for the Irani-American rapprochement.

Notes

Introduction

1 James Morris, *Farewell the Trumpets: An Imperial Retreat* (London: The Folio Society, 1992), 429–30.

2 Butler to Douglas-Home, April 20, 1964, Prime Minister's Records (PREM), 11/4718, The National Archives, Kew, England.

3 Asadollah Alam, *The Shah and I: The Confidential Diary of Iran's Royal Court, 1969–1977* (London: I.B. Tauris, 1991); 234.

4 James E. Noyes, *The Clouded Lens: Persian Gulf Security and U.S. Policy* (Stanford: Hoover University press, 1979), 21.

5 But in reality there was not much to be afraid of: Saudi Arabia was almost completely untouched by modern life until after the oil embargo. On this, see for instance Sandra Mackey, *The Saudis: Inside the Desert Kingdom* (Boston: Houghton Mifflin Company, 1987). More on Buraimi in my chapters on Saudi Arabia.

6 Christa Salamandra, "Cultural Construction, the Gulf and Arab London", in Paul Dresch and James Piscatori (eds.), *Monarchies and Nations: Globalisation and Identity in the Arab States of the Gulf* (London: I.B. Tauris, 2013): 73–95.

7 Thatcher's first visit to president Carter was in December 1979, just after American diplomats had been taken hostage in Iran in November 1979. In this national crisis, the prime minister sought to reassure the Americans: "At times like these you are entitled to look for to your friends for support. We are your friends, we do support you," in Robert Renwick, *A Journey with Margaret Thatcher: Foreign Policy under the Iron Lady* (London: Biteback Publishing, 2013), 123.

8 See for instance, Peter Byrd (ed.), *Foreign Policy under Thatcher* (Oxford: Philip Alan, 1988); Paul Sharp, *Thatcher's Diplomacy: The Revival of British Foreign Policy* (London: Macmillan, 1997).

9 This Nixonian attempt is discussed in detail in Tore T. Petersen, *Richard Nixon, Great Britain and the Anglo-American Alignment in the Persian Gulf and Arabian Peninsula: Making Allies out of Clients* (Brighton & Portland: Sussex Academic Press, 2009).

10 Jonathan Aitken, *Margaret Thatcher: Power and Personality* (London: Bloomsbury, 2013), 426.

I The Nixonian Foundations of American Foreign Policy

1 Richard Nixon in January 1991 on the belief in an emerging new world order in Monica Crowley, *Nixon in Winter* (New York: Random House, 1998), 236. Emphasis in the original.

2 Richard Nixon, *Public Papers of the Presidents of the United States, 1973* (Washington: GPO, 1975), 956.

3 Fawn M. Brodie, *Richard Nixon: The Shaping of His Character* (New York: W.W. Norton & Company, 1981), 17, 504.

4 Stephen E. Ambrose, *Nixon: Ruin and Recovery 1973–1990* (New York: Touchstone, 1991), 268, for comments on the finances see pp. 271–72.

5 Keith W. Olson, *Watergate: The Presidential Scandal that Shook America* (Lawrence: University Press of Kansas, 2003), 180.

6 Stephen E. Ambrose, *Nixon: Ruin and Recovery, 1973–1990* (New York: Simon & Schuster, 1991), 165, 294. W. Quandt is also of the same opinion, by March/April 1973: "Increasingly, Nixon was obliged to devote his time and energies to the Watergate crisis", see *Peace Process: American Diplomacy and the Arab–Israeli Conflict since 1967* (Los Angeles: University of California Press, 1993), 140. This seems to be the standard scholarly consensus, to quote one recent example. According to Asaf Siniver, the 1973 October war occurring simultaneously with American domestic crises caused by Watergate "catapulted Kissinger (. . .) to a position of unparalleled power in projecting American influence abroad." See Asaf Siniver, "US Foreign Policy and the Kissinger Stratagem", in Asaf Siniver (ed.), *The October 1973 War: Politics, Diplomacy, Legacy* (London: Hurst and Company, 2013): 85– 99.

7 But Nixon was far from the only major politician with a touch of the grandiloquent, Margaret Thatcher's leadership style became increasingly regal using the royal plural, most famously in "We have become a grandmother." See John Campell, *The Iron Lady: Margaret Thatcher from Grocer's Daughter to Prime Minister* (New York: Penguin Books, 2009), 362–3.

8 For this, see Tore T. Petersen, *Richard Nixon, Great Britain and the Anglo-American Alignment in the Persian Gulf and Arabian Peninsula* (Brighton and Portland: Sussex Academic Press, 2009).

9 Richard Nixon, *RN: The Memoirs of Richard Nixon*, vol. I (New York: Warner Books, 1978), 452.

10 Richard Nixon, inaugural speech, January 20, 1969, *FRUS, 1969–1976*, vol. I *Foundations of Foreign Policy, 1969–1972* (Washington: GPO, 2003), 53. Here Nixon employs the technique of chiasmus which is the figure of speech in which two or more clauses are related to each other through a reversal of structures to make a larger point. Nixon, of course, is not the only American president to do this, to quote one famous example from Kennedy: "Let us never negotiate out of fear. But let us never fear to negotiate." Chiasmus is thus often a neat rhetorical device, but far too often devoid of serious content. See, Mark Forsyth, "Save the Soundbite", *The Spectator*, November 23, 2013.

11 Richard Nixon, "U.S. Foreign Policy for the 1970's: A New Strategy for Peace", A Report to Congress, February 18, 1970 (Washington: GPO, 1970), p. 4. Kissinger describes the president's annual foreign policy report in this way: "It was to serve as a conceptual outline of the President's foreign policy, as a status report, an as an agenda for action. It could simultaneously guide our bureaucracy and inform foreign governments about our thinking." Hype was not restricted to the president only in the Nixon administration, Kissinger lavishly praised the annual reports. "Once the President's annual review became established, it produced some of the most thoughtful government statements of foreign policy." [Henry Kissinger, *White House Years* (Boston, Little, Brown and Company, 1979), 158–59.] The author of the annual reviews was, of course, Kissinger.

12 Richard Nixon, "President's Nixon's Foreign Policy Report to Congress February 25, 1971", United States Information Service (Washington: GPO, 1971), pp. 3, 4-5, 6, 10, 21.

13 Richard Nixon, *Beyond Peace* (New York: Random House, 1994), 35. For the former president this was obviously an utterance of the gravest significance as it first appears in Richard Nixon, *1999: Victory without War* (New York: Simon and Schuster, 1988), 24.

14 Richard Nixon, *Leaders* (New York: Warner Books, 1982), 239. Again, a Delphic utterance by the former president, recycled in Richard Nixon, *1999: Victory without War* (New York: Simon & Schuster, 1988), 259, and in Richard Nixon, *Beyond Peace* (New York: Random House, 1994), 4. Richard Nixon seems endlessly fascinated with his own rhetoric.

15 Richard Nixon, *RN: The Memoirs of Richard Nixon*, volume II (New York: Warner Books, 1978), 595.

16 Nixon, *Memoirs*, vol. II, 680

17 Richard Nixon, *Real Peace* (Boston: Little, Brown and Company, 1984).

18 Stephen E. Ambrose, *Nixon: Ruin and Recovery, 1973–1990* (New York: A Touchstone Book, 1991), 550.

19 *Newsweek*, May 19, 1986.

20 Richard Nixon, *Leaders* (New York: Warner Books, 1982), 1. p. 53.

21 Henry Kissinger, *Years of Renewal* (New York: Simon & Schuster, 1999), 46.

22 Saunders to Kissinger, May 18, 1972, Nixon Tehran, briefing book [2 of 2], RNNSC, box 479 (emphasis in the original). This was, incidentally, the theme Nixon had also pursued in Moscow, observing to Kissinger while in the Soviet capital: "we would seek to usher in a period of genuine power restraint", Henry Kissinger, *White House Years* (Boston: Little, Brown & Company, 1979), 1209.

23 "Joint US–Iranian Communique", May 31, 1972, *FRUS, 1969–1976*, volume E-4, *Documents on Iran and Iraq, 1969–1972*, PDF version; Peter Ramsbothan, UK ambassador to Tehran, to Home, June 1, 1972, FCO 8/1884/NPB 3/304/1.

24 John Lewis Gaddis, *Strategies of Containment: A Critical Appraisal of Postwar American National Security Policy* (New York: Oxford University Press, 1982), 298–99.

25 Nixon to Kissinger, February 10, 1970, The President's Annual Review of U.S. Foreign Policy, 2/8/70 Vol. I [2 of 3], Richard Nixon Presidential materials Staff, National Security File (hereafter cited as RNNSC), box 325, National Archives, College Park, Maryland. When describing the Nixon Doctrine in his memoirs, most of the space is occupied to how Kissinger himself furnished the president with the basic ideas and concepts, but not the Doctrine itself. On the Doctrine's announcement in Guam July 25, 1969, Kissinger observes: "To this day I do not think that Nixon intended a major policy pronouncement in Guam." See Henry Kissinger, *White House Years* (Boston: Little, Brown and Company, 1979), 224. Nixon himself gives Kissinger no role or credit for developing the Doctrine, Richard Nixon, *The Memoirs of Richard Nixon*, vol. I (New York: Warner Books, 1978), 488, 490).

26 These issues are explored in Tore T. Petersen, *Richard Nixon, Great Britain and the Anglo-American Alignment in the Persian Gulf and Arabian Peninsula* (Brighton & Portland, Sussex Academic Press, 2009).

27 Monica Crowley, *Nixon off the Record* (New York: Random House, 1996), 223.

28 Nixon to Carter, December 20, 1978, Post-presidential Correspondence with Jimmy Carter, Richard Milhous Nixon Library, Yorba Linda California (hereafter cited as RMNL).

29 Carter to Nixon, December 22, 1978, Post-presidential Correspondence with Jimmy Carter, RMNL.

30 Nixon to Carter, July 23, 1979, Post-presidential Correspondence with Jimmy Carter, RMNL.

31 Richard Nixon, *The Real War* (New York: Warner Books, 1980).

32 Stephen Ambrose, *Nixon: Ruin and Recovery, 1973–1990* (New York: A Touchstone Book, 1992), 532.

33 Meese to Nixon, November 26, 1980, Post-presidential correspondence with Ronald Reagan, RMNL.

34 Nixon to Reagan, November 17, 1980, Post-presidential Correspondence with Ronald Reagan, RMNL.

35 Reagan to Nixon, November 22, 1980, Post-presidential Correspondence with Ronald Reagan, RMNL.

36 Nixon to Michael Deaver, January 15, 1981, Post-presidential Correspondence with Ronald Reagan, RMNL.

37 Nixon to Reagan, March 26, 1981, Post-presidential Correspondence with Ronald Reagan, RMNL. On Haig's remarks, see Tom Mathews et al., "A Strategy of Tough Talk", *Newsweek*, March 30, 1981.

38 Reagan, *An American Life*, 360.

39 Alexander Haig, *Caveat: Realism, Reagan, and Foreign Policy* (New York: Macmillan, 1984), 85.

40 For the Nixon White House as a shark tank, see Jerald A. Combs, *The History of American Foreign Policy, vol. II, Since 1900* (New York: Alfred A. Knopf, 1986), 405; for Haig given up daily access to Reagan, see Haig, *Caveat*, 84; for suggestions of Haig as deep throat, see Len Colony and Robert Gettlin, *Silent Coup: The Removal of a President* (New York: St. Martin's paperbacks, 1991), 294–297 (see also pp. 43–44 and 447–448 for deviousness of Haig); and, Jonathan Aitken, *Nixon: A Life* (Washington: Regnery Publishing, 1993), 512.

41 Carrington's impression of Haig in private secretary GGH Walden to Martin Berthoud, May 14, 1981, FCO 82/1085/AMU 011/2.

42 J.S. Wall (UK embassy, Washington) to Sheila Griffith-Jones, November 9, 1981, FCO 82/1086/Amu 011/2.

43 Mc Clark and Carrington, December 3, 1981, FCO 82/1117/Amu 026/32.

44 Clark to Reagan, September 25, 1982, Post-presidential Correspondence with Ronald Reagan, RMNL.

45 Nixon memorandum to Reagan, n.d., 820625, National Security Affairs, Office of Assistant to the President for National Security Affairs, Chron Files, box 3, Ronald Wilson Reagan Library, Simi Valley, California (hereafter cited as RWRL). Emphasis in the original.

46 Nixon to Reagan, November 1, 1982, Post-presidential Correspondence with Ronald Reagan, RMNL. Emphasis in the original.

47 Richard Nixon, *Leaders* (New York: Warner Books, 1982).

48 Jonathan Aitken, *Nixon: A Life* (Washington: Regency Publishing, 1993).

49 Newsweek, May 19, 1986 frontcover and Larry Martz et al., "The Road Back."

50 Richard Nixon, *Leaders* (New York: Warner Books, 1982), 336.

51 Reagan to Nixon, March 11, 1983, Post-presidential Correspondence with Ronald Reagan, RMNL

52 Henry Mitchell, "Pardon, but Isn't that Saint an Ex-President", *The Washington Post*, November 12, 1982.

53 Nixon draft letter to Reagan, n.d., Post-presidential Correspondence with Ronald Reagan, RMNL.

54 Nixon, "Elements for a Joint Communique", n.d., Post-presidential Correspondence with Ronald Reagan, RMNL.

55 Nixon to Reagan, October 7, 1985, Post-presidential Correspondence with Ronald Reagan, RMNL. Emphasis in the original.

56 Reagan to Nixon, October 29, 1985. Exex. Sec, NSC: System File, 8508407, box 4, RWRL.

57 Nixon to Reagan, Janaury 13, 1987, Presidential Handwriting File (1/13/87-1/15/87), box 274, RWRL.

2 Jimmy Carter in the Oval Office

1 Jimmy Carter, *Keeping Faith: Memoirs of a President* (New York: Bantam Books, 1982), 50.

2 See, "The Daily Diary of President Ronald Reagan", http://www.reaganfoundation.org/white-house-diary.aspx. Incidentally, Reagan himself claimed that he and his wife Nancy began at seven thirty in the morning, see Ronald Reagan, *An American Life* (London: Hutchinson, 1990), 249. The First Lady insists on a seven-thirty start of the day; see Nancy Reagan, *My Turn: The memoirs of Nancy Reagan* (New York: Random House, 1989), 244.

3 Zbigniew Brzezinski, *Power and Principle: Memoirs of the National Security Adviser, 1977–1981* (New York: Farrar, Straus and Giroux, 1983), 29.

4 Jimmy Carter, *White House Diary* (New York: Farrar, Straus and Giroux, 2010), 11, 12. *Newsweek* portrayed the president on May 2, 1977; the day "begins promptly at 6:30 most mornings with a single ring of the telephone – enough to rose him but not Rosalynn from their double bed – and the brisk voice of an Army Signal Corpsman announcing the time, the temperature and the weather forecast. Carter showers, shaves, dresses, downs a glass of orange juice, inspects the crab apples and magnolias outside, and repairs to his study off the Oval Office, all within the first half hour of the day. A steward serves him coffee at 7, and his secretary, Susan Clough, puts on the day's first classical recording – something soothing from Vivaldi or Bach – at 7:15. Nothing else intrudes on Carter's first 90 minutes of 'quiet time' ". Written by Mel Elfin, Eleanor Clift and Thomas M. DeFrank.

5 Jim Kuhn, *Ronald Reagan in Private: A Memoir of My Years in the White House* (New York: Sentinel, 2004), 137.

6 James Fallows, "The Passionless Presidency", *The Atlantic Monthly* (May, 1979).

7 Carter, *Diary*, 267 (workload and medical problem), 24 (for speedreading), 15 (Spanish), 126 (Camp David). Carter claimed that his reading speed quadrupled: "afterward, only special study of an issue would require me to work after supper, and I was usually free to read, watch a movie, or just relax with my family", in *Keeping Faith*, 57.

8 Carter, *Diary*, 52.

9 Staff Offices, Speechwriters-Subject File [Crisis of Confidence [Speech], 7/15/79,

5/1/79-8/31/79 RH], Jimmy Carter Library , Atlanta, Georgia (hereafter cited as JCL).

10 Jimmy Carter, *Keeping Faith: Memoirs of a President* (New York: Bantam Books, 1983), 26.

11 Plains File, "President's Comments on Memos, Incomplete, 6/78 – 8/80, "box 33, JCL.

12 James P. Pfeiffer, "White House Staff Versus the Cabinet: Centripetal and Centrifugal Roles", *Presidential Studies Quarterly* XVI: 4 (Fall, 1986): 666–90.

13 H.R. Haldeman, *The Haldeman Diaries: Inside the Nixon White House* (New York: G.P. Putnam's Sons, 1994), 309.

14 Robert A. Strong, "Recapturing Leadership: The Carter Administration and the Crisis of Confidence", *Presidential Studies Quarterly* XVI: 4 (Fall, 1986): 636–50.

15 Zbigniew Brzezinski, "Foreign Policy Making, "Donated Zbigniew Brzezinski, Subject File, [National Security Council; 1/77-10/80], box 34, JCL.

16 Carter, *Diary*, 295.

17 Rosalynn Carter, *First Lady from Plains* (Fayetteville: University of Arkansas Press, 1994), 162. In their memoirs the Carters cannot agree when they met for lunch, the president claims Thursday for their meetings; *Keeping Faith*, 56.

18 Loyd E. Ambrosius, "Woodrow Wilson and George W. Bush: Historical Comparisons of Ends and Means in Their Foreign Policies." *Diplomatic History,* 30: 3 (June, 2006): 509–19.

19 Walter Mondale quoted from the exhibition in the Jimmy Carter Library, Atlanta, Georgia.

20 Carter, *Diary*, 79.

21 Zbigniew Brzezinski, *Power and Principle: Memoirs of the National Security Adviser, 1977–1981* (New York: Farrar, Straus and Giroux, 1983), xiv.

22 Zbigniew Brzezinski, *Power and Principle: Memoirs of the National Security Adviser, 1977–1981* (New York: Farrar, Straus and Giroux, 1983), 74.

23 Brzezinski, *Power and Principle*, 22, 23, 526.

24 Brzezinski to Carter, December 28, 1978, "NSC Weekly Report # 83", Plains File, box 29, JCL.

25 Brzezinski to Carter, December 28, 1978, "NSC Weekly Report # 83", Plains File, box 29, JCL. Emphasis in the original. Carter put much faith in his national security advisor (and the NSC staff): "They were particularly adept at incisive analyses of strategic concepts, and were prolific in the production of new ideas, which they were always eager to present to me. (. . .) Zbig was a first-rate thinker, very competent in his choice of staff members and able to work harmoniously with them." See Jimmy Carter, *Keeping Faith* (New York: Bantam Books, 1982), 53.

26 Harold Saunders to Kissinger May 18, 1972, Nixon Tehran, briefing book [2 of 2], Nixon Presidential Materials Staff, National Security Files, Subject Files, box 479: Nixon's papers as president was located in the National Archives, College Park, MD when I accessed them. They have since been moved to his library in Yorba Linda, CA. See also Tore T. Petersen, *Richard Nixon, Great Britain and the Anglo-American Alignment in the Persian Gulf and Arabian Peninsula* (Brighton & Portland: Sussex Academic Press, 2009).

27 Vance to Carter, December 20, 1978, NLC-15-119-6-9-9, JCL.

28 Jimmy Carter, *Keeping Faith: Memoirs of a President* (New York: Bantam Books, 1982), 444–5.

29 Carter to Callaghan, January 6, 1979, Plains File, JCL.

30 Brzezinski to Carter, February 28, 1979, Donated Historical Material, Zbigniew Brzezinski Collection, Goegraphic File, Southwest Asia/Persian Gulf [2/79-12/79], JCL.

31 Henderson to Carrington, December 31, 1979, FCO 82/1022/AMU 14/3.

32 Richard Thornton, *The Carter Years: Toward a New Global Order* (New York: Paragon House, 1991), 421.

33 Jimmy Carter, *Keeping Faith: Memoirs of a President* (Toronto: Basic Books, 1982), 96.

34 Linda Blandford, *Oil Sheiks: Inside the Supercharged World of the Petrodollar* (London: W. Allen & Co. Ltd., 1984), 1, backcover.

35 John, Dumbrell, *The Carter Presidency: A Re-evaluation* (Manchester: Manchester University Press, 1995), 169.

36 Robert M. Gates, *Duty: Memoirs of a Secretary at War* (New York: Alfred A. Knopf, 2014), 185.

37 Mark Bowden, *Guests of the Ayatollah: The First Battle in the West's War with Militant Islam* (London: Atlantic Books, 2006), 29–30. See also David Farber, *Taken Hostage: The Iranian Hostage Crisis and America's First Encounter with Radical Islam* (Princeton: Princeton University Press, 2005).

38 Marc J. O'Reilly, *Unexceptional: America's Empire in the Persian Gulf, 1941–2007* (New York: Lexington Books, 2000), 150.

39 See Brzezinski interview in the *Le Nouvel Observateur*, Paris 15–21 January 1988. I am grateful to my former MA student Thomas Kirkslett for bringing this to my attention, see *Amerikansk Afghanistan-politikk februar 1979 til januar 1980* [American Policy towards Afghanistan February 1979 to January 1980], MA thesis, Norwegian University of Science and Technology, 2011.

40 Brzezinski to Carter, December 26, 1979, Donated ZB, Geographic file, Soutwest Asia/Persian . . . Afghanistan [12/26/79-1/4/80], JCL.

41 Vance to Carter, "Blueprint for Implementation of Your State Union Message", January 29, 1980, NLC-25-99-18-7-0.

42 Speech by Carter, February 7, 1980, in Jimmy Carter, *The Public Papers of the Presidents of the United states, 1980–81, Book I* (Washington: GPO, 1981), 284. See also Niall Ferguson, "Obama's Mideast Meltdown: The President Fiddles as the World Burns", *Newsweek*, September 24, 2012. On June 4, 2009, president Barak Obama spoke in Cairo: "I've come here . . . to seek a new beginning between the United States and Muslims around the world, one based on mutual interest and mutual respect, and one based on the truth that America and Islam are not exclusive and need not be in competition. Instead, they overlap, and share common principles – principles of justice and progress, tolerance, and the dignity of all human beings . . . Let there be no doubt: Islam is part of America."

3 Margaret Thatcher takes Charge

1 John Campbell, *The Iron Lady: Margaret Thatcher from Grocer's Daughter to Prime Minister* (New York: Penguin Books, 2011), 80–82.

2 Mc Thatcher and American legislators, December 17, 1979, PREM 19/127.

3 Briefing paper for the president, "United Kingdom", n.d., NLC-133-182-5-13-3, JCL.

4 Department of state, bureau of intelligence and research, "French, British, and

West German Conventional Arms Transfer Policy", January 31, 1979, NLC-21-7-1-13-6, JCL.

5 John Campbell, *The Iron Lady: Margaret Thatcher from Grocer's Daughter to Prime Minister* (New York: Penguin Books, 2009), 124–125. See also Margaret Thatcher, *The Downing Street Years* (London: HarperCollins, 1993), 20: "There was an intensity about the job of being Prime Minister which made sleep seem a luxury."

6 Jonathan Aitken, *Margaret Thatcher: Power and Personality* (London: Bloomsbury, 2013), 279.

7 Richard Reeves, *President Nixon: Alone in the White House* (New York: Simon & Schuster, 2001), 29.

8 Frank Brenchley, *Britain and the Middle East: An Economic History 1945–87* (London: Lester Crook Academic Publishing, 1989), 325.

9 Chrissie Hirst, *The Arabian Connection: The UK Arms Trade to Saudi Arabia* (London: Campaign Against Arms Trade [CAAT], 2000), introduction page 1.

10 Mark Phythian, *The Politics of British Arms Sales since 1964: 'To Secure Our Rightful Share'* "(Manchester: Manchester University Press, 2000), 217–18. The AWACS sale is discussed from American perspective in chapter V, "Ronald Reagan: Leadership Style and Foreign Policy."

11 On this, see Tore T. Petersen, *The Decline of the Anglo-American Middle East 1961–1969: A Willing Retreat* (Brighton & Portland: Sussex Academic Press, 2006).

12 Michael Alexander to Paul Lever, FCO, December 22, 1980, FCO 8/3518/NBE 087/1.

13 Thatcher to Zaid, December 22, 1980, FCO 8/3518, NB3 087/1.

14 P.J. Roberts, defence department, to Gillmore, May 7, 1981, FCO 8/3851/ NB 087/4. Thatcher had instructed the relevant UK departments: "To continue to seek as a matter of high priority to increase the present level of overseas defence sales", see Defence Department, "Defence Sales Policy: Middle East", February 9, 1981, FCO 8/3850/NB 087/4.

15 Foreign and Commonwealth Office, "Foreign Policy Aspects of Overseas Arms Sales", February 24, 1981, FCO 8/3850/NB 087/4. See also Mark Phythian, *The Politics of British Arms Sales since 1964* (Manchester: Manchester University press, 2000).

16 Margaret Thatcher, *The Downing Street Years* (London: HarperCollins, 1993), 8, 9.

17 Michael Alexander, private secretary to Thatcher, to Paul Lever; FCO, December 22, 1980, FCO 8/3518/NBE 087/1.

18 Roberts to Carrington, "British Relations with the United Arab Emirates (UAE)", November 16, 1980, FCO 8/3509/NB 020/2.

19 Miers to Moberly, December 9, 1980, FCO 8/3469/NBC 020/2.

20 Roberts, Annual Review UAE, 1980, December 31, 1980, FCO 8/3908/NBE 014/4.

21 Private secretary to Alexander, February 11, 1981, FCO 8/3917/BBE 026/1.

22 Mc Keith Haskell (UK) and Polad Lowrie; January 11, 1984, United Kingdom 11/1/83-6/30/84 [2 of 3], Executive Secretary, NSC, Country File, box 36, RWRL.

23 Michael Palliser to Robert Armstrong, March 10, 1981, FCO 8/3319/ NBO 26/4. Miers of the Foreign and Commonwealth Office also saw the purpose of

Thatcher's visit in this light: "I start from the assumption that the Prime Minister's visit should be used to proclaim an identity of interest with the countries visited, and to offer cooperation between them and the UK in a way calculated both to advance our political interests and to win us concrete advantage in the field of defence sales and commercial contracts," Miers to Hurd, February 17, 1981, FCO 8/3818/NB 026/4.

24 Thatcher, *The Downing Street Years*, 163, 164.

25 Mc Thatcher and Khalifa, April 22, 1981, FCO 82/1099/ AMU 21/2.

26 Mc Thatcher and Qaboos, April 23, 1981, FCO 82/1099/AMU 21/2.

27 Mc Thatcher and prince Fahd, April 20, 1981, FCO 82/1099/ AMU 21/2.

28 Douglas Hurd, *Memoirs* (London: Little Brown, 2003), 276.

29 Mc Thatcher and Khalifa, Qatar, April 25, 1981, FCO 8/1099/ AMU 21/2.

30 Thatcher to Reagan, April 27, 1981, FCO 82/1099/ AMU 21/2.

31 American embassy, Manama, March 8, 1978, NLC-129-13-2-3-9.

32 Saunders to Vance, December 6, 1978, NLC-132-118-19-5-9, JCL.

33 Mc Carter and Thatcher, December 19, 1979, PREM 19/127.

34 Parsons, "Tour of Saudi Arabia, the Gulf and Oman", June 15, 1979, FCO 8/NB 021/10 (emphasis in the original).

35 Anthony Parsons to John Wilton, "UK Policy towards Arabia and the Gulf in the Wake of the Iran Crisis, "April 2, 1979, FCO 8/3281/NB 021/2.

36 Christopher Shoemaker to Richard V. Allen, January 27, 1981, Chron 01/27/1981-01/28/1981, Nance, James: Files, box 1, RWRL.

37 David Reynolds, *Britannia Overruled: British Policy World Power in the 20th Century* (London: Longman, 1996); John Campbell, *The Iron Lady: Margaret Thatcher, from Grocer's Daughter to Prime Minister* (New York: Penguin, 2011), 232.

38 Alan P. Dobson, *Anglo-American Relations in the Twentieth Century: Of Friendship, Conflict and the Rise and Decline of Superpowers* (London: Routledge, 1995), 150.

39 Ronald Reagan, "My Heart was with Her", *Newsweek*, December 3, 1990

40 Richard Aldhous, *Reagan &Thatcher: The Difficult Relationship* (London: Hutchinson, 2012), 64–65.

41 Mc Thatcher and Reagan et al., July 20, 1981, FCO 82/1093/AMU 20/12. Cf. Geoffrey Smith , *Reagan and Thatcher* (London: The Bodley Head, 1990): "It is hard to believe that there will ever again be an American president and a British prime minister who will form such close a personal association, " p. 265.

42 John Dumbrell, *A Special Relationship: Anglo-American Relations in the Cold War and After* (London: Palgrave Macmillan, 2001), 63.

43 On this, see Tore T. Petersen, *The Decline of the Anglo-American Middle East 1961–1969: A Willing Retreat* (Brighton & Portland: Sussex Academic Press, 2006), 61.

44 Alexander Haig, *Caveat: Realism, Reagan, and Foreign Policy* (New York: Macmillan, 1984), 274.

45 Richard Aldhous, *Reagan & Thatcher: The Difficult Relationship* (London: Hutchinson, 2012), 64–65.

46 Telephone conversation Thatcher and Reagan, May 31, 1982, United Kingdom (4/26/82-9/29/82) [Too Late to File], Executive Secretary; NSC, Country File, box 20, RWRL.

47 Geoffrey Howe, *Conflict of Loyalty* (London: Macmillan, 1994), 331.

48 Percy Craddock, *In Pursuit of British Interests: Reflections on Foreign Policy under Margaret Thatcher and John Major* (London: John Murray, 1997), 57.

49 Henderson to Michael Palliser, permanent undersecretary of state, November 27, 1981, FCO 8/1092/AMU 20/3.

50 McFarlane to Armstrong, November 7, 1983, United Kingdom 11/1/83-6/30/84 [3 of 3] Executive Secretary, NSC, Country File, box 36, RWRL.

51 Robert Armstrong to Alexander, February 2, 1981, PREM 19/600, TNA. Incidentally, the Foreign and Commonwealth Office was well aware of the nature of the US–Saudi relationship, noting in a brief for the prime minister: "The US/Saudi special relationship is under strain. Saudis feel their helpfulness on supply and price of oil should be matched by US willingness to sell arms (e.g. F-15) and make progress on Arab/Israel (by pressure on Israel) if only to safeguard Saudis' domestic position," FCO brief for Thatcher's Washington visit, February 18, 1981, FCO 82/1110.

52 Harold Macmillan, *Pointing the Way, 1959–1961* (London: Macmillan, 1972), 308.

4 Ronald Reagan: Leadership Style and Foreign Policy

1 Reagan's biography, failing to understand his subject. Morris even invented fictional characters in an effort to describe the president. See Edmund Morris, *Dutch: A Memoir of Ronald Reagan* (New York: Random House, 1999). Morris' failure to understand Reagan, even with privileged access, is hardly an excuse for serious historians not to grapple with the late president. Morris was Reagan's 'official' historian, meeting regularly with the president.

2 Michael Schaller, *Reckoning with Reagan: America and Its President in the 1980s* (New York: Oxford University Press, 1992), preface viii; John Lewis Gaddis, *The United States and the End of the Cold War: Implications, Reconsiderations, Provocations* (New York: Oxford University Press, 1992), 130–132.

3 Alan Ehrenhalt, *The United States of Ambition: Politicians, Power, and the Pursuit of Office* (New York: Times Books, 1991), has interesting observations of the fragmentation of the American political system; Michael Duffy & Dan Goodgame, *Marching in Place: The Status Quo Presidency of George Bush* (New York: Simon & Schuster, 1992).

4 David Stockman, *The Triumph of Politics* (New York: Harper & Row, 1986); Alexander M. Haig, Jr., *Caveat: Realism, Reagan and Foreign Policy* (New York: Macmillan, 1984); Donald T. Regan, *For the Record: From Wall Street to Washington* (London: Hutchinson, 1988).

5 Ronald Reagan, *An American Life: The Autobiography* (London: Hutchinson, 1990), 393–394; Richard Ben Cramer, *What it Takes: The Way to the White House* (New York: Random House, 1992), 27.

6 Duffy and Goodgame, *Marching in Place*, 11, 21 describes Bush as president: "He wasn't passive or indolent, but he was a deeply reactive man who has always been less interested in doing anything specific than just *being* president. He had entered politics without a desire to accomplish anything, but rather just to *serve*," 26, 38, Reagan, *For the Record*, 248 (for quote), George F. Will, "Bush Should Withdraw from the Ticket, *Guardian Weekly*, August 9, 1992.

7 Lou Cannon, *President Reagan: The Role of a Lifetime* (New York: Simon & Schuster, 1991), 88, 498–500; Regan, *For the Record*, 248 (for quote); Michael K.

Deaver, *Behind the Scenes* (New York: William Morrow and Company, 1987), 74. Incidentally, John F. Kennedy pursued the same strategy in the 1960 campaign: "All I have to do is to show up", Theodore C. Sorensen, *Kennedy* (New York: Smithmark, 1995), 171.

8   Garry Wills, *Reagan's America: Innocents at Home* (New York: Doubleday & Company, 1987), 138–139.

9   David Mervin, *Ronald Reagan & The American Presidency* (London: Longman, 1990), 4–5.

10 Cannon, *Reagan*, 559–560; Don Oberdorfer, *The Turn: From Cold War to a New Era* (New York: Simon & Schuster, 1992), 262–263; Martin Anderson, *Revolution* (New York: Harcourt Brace Jovanovich, 1988), 291–292. While *Revolution* has much to commend to it, Anderson with his wife Annelise is churning out books on Reagan as a veritable cottage industry, coming close to hagiography in some of their later works on the president.

11 Duffy & Goodgame, *George Bush*, 112.

12 Cannon, *Reagan*, 719, 726–733; Regan, *For the Record*, 255, 373; Edwin Meese, *With Reagan: The Inside Story* (Washington: Regnery Gateway, 1992), 106, 112–114 (called Baker the biggest leaker in Washington), Peggy Noonan, *Life, Liberty and the Pursuit of Happiness* (New York: Random House, 1994), 123; when one of the major members of Reagan's economic team, David Stockman, indiscreetly allowed himself to by openly critical of the administration economic policy, by talking to editor William Greider, published as "The Education of David Stockman", in the now famous *Atlantic* article in December, 1981, only Baker prevented Stockman from being fired. Cannon observed: "Baker was furious with Stockman not for talking to Greider but for the naïveté of permitting himself to be quoted. Baker himself held many candid conversations with reporters, but he protected himself with ground rules that guaranteed his anonymity". [Cannon, *Reagan*, 262]; Reagan's press secretary is also critical of Cannon, see Larry Speakes, *Speaking Out: The Reagan Presidency from Inside the White House* (New York: Avon Books, 1988), 281.

13 H. R. Haldeman, *The Haldeman Diaries: Inside the Nixon White House* (New York: G.P. Putnam's Sons, 1994), p. 7 (Ambrose's observation), p. 309.

14 Quoted from John Tower et al., *The Tower Commission Report*. The full text of the President's Special Review Board (*A New York Times Special*, New York, 1987), 81 (hereafter cited as the Tower report); Ann Wroe, *Lives, Lies and the Iran-Contra Affair* (London: I.B. Tauris, 1991), 155.

15 Mervin, *Ronald Reagan* (London, 1990), 150–161; Jacob V. Lamar, Jr., and Michael Duffy, "The Good Soldier", *Time*, May 25, 1987, pp. 32–34; Robert C. McFarlane, *Special Trust* (New York: Cadell & Davies, 1994), 31, 349. The Independent Counsel in the Iran/Contra investigation is emphatic that Reagan was portrayed as out of control to avoid impeachment, rather than the authority behind the initiatives, see: Lawrence E. Walsh, *Firewall: The Iran-Contra Conspiracy and Cover-Up* (New York: W.W. Norton & Company, 1997), 24. See also: Peter J. Wallison, *Ronald Reagan: The Power of Conviction and the Success of His Presidency* (Cambridge, MA: Westview Press, 2003).

16 The Tower report, 79, 81–82; George P. Shultz, *Turmoil and Triumph: My Years as Secretary of State*, (New York: Charles Scribner's Sons, 1993), 785; Theodore

Draper, *A Very Thin Line: The Iran-Contra Affairs* (New York: Hill And Wang, 1991), 596.

17 Regan, *For the Record*, 378.

18 David Stockman, *The Triumph of Politics: The Crisis in American Government and How it Affects the World* (London: Coronet Book, 1986), 245–246.

19 Mervin, *Reagan*, 122, 184–185; Ronald Reagan, *An American Life* (London: Hutchinson, 1990), 314–315; Regan, *For the Record*, 156; Cannon, *Reagan*, 134–135; Meese, *With Reagan*, 134–142.

20 Haig, *Caveat*, 174–190, (the quote is from page 190); Reagan, *An American Life*, 410–412, 414–416; Mitchell Bard, "Interest Groups, the President and Foreign Policy: How Reagan Snatched Victory from the Jaws of Defeat on AWACS", *Presidential Studies Quarterly* XVIII: 3 (Summer, 1988): 583–600.

21 Regan, *For the Record*, 142, 157, 265–269, Regan sometimes contradicts himself when describing the passive president, see for instance pp. 92–93.

22 *Ibid.*, 250; Donald T. Regan, "The Reagan Presidency in Perspective", *Presidential Studies Quarterly* (Summer, 1986): 414–420; Speakes, *Speaking Out*, 143.

23 Wills, *Reagan's America*, 2, 4, 312; Mervin, *Reagan*, 69–74; Reagan, *An American Life*, 186. Schaller, *Reckoning with Reagan*, 5; Cannon, Reagan, 121; Noonan, *What I Saw at the Revolution*, 170, 181; Anderson, *Revolution* (New York, 1988), 162, for 'a warmly ruthless' quote see p. 288. Part of the president's problem was possibly that his detached leadership style did not always inspire loyalty, as his one time personal secretary explains: "President Reagan never really appreciated the importance of who worked for him. Partly, I suppose, this was a consequence of his personal history as an actor, speaker, and then politician; in those roles he was always a free agent who didn't rely on an organization." See Helene Von Damm, *At Reagan's Side* (New York: Doubleday, 1989), 224. Reagan's first chief of staff James Baker observed on Reagan: "He treats us all the same, as hired help." See Richard Reeves, *President Reagan: The Triumph of Imagination* (New York: Simon & Schuster, 2005), 14.

24 Anderson, *Revolution*, 195.

25 Anderson, *Revolution*, 195–204; Pfeiffer, "White House Staff" (for quote); Regan, *For the Record*, 140–141; Cannon, *Reagan*, quote from p. 73, for Haig's appointment see page 82, Meese, *With Reagan*, 57, 63, 128; Stockman, *The Triumph of Politics*, 81; for Reagan's loyalty toward aides, see for instance: Bob Woodward, *Veil: The Secret Wars of the CIA 1981–1987* (London: Simon & Schuster, 1987), 277; McFarlane, *Special Trust*, 107.

26 Anderson, *Revolution*, 167–168; Meese, *With Reagan*, 59; Pfeiffer, "White House Staff", 682–683; Cannon, *Reagan*, 183–183; Wallace Earl Walker and Michael R. Reopel, "Strategies for Governance: Transition and Domestic Policy Making in the Reagan Administration", *Presidential Studies Quarterly* XVI: 4 (Fall, 1986): 734–760 (for quote), see also Terrel H. Bell, *The Thirteenth Man: A Reagan Cabinet Memoir* (New York: The Free Press, 1980), 32, for a positive evaluation of Reagan as a leader and of the Cabinet councils.

27 Walter LaFeber, *America, Russia and the Cold War, 1945–1990* (New York: McGraw-Hill, 1991), 302; Robert J. McMahon, "Review Essay: Making Sense of American Foreign policy During the Reagan Years», *Diplomatic History* 19:2 (Spring, 1995): 367–384; Schaller, *Reckoning with Reagan*, 122, 126; Raymond Garthoff, *The Great Transition: American -Soviet Relations and the End of the Cold*

War (Washington: The Brookings Institution, 1994), 11; *idem, American–Soviet Relations from Nixon to Reagan* (Washington: The Brookings Institution, 1988); Pemberton, *Exit with Honor,* 153 is shallow on the scholarly debate.

28 Reagan, *An American Life,* 267; McFarlane, *Special Trust,* 193–194; Garthoff, *Détente and Confrontation,* 1014, 1022; Dinesh D'Souza, *Ronald Reagan: How an Ordinary Man Became an Extraordinary Leader* (New York: The Free Press, 1997), 2–5 sums up how Reagan challenged the existing orthodoxy on the Soviet Union.

29 Garthoff, *Detente and Confrontation,* 1020; Reagan, *An American Life,* 552; Robert W. Tucker, "Reagan's Foreign Policy", *Foreign Affairs* 68:1 (1989): 1–27; NSDD-75 is in McFarlane, *Special Trust,* 372–380; for more on the policy, see pp. 219–222; Peter Schweizer, *Victory: The Reagan Administration's Secret Strategy that Hastened the Collapse of the Soviet Union* (New York: The Atlantic Monthly Press, 1994), 131–133; Meese, *With Reagan,* 168–170.

30 Cannon, *Reagan,* 314–315.

31 Antony J. Blinken, *Ally vs. Ally: America, Europe and the Siberian Pipeline Crisis* (New York: Praeger, 1987).

32 Shultz, *Turmoil and Triumph,* 135–136; Thatcher, *The Downing Street Years,* 255–256.

33 Shultz, *Turmoil and Triumph,* 137–144; Thatcher, *Downing Street,* 256; McFarlane, *Special Trust,* 221–222; Schweizer, Victory, 106–110; Blinken, *Ally vs. Ally,* 110 argues that the agreement was mostly a face-saving device for the United States to escape the consequences of its own unwise policy.

34 Scwheizer, *Victory,* 31, 105, 243, 262.

35 Daniel Yergin, *The Prize: The Epic Quest for Oil, Money and Power* (New York: A Touchstone Book, 1992), 717–721, 747.

36 Anderson, *Revolution,* 94–98; Tucker, "Reagan's Foreign Policy", Reagan, *An American Life,* 547–548; 586–587; Oberdorfer, *The Turn,* 22–23 'delinks' the 'evil empire' speech and SDI; Anatoly Dobrynin, *In Confidence: Moscow's Ambassador to America's Six Cold Presidents* (New York: Times Books, 1995), 528; McFarlane, *Special Trust,* 231–235; Garthoff, *The Great Transition,* 516 on the Soviets expecting declining military expenditure; Thatcher, *The Downing Street* Years, 467. For an opposing view of SDI, see Frances Fitzgerald, *Way Out there in the Blue: Reagan, Star Wars and the End of the Cold War* (New York: Simon & Schuster, 2000), claims, "In fact the president played almost no role in working out the policies of his administration" (p. 17).

37 Mervin, Reagan, 171.

38 Mohammed Yousaf & Mark Adkin, *The Bear Trap: Afghanistan's Untold Story* (London: Leo Cooper, 1992), 6, 189; Garthoff, *The Great Transition,* 270, 713, 721, 723, 731; Torbjørn L. Knutsen, "The Reagan Doctrine and the Lessons of the Afghan War", *The Australian Journal of Politics & History* 38:2 (1992): 193–205.

39 Garthoff, *The Great Transition,* 696–697 links the Reagan Doctrine and Eastern Europe; on United States–Vatican cooperation, see Carl Bernstein, "The Holy Alliance", *Time,* February 24, 1992, 14–21; Meese, *With Reagan,* 170–171. Tad Szulc in his biography on pope John Paul II discounts the United States/Vatican alliance to help Solidarity, but then goes on to describe precisely the cooperation outlined in this text. Checking his footnotes, Szulc's documentation on this episode

seems exceedingly thin. [Tad Szulc, *Pope John Paul II: The Biography* (New York:Scribner, 1995), 379–381].

40 Garthoff, *The Great Transition*, 273; 700–701; Sam Seibert et al., "How Afghans Say 'Thanks': Making War Against Foreign Relief Workers", *Newsweek*, July 30, 1990, 25; Judith Miller, *God Has Ninety-Nine Names: Reporting from a Militant Middle East* (New York: Simon & Schuster, 1996), 469; Joseph E. Persico, *Casey: The Lives and Secret of William J. Casey: From the OSS to the CIA* (New York: Penguin, 1990), 301; former CIA director Robert Gates notes, "We expected post-Soviet Afghanistan to be ugly, but we never considered that it would become a haven for terrorists operating worldwide", Robert Gates, *From the Shadows: The Ultimate Insider's Story of Five Presidents and How They Won the Cold War* (New York: Simon & Schuster, 1996), 349. The National Commission on Terrorist Attacks upon the United States, *The 9/11 Commission Report* (New York: W.W. Norton & Company, 2004). As the report shows it is unfair to blame this on Reagan. See also: Richard A. Clarke, *Against All Enemies: Inside America's War on Terror* (New York: Free Press, 2004).

41 Joseph T. Stanik, *El Dorado Canyon: Reagan's Undeclared war with Qaddafi* (Annapolis: Naval Institute Press, 2003), ix (for quote) and page 90.

42 Oberdorfer, *The Turn*, 33; Garthoff, *The Great Transition*, 113–114; Schweizer, *Victory*, 166; Pemberton, *Exit with Honor*, 153, 154 (for other historians advancing the same arguments, see note 29); see also: William D. Jackson, "Soviet Behavior in the Cold War", *The International History Review* XX: 2 (June, 1998): 389–401; Martin Malia argues that Gorbachev pursued reform to maintain the system: "revived Soviet economy was the indispensable precondition for maintaining superpower status. Thus the Soviet Union needed a 'breathing space' from international competition in order to regroup internally before returning to the contest of capitalism", *The Soviet Tragedy: a History of Socialism in Russia* (New York; The Free Press,1994), 413; see also: Jack F. Matlock, *Autopsy of an Empire: The American Ambassador's Account of the Collapse of the Soviet Union* (New York: Random House, 1995), 52, 101; for Reagan pursuing an essentially cautious foreign policy, see: Haig, *Caveat*, 109; Reagan, *An American Life*, 466; Caspar Weinberger, *Fighting for Peace: Seven Critical Years at the Pentagon* (London: Michael Joseph, 1990), 128, 282; Coral Bell, *The Reagan Paradox: U.S. Foreign Policy in the 1980s* (New Jersey: Rutgers University Press, 1989), 86.

43 Chester A. Crooker, *High Noon in Southern Africa: Making Peace in a Rough Neighborhood* (New York: W.W. Norton 6 Company, 1992).

44 David C. Wills, *The First War on Terrorism: Counter-Terrorism Policy during the Reagan Administration* (New York Rowan and Littlefield Publishers, 2003).

5 Iran: The Pillar Crumbles

1 Hamilton Jordan, *Crisis: The Last Year of the Carter Presidency* (New York: G.P. Putnam's Sons, 1982), 88–9.

2 Jimmy Carter, *White House Diary* (New York: Farrar, Straus and Giroux, 2010), 137, describes the shah as "quite embarrassed, " p. 137. The shah had invented *shahanshah* (king of king's) and *Aryamehr* (light of the Aryans) for himself, a rather lofty transition for a son of Cossack sergeant that later became the first shah of the Pahlavi house.

3   Hamilton Jordan, *Crisis: The Last Year of the Carter Presidency* (New York: G.P. Putnam's Sons, 1982), 89.

4   Jimmy Carter, *Keeping Faith: The Memoirs of a President* (New York: Bantam Books, 1982), 436–37.

5   Shah of Iran in *Newsweek*, March 14, 1977.

6   James A. Bill, *The Eagle and the Lion: The Tragedy of American–Iranian Relations* (New Haven: Yale University Press, 1988), 202–203; J. B. Kelly, *Arabia, the Gulf and the West* (London: Weidenfeld and Nicolson, 1980), 300–9.

7   Jimmy Carter, *White House Diary* (New York: Farrar, Straus and Giroux, 2010), 74–75.

8   Scott Kaufman, *Plans Unraveled: The Foreign Policy of the Carter Administration* (Dekalb, Illinois: Northern Illinois University Press, 2008), 154.

9   Zbigniew Brzezinski, *Power and Principle: Memoirs of the National Security Adviser, 1977–1981* (London: Weidenfeld and Nicolson, 1983), 354, 355. The officer in charge of Iran at the National Security Council, Gary Sick, agrees with Brzezinski and has the same cast of suspects as his boss: Precht, the State Department and William Sullivan (US ambassador to Tehran appointed by president Carter); see *All Fall Down: America's Tragic Encounter with Iran* (New York: Random House, 1985), 66, 69. But as Sick readily admits, the United States had but few options even under the Carter administration to support the shah: "It was also evident that the United States had no visible strategic alternative to a close relationship with Iran," p. 22.

10 Brzezinski, *Power and Principle*, 379.

11 Henry Precht, *A Diplomat's Progress: Ten Tales of Diplomatic Adventure in and Around the Middle East* (Savannah, Georgia: Williams & Company Publishers, 2005), 129–30.

12 James A. Bill, *The Eagle and the Lion: The Tragedy of American–Iranian Relations* (New Haven: Yale University Press, 1988), 246.

13 Mohammed Reza Pahlavi, *Answer to History* (New York: Stein and Day, 1980), 12, 15.

14 Jimmy Carter, *Keeping Faith: Memoirs of a President* (New York: Bantam Books, 1982), 446.

15 William H. Sullivan, *Mission to Iran* (New York: W. W. Norton & Company, 1981), 225.

16 David Owen, *Time to Declare* (London: Michael Joseph, 1991), 386–7.

17 Kaufman, *Plans Unraveled*, 160.

18 Burton I. and Scott Kaufman, *The Presidency of James Earl Carter Jr.* (Lawrence: University Press of Kansas, 2006), 43.

19 State Department, "Mohammad Reza Pahlavi", January 11, 1977, NLC-25-28-2-1-1, JCL.

20 Marc J. O'Reilly, *Unexceptional: America's Empire in the Persian Gulf, 1941–2007* (New York: Lexington Books, 2008), 139. O'Reilly argues that the shah held the upper hand in his relationship with Carter: "Years of reliance on the Pahlavi thus yielded a form of indenture; without the Shah, the United States risked forfeiting influence in a country of strategic import," p. 141.

21 Rick Inderfurth to Brzezinski, January 24, 1977, NLC-6-28-6-4-5.

22 Parviz C. Radji, *In the Service of the Peacock Throne: The Diaries of the Shah's Last Ambassador to London* (London: Hamish Hamilton, 1983), 16, 101–2.

23 James Callghan, *Time and Change* (London: Collins, 1987), 388.

24 Gary Sick to Inderfurth, January 28, 1977, National Security Affairs, Brzezinski Material, Country File [hereafter cited as NSABMCF], Iran 1-7/77, box 28, Jimmy Carter Library [hereafter cited as JCL].

25 William H. Sullivan, *Mission to Iran* (New York: W.W. Norton & Company, 1981), 20.

26 American embassy, Tehran, February 24, 1977, NLC-21-44-4-15-0, JCL:

27 Situation room to Brzezinski, May 6, 1977, NSABMPDRF [President's Daily Report File], JCL.

28 Brzezinski to Carter, October 14, 1977, Iran [10/1/77-10/15/77], NSABMPDRF, JCL.

29 Vance to Carter May 13, 1977, NLC-128-12-8-7-1, NLC. But Vance knew that all was not well in Iran, the CIA reported on May 6, 1977 that Iranian officials and American citizens in Iran faced a high risk from potential terrorist attacks: "terrorist organizations do not pose a threat to the stability of the regime at this time, but they do remain a major security problem." Situation room for Brzezinski, May 6, 1977, NSABM, PDRF [President's Daily Report File], JCL.

30 William H. Sullivan, *Mission to Tehran* (W.W. Norton & Company, 1981), 54.

31 Brzezinski (reporting conversation between shah and Sullivan) to Carter, June 21, 1977, Iran [6/21/77-6/30/77], NSABMPDRF, JCL.

32 Mc Sullivan and Shah, August 1, 1977, Iran [folder 8/1/77-8/10/77], NSABM, PFRF, JCL.

33 Secretary of treasury Michael Blumenthal (reporting conversation with the shah) to Carter, October 28, Iran [Iran 10/16/77-10/31/77], October 28, 1977, NSABM-PDRF, JCL. Still the shah could not resist blowing hot and cold on his American interlocutors, to Blumenthal the "Shah said Iran had begun to resent being classi-fied by the Congress as just 'another Persian Gulf country,' followed by the usual repartee; the Speech and the standard threat; if need be he could turn to other sources of military equipment than the United States." See: Blumenthal to Carter, October 28, 1977, NLC-16-109-3-1-0.

34 John C. Campbell, "Oil Power in the Middle East", *Foreign Affairs* 56: 1 (October, 1977): 89–110.

35 Asadollah Alam, *The Shah and I: The Confidential Diary of Iran's Royal Court, 1969–1977* (London: I.B. Tauris, 1991), 429, 430 note 1.

36 Peter Tarnoff to Brzezinski, November 2, 1977, Iran, Shah, 11/15-16/77, NSAB-MVIP visit file, JCL. In his diary the president observed: "in my opinion [he] has done an excellent job." See Jimmy Carter, *White House Diary* (New York: Farrar, Straus and Giroux, 2010), 136.

37 Vance to Carter, November 10, 1977, Iran, Shah, 11/15-16/77, NSABMVIP visit file, JCL. Aspects of Israel's secret relations with other powers are explored in Clive Jones and Tore T. Petersen (eds.), *Israel's Clandestine Diplomacies* (London and New York: Hurst & Company and Oxford University Press, 2013).

38 Denis Clift to Walter Mondale, Mondale Papers, "Taking Points for Foreign Policy Breakfast, 1977", box 2, JCL.

39 Crawaith, Swaine and More, Chronology, volume 1 of 3 [II], 12/77, Staff offices Counsel, Cutler, JCL.

40 Sick to Inderfurth, December 16, 1977, Trip Files, JCL.

41 Toast by Carter to shah, Tehran, December 31, 1977 in Jimmy Carter, *Public*

Papers of the Presidents of the United States, 1977. Book II – June 25 to December 31, 1977 (Washington: Government Printing Office, 1978), 2221.

42 Brzezinski to Carter, December 5, 1977, [12/1/77-12/8/77], NSABMPDRF, JCL.

43 *The Washington Post* quoted from U.S. Congress, *Report of the Congressional Committees Investigating the Iran-Contra Affair*, 100th Cong.: 1st Sess, November 17, 1987 (Washington: GPO, 1987), 157.

44 Parsons to Owen, "Annual Review for Iran 1977", January 4, 1978, FCO 8/3191/NBP 014/1.

45 Brzezinski to Carter, January 31, 1978, Iran [1/16/78-1/31/78], NSABMPDRF, JCL.

46 Brzezinski to Carter, May 10, 1978, Iran [5/1/78-5/10/78], NSABMPDRF, JCL.

47 Warren Christopher to Carter (with the president's handwritten comments), October 24, 1978, Plains File, State Department Evening Reports 10/78, JCL. This may, perhaps, point to the weakness of the president's leadership style. In his memoirs, the president wrote that he was concerned about saving time: "Instead of holding a five- or ten-minute conversation (at last), I could read a brief memorandum and make a decision in a matter of moments; and I could do this at odd times during the day, see: *Keeping Faith*, 56. A leadership style that was, perhaps, time efficient for the president, but superficial for most practical purposes. Parsons reported from the same meeting with the shah: "He simply did not know what to do," Parsons to FCO, October 25, 1978, PREM 16/1719.

48 Anthony Parsons, *The Pride and the Fall: Iran, 1974–79* (London: Jonathan Cape, 1984), x.

49 Glen Balfour-Paul, *The End of Empire in the Middle East: Britain's Relinquishment of Power in Her Last Three Arab Dependencies* (Cambridge: Cambridge University Press, 1991), 122, 223 note 68.

50 Clive Jones, *Britain and the Yemen Civil War, 1962–1965: Ministries, Mercenaries and Mandarins: Foreign Policy and the Limits of Covert Action* (Brighton & Portland: Sussex Academic Press, 2004), 11.

51 State Department, Bureau of Intelligence and Research, "Iran: The Unending revolution", June 11, 1985, Iran – Sensitive (3), Teicher, Howard: Files, box 8, RWRL.

52 William H. Sullivan, *Mission to Iran* (New York: W. W. Norton & Company, 1981), 156–7.

53 Brzezinski to Sullivan, November 3, 1978, NLC-SAFE 39 C-11-23-1-1.

54 Brzezinski, *Power and Principle*, 361.

55 Brzezinski to Carter, November 17, 1978, NLC-17-87-4-8-6.

56 Arthur Callahan to Brzezinski, November 17, 1978, NLC.17-87-4-8-6.

57 PDB, December 8, 1978, NLC-2-15-4-1-8.

58 Stansfield Turner to National Security Council, November 29, 1978, NCL-25-33-9-1-8.

59 CIA, "The Gulf Arabs and Iran", December 8, 1978, Iran 11/78, NSABMCF, JCL.

60 Anthony Parsons, *The Pride and Fall: Iran, 1974–1979* (London: Jonathan Cape, 1984), 37, 40, 48, 140.

61 David Owen, *Time to Declare* (London: Michael Joseph, 1991), 322, 390, 392.

62 Cabinet Committee on Economic Strategy, "Iran; Economic and Political Implications", November 10, 1978, CAB 134/4215.

63   C.A. Jampole to Gary Sick, "Iran study paper", September 25, 1980, NLC-15-99-8-1-8, JCL.

64   Brzezinski to Carter, September 29, 1980, NCL-1-17-1-21-8.

65   Rosalynn Carter, *First Lady from Plains* (Fayetteville: The University of Arkansas Press, 1994), 331.

66   Mc Carter, Callaghan, Schmidt and Giscard, January 6, 1979, PREM 16/2050.

67   Carter, *White House Diary*, February 27, 1979, p. 296.

68   Brzezinski, *Power and Principle*, 474, 475.

69   "The Hostage Crisis in Iran: 1979–81", January 20, 1981, Plains File, Folder Iran Report, 1/81, box 25, JCL.

70   Richard Thornton, *The Carter Years: toward a New Global Order* (New York: Paragon House, 1981), 445.

71   American embassy, London to state department, February 21, 1979, NLC-16-15-6-6-6, JCL.

72   Prime minister's private secretary to George Walden, FCO, May 14, 1979, FCO 8/3392/ NBP 243/2.

73   "The Huyser mission in Iran, " Brzezinski donated material [Meetings Vance/Brown/Brzezinski, 3/80-9/80], JCL.

74   State Department Intelligence and Research, "The Collapse of the Iranian Armed Forces", June 25, 1979 (on Brzezinski's letter of transmittal), NLC-21-18-10-1-7, JCL.

75   Stansfield Turner to Carter, Iran 11/17-20/79, NSABMCF, box 30, JCL.

76   Cyrus Vance, *Hard Choices: Critical Years in America's Foreign Policy* (New York: Simon & Schuster, 1983), 371.

77   J. B. Ure to Mallaby planning staff, January 27, 1981, FCO 8/4029/NB 020/8.

78   Anthony Parsons in FCO paper commissioned by David Owen, "British Policy in Iran, 1974–1978", FCO 8/4029/BNP 020/28.

6   Iran: Getting Stuck in the Rubble

1   Brzezinski to Carter, February 28, 1979, ZBDHM, Geographic File, Southwest Asia/Persian Gulf [2/79-12/79], JCL.

2   Khomeini statement, February 12, 1979, Iran 2-3/79, NSABMCF, box 29, JCL.

3   No author, "The Hostage Crisis in Iran: 1979–81", January 20, 1981, Plains File, Iran report, pp. 9–10, 1/81, box 25, JCL.

4   Paul B. Ryan, *The Iranian Rescue Mission: Why it Failed* (Annapolis: Naval Institute Press, 1985), 8.

5   No author, "The Hostage Crisis in Iran: 1979–81", January 20, 1981, Plains File, Iran report, pp.10, 11, 15, 1/81, box 25, JCL.

6   Mc Thatcher, Carter and Giscard, November 19, 1979, PREM 19/76.

7   Mc Thatcher and American legislators, December 17, 1979, PREM 19/127.

8   Carter to Thatcher, nd. NLC-128-10-5-7-6, JCL.

9   Statement by Khomeini, November 21, 1979, CIA daily briefs to president, JCL, emphasis in the original. On January 10, 1939 comrade Stalin informed the top echelons of the Soviet leadership: "The VKP CC affirms that the use of physical pressure in the work of the NKVD has been permitted since 1937 in accordance with a resolution of the VKP CC. (. . .) It is known that all bourgeois secret services use physical pressure against representatives of the socialist proletariat and rely on specially savage methods of it. We might therefore ask why a socialist secret

service should be any more humane in relation to inveterate agents of the bourgeoisie and sworn enemies of the working class and collectivized farmers," http://www.marxist.org/reference/archive/stalin/worksw/1939/01/10.htm.

10 No author, "The Hostage Crisis in Iran: 1979–81", January 20, 1981, Plains File, Iran report, pp. 29–30, 1/81, box 25, JCL.

11 Carter to Jordan, February 15, 1980, chief of Staff Jordan, Iran, 2/80, box 34B, JCL.

12 Carter to Thatcher, March 13, 1980, PREM 19/275.

13 On this see Saki Dockrill, *Britain's Retreat from East of Suez: The Choice between Europe and the World?* (New York: Palgrave Macmillan, 2002), 114, 116.

14 Thatcher to Carter, March 25, 1980, PREM 19/275.

15 Carter press announcement, April 7, 1980, Iran 4/1-18/80, NSABMCF, box 30, JCL.

16 US embassy London, "Aide Memoire", April 8, 1980, PREM 19/275.

17 Phone conversation Thatcher and Carter, April 19, 1980, PREM 19/276.

18 No author, "The Hostage Crisis in Iran: 1979–81", January 20, 1981, Plains File, Iran report, pp. 29–30, 1/81, box 25, JCL.

19 No author, "The Hostage Crisis in Iran: 1979–81", January 20, 1981, Plains File, Iran report, p, 37 1/81, box 25, JCL.

20 Richard Thornton, *The Carter Years: Toward a New Global Order* (New York: Paragon House, 1991), 504, 505.

21 Carter to Thatcher, April 25, 1980, PREM 19/2/6.

22 Carrington interviewed by Peter Snow, Friday April 25, 1980, PREM 19/276.

23 Muskie to Carter, "A Strategy for the New Phase in Iran", July 31, 1980, in papers of vice president Walter Mondale, Foreign Policy Breakfasts, [7/80-12/80], box1, JCL; see also "The Hostage Crisis."

24 Herbert A. Cohen, "Negotiating the Iranian Crisis, " NLC-25-42-8-1-9, JCL.

25 Khomeini statement, September 12, 1980, in CIA daily brief, JCL.

26 Carter, formal declaration, November 8, 1980, Plains File, Iran, 11/1-23/80, box 24, JCL.

27 Carter to Reagan, January 20, 1981, Plains File, Iran 1/21/81 [1], box 24, JCL.

28 Steven Strasser, Paul Martin et al., "A Grim Tale of Brutality", *Newsweek* February 2, 1981.

29 See for instance: Mark Bowden, *Guests of the Ayatollah: The First Battle in the West's War with Militant Islam* (London: Atlantic Books, 2006), 577: "what Reagan would do was anybody's guess."

30 Ann Wroe, *Lives, Lies and the Iran-Contra Affair* (London: I.B. Tauris, 1991), 3.

31 Iran-contra Report quoted from Peter Kornbluh and Malcolm Byrne (eds.), *The Iran-Contra Scandal: The Declassified History* (New York: New Press, 1993), 215.

32 Peter Kornbluh and Malcolm Byrne, *The Iran-Contra Scandal: The Declassified History* (New York: The New Press, 1993), 251–2.

33 In his memoirs Reagan stated: "Nothing is so good for the inside of a man as the outside of a horse," Ronald Reagan, *An American Life* (London. Hutchinson, 1990), 74.

34 James G. Roche to Lawrence Eagleburger, March 23, 1982, Iran (05/29/1981–12/31/1983), Fortier, Donald Files, box 1, RWRL.

35 Henry S. Rowen, "The Iranian Threat to American Interest in the Persian Gulf", July 20, 1982, Iran/Iraq, July 1982, Kemp, Geoffrey Files, box 4, RWRL; Peter

Hahn, *Caught in the Middle East: U.S. Policy toward the Arab–Israeli Conflict, 1945–1961* (Chapel Hill and London: The University of North Carolina Press, 2004).

36   Clark to Reagan, n.d., Iran/Iraq, Jan–Jun 1982, Kemp Geoffrey: Files, box 4, RWRL.

37   Con Coughlin, *Saddam: The Secret Life* (London: Macmillan, 2002), 216–17.

38   McFarlane to Shulz and Weinberger, June 17, 1985 in Peter Kornbluh and Malcolm Byrne, *The Iran-Contra Scandal: The Declassified History* (New York: The New Press, 1993), 220–26.

39   US Congress, *Report of the Congressional Committees Investigating the Iran-Contra Affair,* " 100th Cong.: 1st Sess, November 17, 1987 (Washington: GPO, 1987), 17.

40   Bruce W. Jentleson, *With Friends Like These: Reagan, Bush, and Saddam, 1982–1990* (New York: W.W. Norton & Company, 1994), 58–59.

41   US Congress, *Report of the Congressional Committees Investigating the Iran-Contra Affair,* " 100th Cong.: 1st Sess, November 17, 1987 (Washington: GPO, 1987), 157,

42   John Tower, et al., *The Tower Commission Report* (New York: Bantam Books, 1987), 503.

43   Lawrence E. Walsh, *Firewall: The Iran-Contra Conspiracy and Cover-Up* (New York: W.W. Norton & Company, 1997), 352. Words in brackets added by Walsh.

44   Reagan to Joseph F. Banashek, December 22, 1986, 0071 (Iran) WHORM subject File, box 92, RWRL. Emphasis in the original.

7   Saudi Arabia: The Myth of Independence

1   Jimmy Carter, *White House Diary* (New York: Farrar, Straus and Giroux, 2010), February 6, 1980, p. 398.

2   Buraimi was a remote oasis on the south-east tip of the Arabian Peninsula, and seemed in the early 1950s an unlikely spot for an international confrontation; few Americans knew it even existed. Roughly circular, and about six miles across, it had a population of between six and ten thousand inhabitants clustered in nine villages, three of them controlled by Abu Dhabi, and the rest by the sultan of Muscat and Oman. Buraimi was blessed with abundant water and a fertile soil, which provided the villagers with a variety of fruits and crops and pasture for their livestock. Most important, however, was its strategic location at important cross-roads; whoever held it controlled the approaches to Muscat and Oman. These facts were well known to the king of Saudi Arabia, Ibn Saud, who, in August 1952, supported by the Arabian American Oil Company (ARAMCO), sent his troops to occupy the oasis. Like most of its Persian Gulf neighbors, Buraimi held the promise of new oil reserves. For Britain, it was yet another example of the United States poaching on their turf using local leaders and rulers, undermining the British position as had taken place in Egypt and Iran, simultaneously with the troubles on the Arabian Peninsula. Britain would later reoccupy the oasis and forcibly evict the Saudis in October 1955. Buraimi thereafter was a continuing eyesore for then crown prince and later king Faisal, who until the dispute was finally resolved in 1974 would demand satisfaction from the British and assistance from the Americans. Needless to say, disagreements over Buraimi would particularly in the

1950s cause Anglo-American friction. On this, see: Tore T. Petersen, "Anglo-American Rivalry in the Middle East: The Struggle for the Buraimi Oasis, 1952–1957", *The International History Review* XIX: 4 (November, 1992): 71–91.

3 One tenured faculty confided in me that after Clinton's retirement they had no expectation to see the resumption of Saudi munificence at the University of Arkansas, Little Rock.

4 Pariz C. Radji, *In the Service of the Peacock Throne: The Diaries of the Shah's Last Ambassador to London* (London: Hamish Hamilton, 1983), 72.

5 This is discussed in Tore T. Petersen, *Richard Nixon, Great Britain and the Anglo-American Alignment in the Persian Gulf and Arabian Peninsula* (Brighton & Portland: Sussex Academic Press, 2009), 109.

6 G.G. Arthur to Anthony Parsons, March 21, 1971, FCO 8/1573/NB 3/304/1/4.

7 CIA memorandum, "Saudi Arabia: An Assessment, " January 12, 1977, NCC-6-67-4-6-2; JCL.

8 Assistant secretary of state Benjamin Read to Mc George Bundy, May 24, 1962, 611.86B/5-2462, State Department Decimal File, United States National Archives, Record Group 59, College Park, Maryland.

9 CIA memorandum, "Saudi Arabia: An Assessment", January 12, 1977, NCC-6-67-4-6-2, JCL.

10 See for instance Peter Tarnoff to Brzezinski, June 10, 1977, Saudi Arabia 1-8/77, NSABMCF, box 67, JCL; "suggested toast for president to crown prince Fahd, May 24, 1977, Crown Prince Fahd, 5/24/77, NSABM, VIP visit File, box 12, JCL; "The Kingdom of Saudi Arabia has been steadfast in its friendship toward the United States through difficult periods in the Middle East."

11 Briefing papers, "President's Carter's Visit to Poland, Iran, India, Saudi Arabia, France, and Belgium", Dec. 29, 1977–Jan. 1978, NSABM, Trip File, JCL.

12 On the Anglo-American air consortium, see T.T. Petersen, *Willing Retreat.* In contrast to often tempestuous Anglo-American relations over Saudi Arabia in the 1950s, the relationship was patched up in the mid 1960s. The United States let Britain in on the Saudi air consortium in 1965, in part as an inducement for Britain to remain east of Suez. In addition, fearing the consequences of a revolutionary regime in neighboring Yemen, supported by Nasser, Saudi Arabia resumed diplomatic relations with Britain in January 1963. Thereafter the British did their utmost to exploit the possibilities of the Saudi military and civilian market.

13 Mc Judd (UK) and Muhammed Abdul Latif Al-Milhelm, minister of state, Saudi Arabia ministry of defense. November 16, 1978, FCO 8/3109, 'Saudi Arabian Air Defence Scheme,' TNA.

14 John Wilton, UK ambassador Saudi Arabia, "Annual Review 1978", January 15, 1979, FCO 8/3416/NBS 014/1, TNA.

15 Senator Frank Church on behalf of the Senate Foreign Relations Committee to Vance, January 24, 1978, SA 1-5/78; Harold Brown to Clement J. Zabloski, May 9, 1978, Saudi Arabia 6-7/80; both in NSABMCH, JCL. Carter informed king Khalid ibn Abd al-Aziz Al Saud on May 16, 1978 that the Senate had voted in support of the sale of F-15s to Saudi Arabia in Carter to Khalid, NLC-128R-4-2-86-1, JCL.

16 Kenneth Labich, Paul Martin and Lars-Erik Nelson, "Saudi Power", *Newsweek*, March 6, 1978.

17 Carter to Khalid, April 14, 1978, NLC-128R-4-2-86-1.

18 Tarnoff to Brzezinski, "Listing of Presidential Assurances to Saudi Arabia", January 30, 1979, NLC-132-74-6-13-3, JCL.

19 Michael A. Palmer, *Guardians of the Gulf: A History of America's Expanding Role in the Persian Gulf, 1833–1992* (New York: The Free Press, 1992), 118.

20 Carter to Khalid, September 26, 1978, NLC-128R-4-2-86-1.

21 State Department, president's daily brief, February 6, 1979, NCL-1-9-5-10-5, JCL.

22 Wilton, UK ambassador Jeddah to FCO, February 14, 1979, FCO 8/3420/NBS 020/.

23 R.J.S. Muir, UK embassy Washington to D.E. Tatham, February 9, 1979, FCO 8/3420/NBS 020/1. To which Tatham commented: "It is easy, particularly for those who have no knowledge of the Kingdom to forget how slow and unco-ordinated decision-making usually is, and how loath the Saudis are to move beyond the general Arab consensus or to use their enormous wealth as a political lever." Tatham to Moderly, February 13, 1979, FCO 8/3420/NBS 020/1.

24 John West, background paper on Saudi Arabia, April 27, 1979, NLC-132-74-6-8-9, JCL.

25 J.C. Moberly to A. Parsons, February 14, 1979, FCO 8/3280/NB 021/2.

26 John West, "Saudi Arabia – the Lessons of Iran – After Six Months", July 15, 1979, NLC-15-46-7-31-4, JCL.

27 Vance to Carter, November 28, 1979, NLC-128-14-13-20-8.

28 Jimmy Carter, *White House Diary* (New York: Farrar, Straus and Giroux, 2010), diary entry November 21, 1979, page 371. It is interesting how the president himself reacted to the crisis, the day after Fahd's blood-curling message, Carter noted in his diary at Camp David: "This was the quietest day I've had in a long time, and did some reading, swimming, jogging, and fishing." See: Jimmy Carter, *White House Diary* (New York: Farrar, Straus and Giroux, 2010), diary entry November 22, 1979, p. 372.

29 Jimmy Carter, *White House Diary* (New York: Farrar, Straus and Giroux, 2010), diary entry January 14, 1980, 391–2.

30 Henderson to FCO, November 26, 1979, FCO 8/3419/ NBS 14/5.

31 Carter to Fahd, December 5, 1979, NLC-16-119-2-22-7, JCL.

32 Yaroslav Trofimov, *The Siege of Mecca: The Forgotten Uprising in Islam's Holiest Shrine* (London: Penguin, 2007), 228–29, 239.

33 The president's diaries are mercifully quiet on this; there are no pronouncements in the public papers of Carter; I have not found anything in the current declassified record.

34 Wilton to Carrington, September 12, 1979, FCO 8/3418/NBS 14/4.

35 Rachel Bronson, *Thicker than Oil: America's Uneasy Partnership with Saudi Arabia* (Oxford: Oxford University Press, 2006), 148.

36 Vance to West, December 29, 1979, NLC-16-119-5-3-5, JCL.

37 Miers to Maitland, "Secretary of State's Visit to Saudi Arabia, "January 7, 1980, FCO 8/4055/EN 026/1.

38 Middle East Section, Research Department, FCO, "The Seizure of the Grand Mosque in Mecca", August 21, 1981, FCO 8/3419/NBS 14/5.

39 Brzezinski to Carter, January 11, 1980, NLC-1-13-8-1-7, JCL.

40 Joseph W. Twinham to Hunter, "Saudi Arabian Foreign Assistance", January 12, 1980, NLC-25-83-2-3-8, JCL.

41 West to Carter, March 19, 1980, NLC-128-4-2-1-2, JCL.

42 Carter to West (emphasis in the original), 20 March, 1980, NLC-128-4-2-15-7, JCL. Attached to West's letter to the president was the ambassador's memorandum, "The Six Crisis of Saudi Arabia in 1979", inspired by Nixon's book with the same title, Nixon did not survive politically his seventh crisis (Watergate), how would the Saudis fare? The six crisis were: (1) the fall of the shah, (2) the invasion of North Yemen by PDRY [People's Democratic Republic of Yemen], (3) the signing of the Israeli–Egyptian peace treaty, (4) the occupation of the Mecca mosque, (5) Shi'ite demonstrations in eastern Saudi Arabia, (6) the Soviet invasion of Afghanistan. The Mecca incident was the most frightening to the Saudi royal house: "A large number of the more conservative elements in the country were not unsympathetic to the call for stricter religious observance and a crackdown on permissiveness in the society." The occupation demonstrated the ineptness of Saudi armed forces, needing fifteen days to clear out the occupants. Still, West concluded that the Saudi Arabian government had "withstood these crises well." There were even some indications the royal house had taken the lessons to heart, and that the regimes prospects of survival were good.

43 William E. Griffith to Brzezinski, March 21, 1980, NLC-SAFE 3 C-26-47-1-8.

44 Report of UK defense attaché Jeddah in James Craig, UK ambassador, Saudi Arabia, to Lord Carrington, n.d., FCO 8/3755/NBS 062/2.

45 Brzezinski, "Allied Military Deployment in the Indian Ocean Area", Donated Material, Zbigniew Brzezinski Collection (hereafter ZBDM), Geographical File, Southwest Asia/Persian Gulf – [2/80], JCL.

46 Foreign office memorandum, n.d. (probably April 1980), FCO 8/3737/NBS 020/1.

47 Cabinet discussions, April 25, 1980, CAB 148/189.

48 Richard Williams, "Brief for Minister of State's Visit to Saudi Arabia and Qatar, 7–12 November", November 3, 1980, FCO 8/3753/NBS 061/1.

49 Thatcher to Fahd, April 25, 1980, FCO 8/NBS 020/1.

50 Peter Alexander Rupert Carrington, *Reflect on Things Past: The Memoirs of Lord Carrington* (London: Collins, 1988), 339.

51 The situation room for Brzezinski, July 10, 1980, PDRF, box 16, JCL.

52 Paul Foot (with Ron Smith), *The Helen Smith Story* (Great Britain: Fontana Paperbacks, 1983), 405.

53 Peter Carrington, *Reflect on Things Past: The Memoirs of Lord Carrington* (London: Collins, 1988); Margaret Thatcher, *The Downing Street Years* (London: HarperCollins, 1993).

54 Private secretary Alexander to Graham Smith, June 5, 1980, PREM 19/1126.

55 Douglas Hurd, *Memoirs* (London: Little Brown, 2003), 273–74.

56 Mc Hurd and Faisal, July 27, 1980, FCO 47/973/ GK 026/372/1.

57 Foreign and Commonwealth office, "Visit by Foreign and Commonwealth Secretary to Saudi Arabia, 25–27, August", FCO 8/3752/NBS 026/3.

58 Craig to Carrington, September 3, 1980, FCO 8/3751/NBS026/3.

8   Saudi Foreign Policy: What Foreign Policy?

1 Brzezinski to Carter, May 14, 1980, CIA daily brief, box 27, JCL.

2 Carter to Fahd, May 30, 1980, NLC-128R-4-2-86-1, JCL.

3 West, "Saudi Arabia – an Assessment as of June 1, 1980", June 1, 1980, NLC-128-4-2-2-1, JCL.

4 Staff Offices, November 21 and December 2, 1979, Cutler, Iran 3 of 3 [1], 12, 79, JCL.

5 Tom Morganthau, Carol Honsa and Fred Coleman, "An Embassy Burns", *Newsweek*, December 3, 1979.

6 Saunders to American embassy, Islamabad, December 4, 1979, NLC-16-119-2-11-9.

7 State Department, operations center, Libyan working group, December 2, 1979, NLC-12-28-7-19-1, JCL.

8 Vance to Carter, December 19, 1979, NLC-128-14-14-15-3.

9 Vance to Carter, February 1, 1980, Libya 1/77-1/81, NSABMCF, JCL.

10 Vance to Carter, February 14, 1977, Libya 1/77-1/81, NSABMCF, JCL.

11 Tripp to FCO, "Two Years of Revolution in Libya", September 8, 1971, FCO 39/801/NAL 1/1.

12 Mc Joseph Palmer, US ambassador Libya and Qaddafy, October 30, 1972, POL Libya, US National Archives, College Park, Maryland.

13 Haig to Reagan, March 25, 1981, Libya, 1981–1984 (1 of 6), Fortier, Donald Files, box 7, RWRL.

14 Alexander Haig, *Caveat: Realism, Reagan, and Foreign Policy* (New York: Macmillan Publishing Company, 1984), 109: "In response, [Soviet ambassador to Washington Anatoly] Dobrynin made clear that Libya was an American problem. We received further indications that Qaddafi might be expandable. An American delegation returned from Moscow to report hints from members of the Politburo that they were not sure they could control Qaddafi. An important Soviet diplomat told a high U.S. official that Qaddafi was 'a madman'." In his retirement Haig has clearly softened his view on the Libyan threat.

15 Joseph T. Stanick, *El Dorado Canyon: Reagan's Undeclared War against Qaddafy* (Annappolis: Naval Institute Press, 2003), 44, 77.

16 Caspar Weinberger, *Fighting for Peace: Critical Years at the Pentagon* (London: Michael Joseph, 1990), 124, 125.

17 Ronald Reagan, *An American Life* (London: Hutchinson, 1990), 291.

18 Robert McFarlane, "A Public Affairs's Strategy for Actions against Libya," November 16, 1981 NSC records, box 5, RWRL. Emphasis in the original.

19 Wolfowitz to Clark, November 25, 1981, Libya, 1981–1984 (2 of 6), Fortier, Donald Files, Box 7, RWRL. Emphasis in the original.

20 Alison Pargeter, *Libya: The Rise and Fall of Qaddafi* (New Haven: Yale University Press, 2012), 139.

21 Nixon's oil policies are discussed in Tore T. Petersen, *Richard Nixon, Great Britain and the Anglo-American Alignment in the Persian Gulf and Arabian Peninsula: Making Allies out Clients* (Brighton & Portland: Sussex Academic Press, 2009).

22 West, "Saudi Arabia – An Assessment as of October 1980, " NLC-15-47-1-8-5, JCL.

23 James Craig, "Saudi Arabia: Annual Review for 1980", January 25, 1981, FCO 8/4200/NBS 14/2.

24 Richard Williams, "Brief for Minister of State's Visit to Saudi Arabia and Qatar, 7–12 November", November 3, 1980, FCO 8/3753/NBS 061/1.

25 On this, see for instance mc Sheikh Othman Humaid and Lord Strathcona et al.,

November 10, 1980, FCO 8/3753/NBS 061/1.

26 See for instance mc Thatcher and sheikh Hizam Naser, Saudi minister of planning, March 2, 1981, PREM 19/900.

27 See mc Thatcher and Saudi minister of defense Sultan, April 21, 1981, PREM 19/757. Thatcher wrote prince Abdullah bin Abdul Aziz al Saud after the visit on May 8, 1981: "It was particularly helpful to me to review with you the progress of projects where the UK can help the National Guard make important developments in radio communications, health services and in the equipment of units", PREM 19/1126.

28 Private secretary Alexander to John Rhodes, Department of Trade, May 7, 1981, PREM 19/757.

29 Ministry of defence to Thatcher, May 6, 1981, PREM 19/1126.

30 Mc Nott and Sultan, June 10, 1981, FCO 8/4221/NBS 087/1.

31 Craig to Carrington, June 22, 1981, PREM 19/901.

32 Miltholton (sales FCO, minute, June 25, 1981, FCO 8/4220/NBs 018/2.

33 Haig to Reagan, July 24, 1981, AWACS and Air Materials to Saudi Arabia Vol. I (7 of 8), Meese, Edwin Files, box 5, RWRL.

34 Thatcher to Reagan, October 31, 1981, PREM 19/532.

35 Reagan to Thatcher, December 1, 1981, PREM 19/533.

36 Jason H. Campbell, "The Ties that Bind: The Events of 1979 and the Escalation of the U.S.–Saudi Security Relations during the Carter and Reagan Administration", in Jeffrey R. Macris and Saul Kelly (eds.), *Imperial Crossroads: The Great Powers and the Persian Gulf* (Annapolis, Maryland: Naval Institute Press, 2012): 129–146.

37 Talking points for hearing Senate, in AWACS and Air Materials to Saudi Arabia, vol. I (3 of 8), Edwin Meese Files, box 5, RWRL.

38 Christopher Van Hollen, "Don't Engulf the Gulf", *Foreign Affairs* 59: 5 (Summer, 1981): 1064–1078.

39 Ronald Reagan, *An American Life* (London: Hutchinson, 1990), 410–11.

40 Reagan to king Khalid, February 18 and March 4, 1981, Saudi Arabia: King Khalid – Cables (1/2), Head of State File, Executive Secretary, NSC, box 29, RWRL. These assurances were repeated from time to time, see for instance talking points meeting with prince Bandar, in McFarlane to Reagan June 25, 1985, Chron File June 1985 (5), Teicher; Howard J.: Files, box 6, RWRL.

41 Richard Allen to Reagan, February 18, 1981, Saudi Arabia – General (1 of 3), Meese, Edwin Files, box 3, RWRL.

42 Clark to Reagan, February 27, 1982, Oil (January–March 1982), Executive Secretariat, NSC, RWRL.

43 Mc Carrington and Fahd, November 4, 1981, PREM 19/533. Emphasis in the original.

44 Jane Ridley to John Nott, June 23, 1982, PREM 19/842.

45 Private secretary to Thatcher, April 19, 1983, Thatcher to Fahd, "I was concerned to learn that an inaccurate news item had been carried by the BBC," October 18, 1983; Thatcher to king Fahd bin Abdul Aziz bin Abdul, December 1, 1983; "The close co-operation in economic and trade matters between the Kingdom of Saudi Arabia and the United Kingdom is a reflection of the good relations that between our two countries," all in PREM 19/1126.

46 Thatcher to Fahd, December 12, 1983, PREM 19/1126.

47 Michael Hesseltine to Thatcher, December 21, 1983; Jane Ridley, defence, to Thatcher November 15, 1982; both in PREM 19/1185.

48 Hesseltine to Thatcher, "Quarterly Report on Defence Sales", February 21, 1984, PREM 19/1185.

49 Peter Schweizer, *Victory: The Reagan Administration's Secret Strategy that Hastened the Collapse of the Soviet Union* (New York: The Atlantic Monthly Press, 1994), 219.

50 Robert C. Macfarlane, talking points for president's meeting with prince Bandar, June 25, 1985, Chron File 1985 (5); Teicher, Howard Files, box 6, RWRL.

51 Lawrence E. Walsh, *Firewall: The Iran-Contra Conspiracy and Cover-up* (New York: W.W. Norton, 1997), xiv.

52 Don Gregg to George Bush, April 2, 1986, The Vice President's Trip to the Persian Gulf and Arabian Peninsula, April 3–12, 1986 [Briefing Book] (1), NSC records, box 7, RWRL.

9   Oman: Discretion Required

1 US embassy Muscat to State Department, February 14, 1978, NLC-1-1-25-9, JCL. On his comments to the British embassy's annual review for Oman for 1977, D.C. Beaumont noted that British exports to the Sultanate had increased with over 50 per cent from 1976. See Beaumont to Lucas, January 18, 1978, FCO 8/3165/NBL 14/1.

2 Lucas to Weir, October 20, 1978, FCO 8/3145/NBE 020/2.

3 On this see following folder in the Foreign and Commonwealth Office, FCO 8/3110; "Loan Service Personnel from UK to Oman."

4 Rory to M.S. Weir, April 24, 1978, FCO 8/3110,NBD 071/8/20.

5 Treadwell, UK embassy Oman to FCO, January 29, 1980, FCO 8/3330/NBL 020/1.

6 R.J.S. Muir, UK embassy Washington, to D.C.B Beaumont, Middle East Department, FCO, FCO 8/3330/NBC 0/20/1.

7 Carter to Qaboos, June 7, 1979, NLC-16-103-5-14-0, JCL.

8 CIA daily brief, January 15, 1980, JCL.

9 Lucas to Carrington, February 19, 1980, FCO 46/227/DP061/2.

10 Lucas annual review 1979, December 30, 1979, FCO 8/3532/NBL 014/2.

11 Memorandum to Carrington, June 26, 1979, DEFE 70/631.

12 Oman, secretary of state to Mod, June 28, 1979, DEFE 70/631.

13 Minister of state for foreign affairs, February 11, 1980, Qais Al-Zawawi, to UK ambaasador Muscat, I.T.M Lucas, February 11, 1980, FCO 8/3547/NBL 071/1.

14 Miers to D. Maitland, January 7, 1980, FCO 28/4055/EN 026/1.

15 Harold Saunders and David Newsom to Vance, n.d., NLC-25-73-7-13-3, JCL.

16 Zawawi to Lucas, February 11, 1980, FCO 8/3547/NBL 071/1.

17 Bailes to Taham, February 22, 1980, FCO 8/3547/NBL 071/1.

18 Report by the defence policy staff, "Loan Service Personnel in Oman", April 2, 1979, FCO 46/222(/DPP 061/2.

19 Lucas to FCO, April 23, 1980, FCO 8/2228/DPP 061/2.

20 Mark Bowden, *Guests of the Aytollah: The First Battle in the West's War with Militant Islam* (London: Atlantic Books, 2006), 29.

21 Mc Reg Bartholomew and Omani foreign minister Zawari, April 9, 1980, NLC-128-15-4-5-4, JCL.

22 See William Odom to Brzezinski (with Carter's handwritten comments on), April 27, 1980, Donated ZB, Geographic File, Southwest Asia/Persian Gulf, 4/80, JCL (emphasis in the original).

23 Tatham to Lucas, reporting on Anglo-American talks on Persian Gulf, April 27, 1980, FCO 8/3536/NBL 020/2.

24 Carter to Qaboos, May 1, 1980, NLC-16-105-5-2-1, JCL.

25 Lucas to Miers, May 3, 1980, FCO 8/3536/NBL 020/2.

26 Adrian Fortesque to Miers, May 13, 1980, FCO 8/3536/NBL 020/2.

27 Carrington to Lucas, May 11, 1980, FCO 8/3535/NBL 020/2.

28 Lucas to Al-Zawawi, May 15, 1980, FCO 8/3537/NBL 071/2.

29 Mc Zawawi and Pym et al. May 29, 1980, FCO 8/3547/NBL 071/9 (emphasis in the original).

30 Tatham to Lucas, July 14, 1980, FCO 8/3536/NBL 020/2.

31 Miers to Lucas, October 3, 1980, FCO 8/3533/NBL 014/3.

32 Moberly to Graham with memorandum of discussion, December 22, 1980, FCO 46/2237/DPP 061/11.

33 Carter to Qaboos, January 14, 1981, Plains File, Heads of State Farewell, box 23, JCL.

34 Report Directors of Defence Policy, "Defence Options in the Gulf, Red Sea and North West Indian Ocean Areas", July 31, 1980, FCO 46/2229/DPP 061/2.

35 UK embassy Muscat to Foreign and Commonwealth office, September 27, 1980, PREM 19/278.

36 Qaboos to the American embassy Muscat, June 18, 1980, President's Daily CIA brief, NSABM, JCL.

37 Phone conversation Thatcher and Carrington, September 27, 1980, PREM 19/278.

38 Tunnel to Carrington, September 27, 1980, PREM 19/278.

39 Muskie to American embassy, Muscat, n.d., NLC-12-46-2-22-2, JCL.

40 Carrington to Muscat, September 28, 1980, PREM 19/278.

41 Lucas, "Annual Review Oman 1980", January 10, 1981, FCO 8/3952/NBL 14/ 2.

42 Brzezinski to Carter, NSC Weekly Report # 156, NLC-128-10-4-9-5, JCL.

43 Henderson to FCO, October 4, 1980, FCO 8/3693/ NBR 020/.

44 Carrington to Pym, December 29, 1980, FCO 46/2237/DPP 061/11.

45 Lucas, "Annual Review Oman 1980."

46 Discussion in Moberly to Miers, December 30, 1980, FCO 8/3535/NBL 020/1.

47 Alexander to Richards, May 6, 1981, FCO 8/3966/NBL 62/1. When meeting Qaboos on April 24, the prime minister went far to accommodate the Sultan, all points raised by the Sultan received a favorable response, Thatcher agreed to try reduce charges for LSP officers, to increase aid to Oman, to support the building of an university in Oman, to give Oman a new line of credit, See mc Thatcher and Qaboos, April 24, 1981, PREM 19, 1981.

48 Tom Mathws et al., "Arming America's Friends", *Newsweek*, March 23, 1981.

49 Mc Richard Burt (US) and Gillmore (UK), December 4, 1981, FCO 8/3804/NB 021 /8.

50 Miers to Lucas, February 5, 1981, FCO 8/3965/ NBL 62/1. (Emphasis in original).

51 Carrington to Thatcher, November 29, 1981, FCO 8/3963/NBL 061/1.

52 Thatcher's private secretary Michael Alexander to Francis Richards, December 1, 1981, FCO 8/3963/NBL 061/1.

53 J.D.S. Dawson, Ministry of Defence, to Alexander, December 1, 1981, FCO 8/3963/NBL 061/!.

54 Miers in US and UK talks on Oman, July 9, 1981, FCO 8/3967/NBL 062/1.

55 FCO brief for Douglas Hurd Oman visit December 1981, November 26, 1981, FCO 8/3962/NBL 26/3.

56 Mc Hurd and Qaboos, December 3, 1981, FCO 8/3962/NBL 26/3.

57 UK embassy Muscat to FCO, December 2, 1981, FCO 8/3962/NBL 26/3.

58 Henderson to Foreign and Commonwealth Office, January 23, 1982, PREM 19/843.

59 Lucas valedictory dispatch, December 3, 1981, FCO 8/3953/NBL 014/3.

60 Thatcher to Qaboos, July 15, 1982, PREM 19/842.

61 A.D, Hutton, *Directives to the Chief of the Defence Staff (Oman) and to the British LSP Service Commanders in Oman*, April 28, 1981, FCO 8/3968/NBL 71/1.

62 Ronald Reagan, *The Reagan Diaries* (New York: HarperCollins, 1997), 144.

63 Reagan to Qaboos, March 27, 1986, The Vice President's Trip to the Persian Gulf and Arabian Peninsula, April 3–12, 1986 [Briefing Book], NSC Records, box 7, RWRL.

64 Simon C. Smith, *Ending Empire in the Middle East: Britain, the United States and Post-War Decolonization, 1945–1973* (London: Routledge, 2012), 126, 211 note 299.

Epilogue

1 Joseph T. Stanick, *El Dorado Canyon: Reagan's Undeclared War with Qaddafy* (Annapolis: Naval Institute Press, 2003), x, 90.

2 Clifford to Rostow, 18 July 19967, Johnson Papers, memorandums to the president, W.W. Rostow vol. 35 [2 of 2], July 16–24, 1967.

3 D. Rusk, *As I Saw It: A Secretary of State's Memoirs* (London, 1990), 332.

4 G. W. Ball and D. B. Ball, *The Passionate Attachment: America's Investment with Israel: 1947 to the Present* (New York, 1992), 57–58.

5 Saddam Hussein to Ronald Reagan, November 18, 1986, Iraq, Teicher, Howard J. Files, box 9, RWRL.

6 Mc Iraqi ambassador Hamdoon and Murphy, Noveber 20, 1986, Iraq, Teicher, Howard J. Files, box 9, RWRL.

7 Ronald Reagan, *An American Life* (London, 1990), 684; G.P. Shultz, *Turmoil and Triumph: My Years as Secretary of State* (New York, 1993), 927; Colin Powell, *My American Journey* (New York, 1995), 512.

8 Harold Lee Wise, *Inside the Danger Zone: The U.S. Military in the Persian Gulf, 1987–1988* (Annapolis: Naval Institute Press, 2007), 47.

9 Testimony Murphy, "U.S: Policy in the Persian Gulf." Hearings before the Committee on Foreign Relations, 100d Cong: 1st sess., May 29, 1987 (Washington: GPO, 1988), 4–7.

10 Testimony Armitage in *ibid*.

Bibliography

The National Archives, Kew
CAB – Records of the Cabinet Office.
The Defence and Oversea Policy Committee (CAB 148).
FO 371-Records of the Foreign Office.
FCO – Records of the Foreign and Commonwealth Office.
PREM – Prime Minister's Office.
DEFE – Ministry of Defence.

Nixon Presidential Materials Staff
Lyndon Baines Johnson Presidential Library, Austin, Texas.
Jimmy Carter Presidential Library, Atlanta, Georgia.
Ronald Reagan Presidential Library, Simi Valley, California.

Newspapers and Periodicals
The Economist.
Time.
Newsweek .

Printed Primary Sources

Alam, Asadollah. *The Shah and I: The Confidential Diary of Iran's Royal Court, 1969–1977* (London: I.B. Tauris, 1991).

Carter, Jimmy. *Public Papers of the Presidents of the United States, 1977. Book II – June 25 to December 31, 1977* (Washington: Government Printing Office, 1978).

Carter, Jimmy. *White House Diary* (New York: Farrar, Straus and Giroux, 2010).

Crowley, Monica. *Nixon off the Record* (New York: Random House, 1996).

——. *Nixon in Winter* (New York: Random House, 1998).

H.R. Haldeman, *The Haldeman Diaries: Inside the Nixon White House* (New York: G.P. Putnam's Sons, 1994).

Kornbluh Peter and Malcolm Byrne (eds.), *The Iran-Contra Scandal: The Declassified History* (New York: New Press, 1993).

Nixon, Richard, *Public Papers of the President of the United States, 1973* (Washington: Government Printing Office, 1975).

——, "U.S. Foreign Policy for the 1970s: A New Strategy for Peace", *A Report to the Congress by Richard Nixon, February 18, 1970* (Washington: GPO, 1970).

——, "President Nixon's Foreign Policy Report to the Congress February 25, 1971", United States Information Service (Washington: GPO, 1971).

——, "U.S. Foreign Policy for the 1970s: The Emerging Structure of Peace", *A Report to the Congress by Richard Nixon, February 9, 1972* (Washington: GPO, 1972).

Radji, Parviz C. *In the Service of the Peacock Throne: The Diaries of the Shah's Last Ambassador to London* (London: Hamish Hamilton, 1983).

Ronald Reagan, *The Reagan Diaries* (New York: HarperCollins, 2007).

Tower, John et al., *The Tower Commission Report* (New York: Bantam Books, 1987).

US Congress, *Report of the Congressional Committees Investigating the Iran-Contra Affair*, "100th Cong.: 1st Sess, November 17, 1987 (Washington: GPO, 1987).

Memoirs

Anderson, Martin, *Revolution* (New York: Harcourt, Brace Jovanovich Publishers, 1988).

Brzezinski, Zbigniew. *Power and Principle: Memoirs of the National Security Advisor, 1977–1981* (London: Weidenfeld and Nicolson).

Carrington, Peter. *Reflect on Things Past: The Memoirs of Lord Carrington* (London: Collins, 1988).

Carter, Jimmy. *Keeping Faith: Memoirs of a President* (New York: Bantam Books, 1983).

Rosalynn Carter, *First Lady from Plains* (Fayetteville: University of Arkansas Press, 1994).

Callaghan, James. *Time & Change* (London: Collins, 1987).

Craddock, Percy. *In Pursuit of British Interests: Reflections on Foreign Policy under Margaret Thatcher and John Major* (London: John Murray, 1997).

Deaver, Michael, *Behind the Scenes* (New York: William Morrow and Company, 1987).

Dobrynin, Anatoly. *In Confidence: Moscow's Ambassador to America's Six Cold War Presidents* (New York: Times Books, 1995).

Gates, Robert M. *From the Shadows: The Ultimate Insider's Story of Five Presidents and How They Won the Cod War* (New York: Simon & Schuster, 1996).

——. *Duty: Memoirs of a Secretary at War* (New York: Alfred A. Knopf, 2014).

Haig, Alexander *Caveat: Realism, Reagan, and Foreign Policy* (New York: Macmillan, 1984).

Helms, Cynthia. *An Ambassador's Wife in Iran* (New York: Dodd, Mead & Company).

Henderson, Nicholas. *Mandarin: The Diaries of an Ambassador 1969–1982* (London: Weidenfeld and Nicolson), 1994.

Howe, Geoffrey. *Conflict of Loyalty* (London: Macmillan, 1994).

Hurd, Douglas. *Memoirs* (London: Little Brown, 2003).

Jordan, Hamilton. *Crisis: The Last Year of the Carter Presidency* (New York: G.P. Putnam's Sons, 1982).

Kissinger, Henry. *White House Years* (Boston, Little, Brown and Company, 1979).

Kuhn, Jim. *Ronald Reagan in Private: A Memoir of My Years in the White House* (New York: Sentinel, 2004.

McFarlane, Robert. *Special Trust* (New York: Cadell & Davis, 1994).

Meese, Edwin, *With Reagan: the Inside Story* (Washington: Regnery, 1992).

Menges C. Constantine, *Inside the National Security Council: The True story of the Making and Unmaking of Reagan's Foreign Policy* (New York: Simon and Schuster, 1988).

Nixon, Richard. *RN: The Memoirs of Richard Nixon*, vol. I (New York: Warner Books, 1978).

Owen, David. *Time to Declare* (London: Michael Joseph, 1991).

Pahlavi, Mohammed Reza. *Answer to History* (New York: Stein and Day, 1980).

Parsons, Anthony. *The Pride and Fall: Iran, 1974–1979* (London: Cape, 1981).

Powell, Jody. *The Other Side of the Story* (New York: William and Company, 1984).

Precht, Henry. *A Diplomat's Progress: Ten Tales of Diplomatic Adventure in and around the Middle East* (Savannah, Georgia: Williams & Company, Publishers, 2005).

Pym, Francis. *The Politics of Consent* (London: Hamish Hamilton, 1984).

Reagan, Ronald, *An American Life: The Autobiography* (London: Hutchinson, 1990).

Regan, Donald T. *For the Record: From Wall Street to Washington* (London: Hutchinson, 1988).

Roosevelt, Selwa. *Keeper of the Gate* (New York: Simon and Schuster, 1990).

Rumsfeld, Donald. *Known and Unknown: A Memoir* (New York: Sentinel, 2011).

Shultz, George P. *Turmoil and Triumph: My Years as Secretary of State* (New York: Charles Schribner's Sons, 1993).

Sick, Gary. *All Fall Down: America's Tragic Encounter with Iran* (New York: Random House, 1985).

Stockman, David. *The Triumph of Politics* (New York: Harper & Row, 1986).

Sullivan, William H. *Mission to Iran* (New York: W. W. Norton & Company, 1981).

Thatcher, Margaret. *The Downing Street Years* (London: HarperCollins, 1993).

Vance, Cyrus. *Hard Choices: Critical Years in America's Foreign Policy* (New York: Simon and Schuster, 1983).

Von Damm, Helene . *At Reagan's Side* (New York: Doubleday, 1989).

Weinberger, Caspar. *Fighting for Peace: Critical Years at the Pentagon* (London: Michael Joseph, 1990).

Wilson, Harold. *Final Term: The Labour Government, 1974–1976* (London: Weidenfeld and Nicolson and Michael Joseph, 1979).

Books

Aitken, Jonathan. *Nixon: A Life* (Washington: Regnery Publishing, 1993).

——. *Margaret Thatcher: Power and Personality* (London: Bloomsbury, 2013).

Aldhous, Richard. *Reagan & Thatcher: The Difficult Relationship* (London: Hutchinson, 2012).

Algar, Hamid. *The Islamic Revolution in Iran* (London: Open Press, 1980).

Ambrose, Stephen E. *Nixon: Ruin and Recovery 1973–1990* (New York: Touchstone, 1991).

Bagevich, Andrew J. *The New American Militarism: How Americans are Seduced by War* (Oxford: Oxford University press, 2005).

——. *The Limits of Power: The End of American Exceptionalism* (New York: Henry Holt and Company, 2009).

Bakhash, Shaul. *The Reign of the Ayatollahs: Iran and the Islamic Revolution* (London: Urwin Paperbacks, 1985).

Balfour-Paul, Glen.*The End of Empire in the Middle East: Britain's Relinquishment of Power in Her Last Three Arab Dependencies* (Cambridge: Cambridge University Press, 1991).

Bill, James A. *The Eagle and the Lion: The Tragedy of American–Iranian Relations* (New Haven: Yale University Press, 1988).

Blackstone, Tessa and William Plowden. *Inside the Think Tank: Advising the Cabinet, 1971–1983* (London: William Heineman, 1988).

Blandford, Linda. *Oil Sheiks: Inside the Supercharged World of the Petrodollar* (London: W. Allen & Co. Ltd., 1984).

Blinken, Anthony J. *Ally vs. Ally: America, Europe and the Siberian Pipeline Crisis* (New York: Praeger, 1987).

Bronson, Rachel. *Thicker than Oil: America's Uneasy Partnership with Saudi Arabia* (Oxford: Oxford University Press, 2006).

Brenchley, Frank. *Britain and the Middle East: An Economic History 1945–87* (London: Lester Crook Academic Publishing, 1989).

Bowden, Mark. *Guests of the Aytollah: The First Battle in the West's War with Militant Islam* (London: Atlantic Books, 2006).

Brodie, Fawn M. *Richard Nixon: The Shaping of His Character* (New York: W.W. Norton & Company, 1981).

Byrd, Peter (ed.), *Foreign Policy under Thatcher* (Oxford: Philip Alan, 1988).

Campbell, John. *The Iron Lady: Margaret Thatcher from Grocer's Daughter to Prime Minister* (New York: Penguin Books, 2011).

Cannon, Lou. *President Reagan: The Role of a Lifetime* (New York: Simon & Schuster, 1991).

Coughlin, Con. *Saddam: The Secret Life* (London: Macmillan, 2002).

Cramer, Richard Ben, *What it Takes: The Way to the White House* (New York: Random House, 1992).

Draper, Theodore. *A Very Thin Line: The Iran-Contra Affairs* (New York: Hill and Wang, 1991).

Duffy, Michael & Dan Goodgame, *Marching in Place: The Status Quo Presidency of George Bush* (New York: Simon & Schuster, 1992).

Dumbrell, John. *The Carter Presidency: A Re-evaluation* (Manchester: Manchester University Press, 1995).

——. *A Special Relationship: Anglo-American Relations from the Cold War to Iraq* (London: Palgrave Macmillan, 2006).

Ehrenhalt, Alan .*The United States of Ambition: Politicians, Power, and the Pursuit of Office* (New York: Times Books, 1991).

Farber, David. *The Iran Hostage Crisis and America's First Encounter with Radical Islam* (Princeton: Princeton University Press, 2005).

Foot, Paul (with Ron Smith). *The Helen Smith Story* (Great Britain: Fontana Paperbacks, 1983).

Gaddis, John Lewis. *The United States and the End of the Cold War: Implications, Reconsiderations, Provocations* (New York: Oxford University Press, 1992),

Gause, F. Gregory III. *The International Relations of the Persian Gulf* (Cambridge: Cambridge University Press, 2010).

Harris, David. *The Crisis: The President, the Prophet, and the Shah-1979 and the Coming of Militant Islam* (New York: Little, Brown and Company, 2004).

Harris, Robin. *Not for Turning: The Life of Margaret Thatcher* (London: Bantam Press, 2013).

Hirst, Chrissie. *The Arabian Connection: The UK Arms Trade to Saudi Arabia* (London: Campaign Against Arms Trade [CAAT], 2000).

Horowitz, Daniel. *Jimmy Carter and the Energy Crisis of the 1970s: The "Crisis of Confidence" Speech of July 15, 1979* (New York: Bedford/St. Martins, 2005).

Jentleson, Bruce W. *With Friends like these: Reagan, Bush, and Saddam, 1982–1990* (New York: W. W. Norton & Company, 1994).

Jones, Clive. *Britain and the Yemen Civil War, 1962–1965: Ministries, Mercenaries and*

Mandarins, Foreign Policy and the Limits of Covert Action (Brighton & Portland: Sussex Academic press, 2004).

Jones, Clive and Tore T. Petersen (eds.). *Israel's Clandestine Diplomacies* (London and New York: Hurst & Company and Oxford University Press, 2013).

Kaufman, Burton I. and Scott Kaufman. *The Presidency of James Earl Carter Jr.* (Lawrence: University Press of Kansas, 2006).

Kaufman, Scott. *Plans Unraveled: The Foreign Policy of the Carter Administration* (DeKalb : Northern Illinois University Press, 2008).

Kelly, J. B. *Arabia, the Gulf and the West* (London: Weidenfeld and Nicolson, 1980).

Laham, Nicholas. *Selling AWACS to Saudi Arabia: The Reagan Administration and the Balancing of America's Competing Interests in the Middle East* (London: Praeger, 2002).

Lacey, Robert. *The Kingdom* (New York: Harcourt Brace Jovanovich, 1982).

Lee, Harold Wise. *Inside the Danger Zone: The U.S. Military in the Persian Gulf, 1987–1988* (Annapolis: Naval Institute Press, 2007).

Mackey, Sandra. *The Saudis: Inside the Desert Kingdom* (Boston: Houghton Mifflin Company, 1987).

Macris, Jeffrey R. and Saul Kelly (eds.), *Imperial Crossroads: The Great Powers and the Persian Gulf* (Annapolis, Maryland: Naval Institute Press, 2012).

Mattson, Kevin. *"What the Heck are You up to, Mr. President?" Jimmy Carter, America's "Malaise" and the Speech that should have changed the Country* (New York: Bloomsbury, 2009).

Mervin, David, *Ronald Reagan & the American Presidency* (London: Longman, 1990).

Morgan, Kenneth O. *Callaghan: A Life* (Oxford: Oxford University Press, 1997).

Morris, Edmund. *Dutch: A Memoir of Ronald Reagan* (New York: Random House, 1999).

Morris, James. *Farewell the Trumpets: An Imperial Retreat* (London: The Folio Society, 1992).

Moore, Charles. *Margaret Thatcher; The Authorized Biography*, volume one: *Not for Turning* (London: Allen Lane, 2013).

Nixon, Richard. *The Real War* (New York: Warner Books, 1980).

——. *Leaders* (New York: Warner Books, 1982).

——. *Real Peace* (Boston: Little, Brown and Company, 1984).

——. *No More Vietnams* (New York: Arbor House, 1985).

——. *1999: Victory without War* (New York: Simon & Schuster, 1988).

——. *In the Arena: A Memoir of Victory, Defeat, and Renewal* (New York: Simon and Schuster, 1990).

——. *Seize the Moment: America's Challenge in a One-Superpower World* (New York: Simon & Schuster, 1992).

—— . *Beyond Peace* (New York: Random House, 1994).

Noonan, Peggy. *Life, Liberty and the Pursuit of Happiness* (New York: Random House, 1992).

——. *What I Saw at the Revolution. A Political Life in the Reagan Era* (New York: Random House, 1990).

Noyes, James E. *The Clouded Lens: Persian Gulf Security and U.S. Policy* (Stanford: Hoover University press, 1979).

Oberdorfer, Don. *The Turn: From Cold War to a New Era* (New York: Simon & Schuster, 1992).

Olson, Keith W. *Watergate: The Presidential Scandal that Shook America* (Lawrence: University Press of Kansas, 2003).

O'Reilly, Marc J. *Unexceptional: America's Empire in the Persian Gulf, 1941–2007* (New York: Lexington Books, 2008).

Owtram, Francis. *A History of Modern Oman* (London: I.B. Tauris, 2004).

Petersen, Tore T. *Richard Nixon, Great Britain and the Anglo-American Alignment in the Persian Gulf and Arabian Peninsula: Making Allies out of Clients* (Brighton & Portland: Sussex Academic Press, 2009).

——. *The Decline of the Anglo-American Middle East 1961–1969: A Willing Retreat* (Brighton and Portland: Sussex Academic Press, 2006).

Palmer, Michael A. *Guardians of the Gulf: A History of America's Expanding Role in the Persian Gulf, 1833–1992* (New York: The Free Press, 1992).

Pearce, Edward. *Denis Healey: A Life in Our Times* (Great Britain: Little Brown).

Phythian, Mark. *The Politics of British Arms Sales since 1964* (Manchester: Manchester University Press, 2000).

Pargeter, Alison. *The Rise and Fall of Qaddafi* (New Haven: Yale University Press, 2012).

Qandt, William B. *Peace Process: American Diplomacy and the Arab–Israeli Conflict since 1967* (Los Angeles: University of California Press, 1993).

Reagan, Ron. *My Father at 100: A Memoir* (New York: Viking, 2011).

Reeves, Richard. *President Reagan: The Triumph of Imagination* (New York: Simon &Schuster, 2005).

Robert Renwick, *A Journey with Margaret Thatcher: Foreign Policy under the Iron Lady* (London: Biteback Publishing, 2013).

Rubin, Barry. *Paved with Good Intentions: The American Experience and Iran* (Oxford: Oxford University Press, 1980).

Ryan, Paul B. *The Iranian Rescue Mission: Why it Failed* (Annapolis, Maryland: Naval Institute Press, 1985).

Schaller, Michael. *Reckoning with Reagan: America and It's President in the 1980s* (New York: Oxford University Press, 1992).

Schweizer, Peter. *Victory: The Reagan Administration's Secret Strategy that Hastened the Collapse of the Soviet Union* (New York: The Atlantic Monthly Press, 1994).

Sharp, Paul. *Thatcher's Diplomacy: The Revival of British Foreign Policy* (London: Macmillan, 1997).

Smith, Gaddis. *Morality, Reason and Power: American Diplomacy in the Carter Years* (New York: Hill and Wang, 1986).

Smith, Geoffrey. *Reagan and Thatcher* (London: The Bodley Head, 1990).

Smith, Simon. *Ending Empire in the Middle East: Britain, the United States and Post-War Decolonization, 1945–1973* (London: Routledge, 2012).

Stanik, Joseph T. *El Dorado Canyon: Reagan's Undeclared War with Qaddafi* (Annapolis: Naval Institute Press, 2003).

Teicher, Howard and Gayle Radley Teicher, *Twin Pillars to Desert Storm: America's Flawed Vision in the Middle East from Nixon to Bush* (New York: William Morrow and Company, 1993).

Trofimov, Yaroslav. *The Siege of Mecca: The Unforgotten Uprising in Islam's Holiest Shrine* (London: Penguin Books, 2007).

Thornton, Richard C. *The Carter Years: Toward a New Global Order* (Paragon House: New York, 1991).

Walsh, Lawrence E. *Firewall: The Iran-Contra Conspiracy and Cover-up* (New York: W.W. Norton, 1997).

Walt, Stephen M. *Taming American Power: The Global Response to U.S. Primacy* (New York: W.W. Norton & Company, 2005).

Wills, Gary, *Reagan's America: Innocents at Home* (New York: Doubleday & Company, 1987).

Woodward, Bob. *Veil: The Secret wars of the CIA 1981–1987* (London: Simon & Schuster, 1987).

Wroe, Ann. *Lives, Lies and the Iran-Contra Affair* (London: I.B. Tauris, 1991).

Yergin, Daniel. *The Prize: The Epic Quest for Oil, Money, and Power* (New York: Simon & Schuster, 1992).

Articles

Loyd E. Ambrosius, "Woodrow Wilson and George W. Bush: Historical Comparisons of Ends and Means in Their Foreign Policies". *Diplomatic History,* 30: 3 (June, 2006): 509–19.

Mitchell Bard, "Interest Groups, the President and Foreign Policy: How Reagan Snatched Victory from the Jaws of Defeat on AWACS", *Presidential Studies Quarterly* XVIII: 3 (Summer, 1988): 583–600.

Brands, Hal. "Saddam Hussein, the United States, and the Invasion of Iran: was there a green light?" *Cold War History* 12: 2 (2012): 319–43.

Campbell, Jason H. "The Ties that Bind: The Events of 1979 and the Escalation of the U.S.-Saudi Security Relations during the Carter and Reagan Administration," in Jeffrey R. Macris and Saul Kelly (eds.), *Imperial Crossroads: The Great Powers and the Persian Gulf* (Annapolis, Maryland: Naval Institute Press, 2012): 129– 146.

Campbell, John C. "Oil Power in the Middle East", *Foreign Affairs* 56: 1 (October, 1977): 89–110.

Greider, William. "The Education of David Stockman", *The Atlantic* (December, 1981).

Fallows, James. "The Passionless Presidency: The Trouble with Jimmy Carter's Administration", *The Atlantic Monthly* (May, 1979): 33–48.

Hughes, Geraint. "From Jebel to the Palace: British military Involvement in the Persian Gulf, 1957–2011", Corbett paper no. 10, Kings College London (March, 2012).

Little, Doug. ""To the Shores of Tripoli: America, Qaddafi, and the Libyan Revolution 1969–89", *The International History Review* 35: 1 (2013): 70–99.

James P. Pfeiffer, "White House Staff versus the Cabinet: Centripetal and Centrifugal Roles", *Presidential Studies Quarterly* XVI: 4 (Fall, 1986): 666–90.

Petersen, Tore T. "Anglo-American Rivalry in the Middle East: The Struggle for the Buraimi Oasis, 1952–1957", *The International History Review* XIX: 4 (November, 1992): 71–91.

Regan, Donald T. "The Reagan Presidency in Perspective", *Presidential Studies Quarterly* (Summer, 1986): 414–420.

Robb, Thomas. "The "Limit of What is Tolerable": British Defence Cuts and the "Special Relationship", 1974–1976", *Diplomacy & Statecraft* 22: 2, pp. 321–37.

Salamandra, Christa. "Cultural Construction, the Gulf and Arab London", in Paul Dresch and James Piscatori (eds.), *Monarchies and Nations: Globalisation and Identity in the Arab States of the Gulf* (London: I.B. Tauris, 2013): 73– 95.

Siniver, Asaf. "US foreign policy and the Kissinger Stratagem", in Asaf Siniver (ed.),

The October 1973 War: Politics, Diplomacy, Legacy (London: Hurst and Company, 2013): 85–99.

Robert A. Strong, "Recapturing Leadership: The Carter Administration and the Crisis of Confidence", *Presidential Studies Quarterly* XVI: 4 (Fall, 1986): 636–50.

Van Hollen, Christopher. "Don't Engulf the Gulf; "*Foreign Affairs* 59: 5 (Summer, 1981): 1064–1078.

Walker, Wallace Earl and Michael R. Reopel, "Strategies for Governance: Transition and Domestic Policy Making in the Reagan Administration", *Presidential Studies Quarterly* XVI: 4 (Fall, 1986): 734–760.

Index